REPROGRAMMING THE

American Dream

REPROGRAMMING THE

American Dream

FROM RURAL AMERICA TO SILICON VALLEY—
MAKING AI SERVE US ALL

Kevin Scott

with Greg Shaw

HARPER
BUSINESS

An Imprint of HarperCollins*Publishers*

HarperCollins books may be purchased for educational, business, or sales promotional use. For information, please email the Special Markets Department at SPsales@harpercollins.com.

FIRST EDITION

Library of Congress Cataloging-in-Publication Data has been applied for.

ISBN 978-0-06-287987-5

20 21 22 23 24 LSC 10 9 8 7 6 5 4 3 2 1

For my dad, Jimmie Scott,
and my kids, Chloe and Connor

Contents

Foreword

————

A couple of years ago, I found myself on the phone with Microsoft Chief Technology Officer (CTO) Kevin Scott. Calls like this happen from time to time: I am in the business of investing in technology companies, and when an important leader of one of the most important technology companies wants to give you a call, you answer.

I didn't realize at the time that Kevin and I came from similar backgrounds. He grew up poor, in a family living on the outskirts of rural Appalachia, and though our stories differed in important ways, I felt like I was talking to a kindred spirit. I spend so much of my life around people who don't understand my background that it was easy to talk to someone whose life bore so much resemblance to my own. We spoke about what he was seeing in his work with Microsoft, what types of companies I had invested in, and my book, *Hillbilly Elegy*. He also asked me about writing a book, something he had apparently thought about doing for some time. So I gave him my views on writing a book while having a full-time job, the upsides and the downsides. The advice was probably useless—worth about what Kevin paid for it—but we promised to stay in touch, and then I hung up the phone.

In the coming months, I'd invite Kevin to accompany my team during some of our investing work, and he graciously agreed. I knew that he continued to work on his book, and eventually I got an email from Kevin with a long Word file. Apparently, Kevin had worked on his book in earnest, and the pages you hold in your hands are the fruit of that labor.

Reprogramming the American Dream is a hybrid of a book. In it, you learn a bit about Kevin's background: where he came from, what his parents did, and how he struggled (and didn't). You learn a bit about his values, and what motivates him. He's never quite gotten over his home in rural Virginia. He still loves it and regrets just a little the fact that he was eventually forced to leave. That's a tension I know well. But it also has some interesting ideas. The core thesis of the book is that AI—artificial intelligence—is coming, and we need to do something about it. We need to understand it—how it will affect our future, what it will require of our educational institutions, and what it will do to our jobs.

I first became interested in AI through my work as an investor. I didn't originally think much about its effect on jobs. In my life as an investor, I'm paid, at a fundamental level, to see things before other people see them. And I became mildly obsessed with the fact that no one spoke about AI as a military technology. Most new technology, after all, has a military application, and there were some obvious ways in which America's global competition recognized the military use of AI. But among many of the technology entrepreneurs I spoke to, they focused on any number of AI applications— drug discovery, early cancer detection, autonomous vehicles, lighting for agriculture, and on and on.

But if you spend enough time reading about AI, for whatever reason, you'll eventually stumble onto a conversation about its effect on jobs. Before too long, I had uncritically accepted the conventional wisdom that automation would lead to a jobs Armageddon, where low- and middle-skilled workers would lose their ability to make a living. But it's not totally clear that's true. To take just one obvious example from recent history: the advent of automated teller machines—ATMs— might have been expected to eliminate all the human tellers. Instead, ATMs reduced the cost of running a brick-and-mortar bank, it freed up human tellers to do other things, and today there are more tellers employed than when the ATM was invented.

This book is such a critical contribution to the conversation because it pushes back against the conventional wisdom. Sometimes AI will destroy jobs, yes, but technology is a core part of how our society improves itself. Diseases are cured and people made healthier through the process of doing things we couldn't do before—in other words, through technology. Technology is hardly the only important part of a growing and vibrant society, but without real technological innovation, it's hard to achieve rising living standards. One of my favorite parts of this book is where Kevin gets a little technical on AI. Kevin knows his stuff and respects his readers enough to not talk down to them. You won't become an AI expert from one book, but you'll gain some passing knowledge of the issues at hand.

I confess to being skeptical that much of what passes for "technology" is inherently either good or bad. Much of it depends on how we use it. The iPhone is unquestionably a significant technological innovation. Some people use it to post hateful memes on Twitter; others use it to speak to and see their children half a world away. Some of our country's neuroscientists are working to create technology to cure dementia; others to addict our kids to gambling applications.

Even if you don't think innovation is always good, and I obviously don't, the change that it brings is an inexorable part of our lives. If Kevin is right, and AI is among the most important technologies of our generation, some people will do very good things with it and some will do very bad things with it. But the easy, and conventional, approach of seeing AI as something that destroys jobs misses more subtle and interesting questions about how we turn AI to useful purposes, how we prepare our workforce for some of the new jobs that will come, and how we protect our communities in the face of disruption that often accompanies dynamism.

Kevin and I agree on a lot, but not on everything. I'm somewhat more skeptical that a fully human style AI (called artificial general intelligence) is around the corner. He seems pretty skeptical of universal basic income (UBI). I am even more skeptical than Kevin.

There is a laziness at the heart of too much discourse, and it is perhaps Kevin's greatest strength in this book that he avoids it. It is the laziness of assuming that historical and economic trends are entirely immune to our choices. AI may be coming, but how we respond to it, and the effects we face—good and bad—require deliberate, thoughtful action. You may not agree with everything he says, but I hope you, like me, appreciate that Kevin finds some balance between the poles of "the robots are coming for our jobs!" and "AI is great, nothing to worry about!" I suspect that, in the coming decades, we'll increasingly recognize the wisdom of that view.

—J.D. Vance

REPROGRAMMING THE

American Dream

Introduction

———

I've always had a thing for stories. It might be a Southern thing. A rural thing. I grew up surrounded by a lively cast of characters with a flair for narrative and sometimes improbable adventures. Every Sunday morning, I got a two-hour dose of the King James Bible through the lens of fire-and-brimstone preaching. When my mom tired of reading me the same stories over and over, I taught myself to read and begged for trips to the library to keep me flush with new material. History. Greek mythology. Dr. Strange and the Doom Patrol. The *World Book Encyclopedia*. *National Geographic*. The *Peterson Field Guide to the Stars and Planets*. I could not get enough stories.

Turns out that storytelling is not just a Southern or a rural thing. It's also a tech thing. In *The Written World*, an inspiring treatise on the power of stories to shape people, history, and civilization, Martin Puchner writes that in order to tell the story of literature he had to focus on both storytelling and creative technologies because their intersection is the starting point. The alphabet is code; paper and the printing press are technologies for communications, just as computer languages are code, and the Internet communicates. Yuval Noah Harari, in his book *Sapiens*, suggests that stories and the cognitive infrastructure that developed tens of thousands of years ago in humans are the most likely reason that *Homo sapiens* superseded the other species of humans existing seventy thousand years ago. Harari posits that our storytelling ability and the stories we choose to tell are the foundations of our society at scale. Everything from companies to our currency to the Constitution and our laws is a story that we share with one another, allowing us to coordinate our individual efforts among billions of other human beings. Stories are shared not just through written text. The rise of podcasts and Amazon's Audible have shown us that the oral tradition lives on. Netflix and HoloLens show that stories can be presented visually in a variety of formats. Jeff Weiner, my former boss at LinkedIn, says that "we are the stories that we tell." And in a very literal sense, he is right.

There are two prevailing stories about AI: for low- and middle-skill workers, we hear a grim tale of steadily increasing job destruction; for knowledge workers and the professional class, we hear an idyllic tale of enhanced productivity and convenience. At one extreme, we have a narrative imagining of a future where livelihoods and lives are at the mercy of inscrutable machines and the elite who control them. At the other is a vision of a world where jobs and income are no longer necessary, and we all retire to a nice beach somewhere and let the robots do all the work. But neither of these captures the whole story, which is, I would argue, a more nuanced, complicated, and hopeful version of the future. I believe that we are in urgent need of a different story, a story of AI's potential to create abundance and opportunity for everyone and to help solve some of the world's most vexing problems. Indeed, in the story I see, with proper safeguards,

AI can be a tool that empowers us to do more of what makes us essentially human.

In his 1931 book *The Epic of America*, James Truslow Adams wrote:

> *The American Dream is that dream of a land in which life should be better and richer and fuller for everyone, with opportunity for each according to ability or achievement. It is a difficult dream for the European upper classes to interpret adequately, and too many of us ourselves have grown weary and mistrustful of it. It is not a dream of motor cars and high wages merely, but a dream of social order in which each man and each woman shall be able to attain to the fullest stature of which they are innately capable, and be recognized by others for what they are, regardless of the fortuitous circumstances of birth or position.*

The American dream is a noble aspiration, one of the ambitions that has inspired citizens and immigrants to the United States long before Adams coined the term. Our belief in this dream has ebbed and flowed over the course of time, and for some has been all but impossible to achieve. But perhaps to a greater extent than any technological revolution preceding it, AI could be used to revitalize the American dream, to reprogram it to support each of us as we seek to be our fullest and best selves.

Right now, the story of technology's future is in flux in ways not known in the West since the tail end of the Industrial Revolution in the early twentieth century. For some, the coming rise of artificial intelligence and robotics is a utopian story, and they can't get to the future fast enough. For others, the story is dystopian, and they have a hard time imagining how anyone would want to live in the world that we are creating for ourselves.

Implicit in too many of these narratives is the story that

rural America and the people who live there no longer matter. Those tending farms and working in agriculture are less than 2 percent of the American population. In March 2017, the *Washington Monthly* reported that the "depressed state of rural America is getting a fresh look as a result of the 2016 election, and rightly so. People are asking how to bring back rural prosperity and restore small-town civic life." In his *Requiem for the American Dream*, Noam Chomsky writes that the ability for everyone to get a decent job, buy a house and car, and have their kids go to school has "collapsed." I share his concern but not his fatalism. *Reprogramming the American Dream* reveals that we're at an inflection point, with the opportunity to shape how that story unfolds. Realizing that potential, ensuring that it helps the communities where people like J.D. Vance, author of *Hillbilly Elegy*, and I grew up, requires a principled approach to the development of AI, one that puts it on the public agenda alongside climate change, health epidemics, and public education.

I've got a different story to tell, one you haven't heard before. It's informed by two formative life experiences. The first is my upbringing in the rural town of Gladys, Virginia, typical of the communities throughout our country that have been—and will continue to be—disrupted by emerging technologies. The second is my current position as chief technology officer of Microsoft, where we're deeply involved in the development of AI applications and mindful every day about their potential impact on the workers of towns like Gladys, which have always depended on low- or middle-skilled workers.

From where I sit, no one is telling the right story, a realistic story, about AI, which is neither utopian nor dystopian. My aim in this book is to help shape that story by explaining, realistically and optimistically, the potential of AI to create prosperity for us all, not just the privileged few. Realizing that potential requires a principled approach to the development of AI and a set of policies designed to democratize AI.

AI must become a platform that any individual or business can use to enhance their creativity and productivity, and that can be used to solve the biggest of the big problems that confront us as a society. In an interview with Semil Shah, venture capitalist Chamath Palihapitiya paraphrased Bill Gates as having said, "A platform is when the economic value of everybody that uses it exceeds the value of the company that creates it."[1] It is not right if the value created by the development of AI is concentrated solely in the hands of a few elite companies and their employees. People should be rewarded for the innovations that they create, but those innovations must create a surplus of value that benefits businesses and workers everywhere, in middle and rural America as well as in coastal, urban innovation centers.

Much of the progress we've made building an AI platform, one that can support more people building more ambitious things every year, has been a direct consequence of publicly funded and widely disseminated research. In addition to accessible research and this rich marketplace of ideas, open source software and the Internet have made it possible for more people with more diverse backgrounds and experiences to make things with AI by making both code and data available for developers and researchers. Most recently, with the advent of cloud computing, corporations operating cloud infrastructure businesses—like Alibaba, Amazon, Google, and Microsoft—all have economic incentives to support as many developers and makers as possible in their individual efforts to build their own cloud-powered AI products and services. This is all well and good, but not enough. *We must ensure that anyone can participate in the development of this AI platform, and can intelligently engage in critical debates about how the platform evolves and is governed.*

One of the best-known memes in science fiction—a genre

no one will be surprised that I love—is based on the 1950 short story by Damon Knight, "To Serve Man." Popularized by an episode of *The Twilight Zone*, and then referenced dozens of times over the years, including in the first "Treehouse of Horror" episode of *The Simpsons*, the story is a play on the dual meaning of the verb *to serve*. In the story, aliens arrive on Earth and provide humanity with unlimited energy, food, a mechanism to disable our weapons of war, and a promise of medicines that would prolong life. One of the human protagonists of the story, a character named Grigori, is skeptical of the motives of the aliens. He learns their language and steals one of their books, *To Serve Man*, which it turns out is not a treatise on service to humanity, but a cookbook.

In our push to advance the state of the art for AI, to build new products, automate processes, and found whole new businesses empowered by AI technologies, we need to be constantly vigilant that all of this effort is focused on serving humans . . . in the beneficial sense of the word. The good news is that AI is a tool that we humans have developed and control. All of us, from the developer and scientist, to the entrepreneur and business exec, to the educator and the policy maker, have permission to make choices about the development of AI only to the extent that those choices are human-centered and serve the public good on balance. And balance is key even though achieving it is nontrivial, given the complexity of how these technologies intersect with society and our daily lives.

Finally, although AI already is, and will likely continue to be, one of the most beneficial technologies that humans have ever developed, we must be realistic that its development will come with negative consequences, as has been the case with many of history's complex technological revolutions. *We must work to prevent as many of those negative consequences as possible, and when they arise, to have compassion for those impacted, and to work as hard as we can to mitigate those impacts as quickly as possible.*

If doctors take an oath to do no harm, so should software engineers. Software engineering is what I do. It's how I think and see the world. Today, as Microsoft's chief technology officer, a father, and a philanthropist, I also think about how that technology will affect people, communities, and society. The one-two punch of ever bigger data and compute power is fueling an artificial intelligence revolution that will make prior industrial revolutions appear piddling in comparison. The AI Revolution will radically impact economics and employment for everyone for generations to come. I am not alone in foreseeing a massive transformation in the nature of work caused by the very machines I've helped to engineer. The bookshelf of science fiction writers, philosophers, economists, and technologists is sagging beneath the weight of doomsayers. My perspective, steeled by an upbringing in a region of the South decimated by the economic tsunami of dying tobacco, textile, and furniture industries, is forged, however, by a sense of tenacity and optimism.

The question this book asks is this: Can business and government work collaboratively to program next-generation technologies and future public policies to keep the American dream alive? In today's atmosphere that question sounds naive or cynical. But what could be more important? Like public health, climate change, and public education, we need international understanding and collaboration on the future of AI and work. This means intellectual inquiry, rational debate, and coming together, not sound bites, sensationalism, and the politics of division. Just as some believe it's too late to reverse the effects of global warming, some observers and even some technologists worry that AI may be on some unalterable path to taking both our work and our dignity. I'm skeptical of that mind-set, but the evidence I see and read—advances in machine learning algorithms, an increasingly complete and robust digital map of the world and human knowledge for training machine learning systems, and rapid expansion of training compute—suggests that the future we are hurtling toward will be very different from the present.

At the far end of the spectrum of concerns about the future of artificial intelligence are theories about what strong AI or artificial general intelligence (AGI) means for us as humans. Most of the AI that we encounter in our daily lives are systems built with the techniques of machine learning that have been trained by human beings to perform very specific, narrow tasks. These tasks might be selecting the ads you see when browsing the Internet, or turning the words you utter into your phone or PC into a text transcript that can then be processed by some other system, or identifying friends and family in the photos that you upload so that they can be tagged and notified. AGI—which no one really knows when we will reach—would be much more humanlike in its capabilities. Some, very worried about what AGI could mean for humanity, imagine futures like those from the Terminator series, where an AGI could become truly autonomous and hostile to humans. Critics of those fears assert that AI is far from passing even weak tests for sapience like the Turing test[2] or Winograd schema challenge,[3] and that human-level AI is some unknowable way off in the future, maybe never to be achieved.

Even though I have neither the expertise nor the crystal ball to predict exactly when AGI might arrive, I've been involved with modern technology long enough, and read enough history, to know that we've often underestimated the speed with which futuristic technology suddenly arrives. AI has historically been limited in what it has been able to accomplish by the amount of compute power we can throw at AI problems, and how much time it takes for humans to encode logic and knowledge into AI algorithms. We now have enormous amounts of compute power in the cloud. And we have enormous databases of digitized human knowledge like YouTube and the Kindle bookstore that can be used to train AI systems. As our modern AI algorithms absorb that human intelligence to accomplish new tasks we imagine for AI-powered systems, we may achieve what Thomas Kuhn defined as a paradigm shift, one in which humans will either be in the loop or out. Which one of these options we reach depends on our actions today, the story we craft, and the principles we assert about what kind of world we want our children to live in tomorrow.

I feel this profound sense of cognitive dissonance: the same thing that can advance humanity can also cause people distress and even harm. This book arises out of a powerful urge I feel to reconcile the two. It is an engineer's tale, not the musings of a philosopher, economist, or screenwriter. As Microsoft's chief technologist, do I have skin in the game? Of course I do. But I'm also the product of rural America, one of the places most vulnerable in the dystopic story of AI. My values and many of my earliest experiences as a budding engineer occurred in a part of America, rural America, that is most at risk. I left the rural South over two decades ago, first for academia and then for Silicon Valley and the tech industry. But at my core I am those people—rural people—and I care about creating a future that values them and their resourcefulness.

I'm no apologist for AI. I am, however, an optimist. The AI future I see needs high-skilled, middle-skilled, and even low-skilled workers involved in building and operating intelligent systems. I'm not alone in this view. Indeed, Microsoft announced in 2018 that it would invest substantially in rural communities to increase local digital skills. Google also announced it would train ten million Nigerians to build digital skills. And start-ups in China and Silicon Valley like BasicFinder, Mada Code, and Scale employ tens of thousands of people to teach machine learning systems how to perform specific tasks. Conversely, Amazon discovered the consequences of not having a skilled workforce when it announced in 2017 it would open an office in East Palo Alto, California, in the heart of Silicon Valley, only to learn that "there aren't enough people with the required skills," according to *Forbes* contributor Bernard Marr.

The story I aim to tell is one of a hopeful future where AI benefits us all equitably, and one where the obstacles standing in the way of this future are not intractable. There's a role for all of us to play in realizing this hopeful future.

For the AI experts it means really thinking through the consequences of the choices you make on an almost daily basis, taking action to avoid bad things like biased models or AI systems that empower or amplify the worst of our human tendencies, and ensuring that your work is having the net positive impact that you intend for your fellow humans. I know from personal experience that it's all too easy to allow yourself to be completely immersed in the details of the incredibly complex and narrowly focused thing on which you're working in AI. In fact, it's almost impossible to do your job if you can't do that! But no matter how absorbing the complexity of your daily work is, understanding your work in context, and thinking through the consequences of the decisions you make, are also parts of your job.

For product developers and entrepreneurs, your role means ensuring that the things you're powering with AI are genuinely beneficial for as broad a swath of humanity as possible; that you are seeking collaborators with a diversity of backgrounds, experiences, and expertise; and that you embrace your responsibility to help mitigate the disruption that you create, whether the disruption was intentional or not.

For investors and allocators of capital, your role means thinking about your AI investments as a Bill Gates thinks about platforms: that they create more economic benefit for others than for you or your enterprise or your portfolio companies. Given the tendency of early-stage disruptive technologies like AI to benefit the owners of expertise and capital disproportionately, this is incredibly important, and given how geographically concentrated AI development is, we investors have a real duty to make sure that we are encouraging diverse and geographically equitable investment.

For policy makers, your role means implementing policies that not only prevent or discourage the negative consequences of bad AI, but more important, incents and accelerates the benefits of good AI. In the United States, we have perhaps the best track record in modern history of government policy making that facilitates disruptive technology rollout for the public good. The entire aerospace industry is a great example of where a judicious blend of direct government funding, incentives, and regulation has facilitated an entire ecosystem of technologies without which modern life would be impossible.

Interestingly, China is now taking pages from the US playbook to bootstrap its own AI industry. The "Three-Year Action Plan for Promoting Development of a New Generation Artificial Intelligence Industry,"[4] adopted at the 19th National Congress of the Communist Party of China in 2017, articulates a very granular strategy for how to build an AI industry in China, asserting:

We should seize the historical opportunity, make breakthroughs in key areas, promote the development of the AI industry, enhance the intelligent manufacturing industry, and promote the in-depth integration of AI and real economy.

In addition to developing a similarly detailed public policy road map for promoting the AI industry in the United States, we may also want to consider the role that the voice of the United States plays in the development of AI policy globally. AI was literally invented in the United States, and since its inception, US research institutions and companies have been among the leaders of its development. We are now at a moment where we either need to choose to lead in AI policy in a way that promotes both our future prosperity and democratic values, or allow the definitive policies for AI to be written elsewhere.

Perhaps the most important role to be played in securing a hopeful AI future for all of us is that of the individual citizen. No matter who you are, what your job is, where you live, or where you are in your life's journey, you need to understand AI's opportunities and pitfalls so that you can help make the right choices about what to study for future generations. You need to understand what AI means for the future of work so that you can prepare yourself for future job opportunities, to know where opportunities might exist for the company you want to start, or even to know what's a good bet for a retirement investment. The public policy debate around AI is going to be complex, and it's going to demand that citizens of democratically elected governments wrap their heads around nontrivial issues and make tough trade-offs. You won't be able to have an effective voice in these debates unless you are at least a little bit informed, and you won't be able to say that you're truly informed unless you are able to look across a bunch of mutually conflicting opinions and points of view and rationally synthesize your own, intelligent opinion.

Even though I experienced poverty and massive loss of industry in the region where I grew up, fulfillment of an American dream was somehow a hope that my friends and I all shared. But for the American dream to be a realistic goal today for everyone, we need more than just belief in it. We need to cultivate it. In the words of a software engineer, we need to reprogram it. This book is my attempt to contribute to that goal, and to show how intelligent technologies, done right, can make it more possible for everyone to attain the full measure of his or her innate capabilities.

To show you the future, I invite you to take a journey with me back to my rural origins in Virginia.

PART I

Where We've Been

CHAPTER 1

When Our Jobs First Went Away

Chances are you've already encountered, more than a few times, truly frightening predictions about artificial intelligence and its implications for the future of humankind. The machines are coming and they want your job, at a minimum. Scary stories are easy to find in all the erudite places where the tech visionaries of Silicon Valley and Seattle, the cosmopolitan elite of New York City, and the policy wonks of Washington, DC, converge—TED Talks, Davos, ideas festivals, *Vanity Fair*, the *New Yorker*, the *New York Times*, Hollywood films, South by Southwest, Burning Man. The brilliant innovator Elon Musk and the genius theoretical physicist Stephen Hawking have been two of the most quotable and influential purveyors of these AI predictions. AI poses "an existential threat" to civilization, Elon Musk warned a gathering of governors in Rhode Island one summer's day.

When the founder of PayPal, Tesla, and SpaceX speaks, I listen. And Musk's words are very much on my mind as the car *I* drive (not autonomously, not yet) crests a hill in the rural southern piedmont of Virginia where I was born and raised. From here I can almost see home, the fields once carpeted by a stunning shade of lush green tobacco leaves and the roads long ago bustling with workers commuting from profitable textile mills and furniture plants. But that economy is no more. Poverty, unemployment, and frustration are high, not unlike our neighbors across the Blue Ridge Mountains in Appalachia and to the north in the Rust Belt. I am driving between Rustburg, the county seat, and Gladys, an unincorporated farming community where my mom and brother still live.

I left this community, located just down the road from where Lee surrendered to Grant at Appomattox Court House, because even as a kid I could see the bitter end of an economy that used to hum along, and I couldn't wait to chase my own dreams of building computers and software. But these are still my people, and I love them. Today, as one of the many tech entrepreneurs on the West Coast, my worldview has feet firmly planted in both urban California and rural Southern soil. I've come home to test those confident, anxiety-producing warnings about the future of jobs and artificial intelligence that I frequently hear among thought leaders in Silicon Valley, New York City, and DC, to see for myself whether there might be a different story to tell.

Like many, I was moved by J.D. Vance's description of a hardscrabble life and poverty-as-family-tradition in *Hillbilly Elegy*. The book got underneath the anger and despair that converted many Democrat-leaning regions of this country to more conservative politics. It provided a narrative unfamiliar to some of my coastal friends trying to understand what's going on in middle America. This book is about technology, not politics. But if I can better understand how the friends and family I grew up with in Campbell County are faring today, a decade after one economic tidal wave swept through, and in the midst of another, perhaps I can better influence the development of advanced technologies that will soon visit their lives and livelihoods.

I pull off Brookneal Highway, the two-lane main road, into a wide gravel parking lot that looks like a staging area for heavy equipment, next to the old house my friends W. B. and Allan Bass lived in when we were in high school. A sign out front proclaims that I've arrived at Bass Sod Farm. The house is now headquarters for their sprawling agricultural operation. It's just around the corner from my mom's house and, in a sign of the times, near a nondescript cinder-block building that houses a CenturyLink hub for high-speed Internet access. Prized deer antlers, a black bearskin, and a stuffed bobcat adorn their conference room, which used to be the family kitchen.

W.B. and Allan were popular back in the day. They always had a nice truck with a gun rack, and were known for their hunting and fishing skill. The Bass family has worked the same plots of Campbell County tobacco land for five generations dating back to the Civil War. Within my lifetime, Barksdale the grandfather, Walter the father, and now W.B. (Walter Barksdale) and brother Allan have worked the land alongside nine seasonal workers, mostly immigrants from Mexico.

Many families in Campbell County used to grow and sell tobacco, but today only two families continue. First came the 1964 surgeon general's report officially recognizing the health risks of tobacco. At the time, about 42 percent of adults in the United States smoked, compared with about 20 percent today. By 1988, smoking was banned on US flights two hours or less, and ten years later all US carrier flights became smoke-free. A 1991 study published in the *Journal of the American Medical Association* found that six-year-olds could just as easily recognize Joe Camel as Mickey Mouse. Big change began to come in 1998 when the tobacco industry agreed to a $206 billion master settlement, the largest in US history, with forty-six state attorneys general to resolve lawsuits that sought to recover the Medicaid costs for tobacco-related illnesses. Finally, in 2004, Congress ended a sixty-six-year-old federal price-support program that had maintained tobacco production and prices. With foreign competition and no federal regulation of quotas, tobacco prices plummeted. Tobacco, a major employer in rural Virginia, evaporated.

The Bass family grew brightleaf tobacco, commonly known as Virginia tobacco. With "bright" you cultivate the leaves only, about eighteen to twenty-two leaves per stalk, for cigarettes. They also sold dark tobacco, which involves cultivating the whole stalk and is used for chewing tobacco and cigars. By 2005 the Bass family saw the writing on the wall for its once valuable operation, and began to transition their land from tobacco to sod, or turf, a grassy product they sell to construction companies for new and refurbished building landscapes, golf courses, and other sports fields. By 2008 they were completely out of tobacco, and today their products are a new shade of green—Bermuda, zoysia, and fescue. They also grow some soybeans.

"People gotta eat, but they won't always need sod," I'm told. Fortunately, they got out of tobacco while the gettin' was still good.

As at any business, the cell phone and PC are ubiquitous at Bass Sod Farm. They also use some automation technology in their heavy machinery, including a Trebro harvester that rolls up the sod, stacks it on a pallet, and ensures minimum waste. It required Allan Bass to take forty hours of training, and he now has put in about three thousand hours of operation. According to Allan, "it's an art and a science" to harvest the sod just right. The Bass brothers recently added global positioning satellite (GPS) technology to their sprayers, exponentially increasing their efficiency and effectiveness. That transition is still a work in progress. "We don't have it down pat yet," Allan admits.

What really bugs them is that technology is not as transparent as it used to be. The problem with self-driving tractors and GPS sprayers is that you can't see what's broken, or at least your average farmer can't. Their biggest worry is not AI, but making sure that the technology they do have is self-healing. "If something fails, you spend lots of time debugging it." And the time Allan spends debugging his farm equipment is a big productivity hit for their small business.

They regard drones, and what I would describe as advanced machine learning or early AI, as something that will be helpful in gathering intelligence on their crops. A drone can take scores of pictures of "hot spots" on their crops to find irrigation problems, insects, and disease. An AI and drones can be trained to spot most potential calamities and provide an early warning system, likely saving many of the human jobs that would have been lost if the problem went undetected and the crops were ruined. Although they feel their human solution is best—"What we've got is working. Humans know what to look for"—it is time-consuming and costly for their small workforce to comb through acres of farmlands, looking for minute details. They'd much rather deploy human capital to expansion, quicker delivery, and product innovation, anything but walking mile after mile.

The Bass boys are optimistic. Business is good, and W.B.'s son chose to remain in Campbell County even though he's become a computer engineer in nearby Lynchburg. The next Industrial Revolution is not far off at Bass Sod Farm.

My next stop is nearby Brookneal, Virginia, to see another friend, Sheri Denton Guthrie, a financial manager at Heritage Hall Nursing Home. Heritage cared for three of my grandparents in their final years. Like at Bass Sod Farm, I want to better understand how AI will one day affect a place

I know all too well, a place that millions of baby boomers will also soon know.

Heritage has seventeen homes scattered across rural Virginia. It has sixty residents and as many as eighty staff depending on occupancy. There are nurses, nursing assistants, housekeepers, a medical secretary, an admissions staff, and a director. Sheri manages the home's books and has an astonishing amount of training on a range of health-care systems, PointClickCare and Toughbook to name a few. Even with all the available technologies, she says it's still too hard. Heritage gets paid based on individual residents' "RUG scores," short for a Resource Utilization Group calculation for Medicare and Medicaid. Staff go around with Toughbooks and log things like minutes of physical, speech, and occupational therapy; a doctor's visit; a mental health consult; an IV; help from the nurse assistants. These services all add up to an overall RUG score for which the nursing home is reimbursed.

Like the Bass brothers, Sheri is less worried about AI and more concerned about mundane things like needing her financial system reports to line up on a printer. A few years ago, hackers stole personal records from their health-care insurance provider, Anthem, so she worries about privacy and security. AI-infused robots could almost certainly be trained to do many tasks in the nursing home, from inputting medical data to providing medications and even treating wounds, though she has one caveat. "For our generation, yes, but not this generation. They'd beat the robot with a cane."

After a quick stop at the Golden Skillet for fried chicken, lima beans, and iced tea, I hurry over to check in on Hugh E. Williams, who manages a small team of workers at American Plastic Fabricators. Hugh E, as all our classmates know him, is a tall, strongly built man with a red beard that is only beginning to hint at his age with a streak of gray down the middle. Hugh E and I grew up together, going to the

same church from the time we were toddlers, and to the same
school as teenagers. He's proud to show me his plant, now located in an abandoned Bassett-Walker textile factory. Started
in 1936 as Bassett Knitting Corporation an hour and a half
west of Brookneal in Bassett, Virginia, the old mill was part
of a storied Southern industry that turned cotton into clothes.
Cotton textiles once dominated the South's economy, but
cheaper labor abroad and automation decimated the workforce. This mill in Brookneal closed with little hope of ever
reopening.

But a local entrepreneur began this modest company to
shape small, precision plastic parts that were needed by a
wide range of customers, from theme parks to defense con-
tractors. The business, essentially a job shop, was hit hard by
the financial crisis of 2008, but began to grow again in the
aftermath by offering competitive pricing on polyethylene
and high-density plastics fabrication. With more than twenty
employees, needing a larger space, they took over the defunct
textile mill. The day I visited, one of the workers was using a sophisticated milling machine controlled by a computer
to create an intricate piece for Disneyland's Jumpin' Jelly-
fish ride. Disney sent Hugh E the specifications, they programmed the machine, and voilà, one by one these young
workers carve plastic into industrial works of art. A machinist
diploma from Southside Virginia Community College and
a little on-the-job training can land a well-paying job in a
small town that was once counted out.

As I've witnessed firsthand, and as many working Americans have experienced personally, manufacturing jobs have
been disappearing for decades now, moving overseas where
things can be built cheaper. What I saw in Brookneal and
what's happening across the country, in rural and urban settings alike, is new manufacturing jobs being created because
AI, robotics, and advanced automation are becoming more

capable and cheaper every day, making it feasible to build things in the United States and other markets where labor costs are high. As automation becomes cheaper and more powerful, it levels the playing field for small companies, allowing them to lower their unit costs of production and to become more competitive, consequently allowing them to grow their businesses and create more and higher-paying jobs.

This pattern of combining the best of human skill with the best of automation can result in incredible prosperity. Look no further than Germany's Mittelstand, small- and medium-size enterprises generating less than 50 million euro in revenue annually, which collectively account for 99.6 percent of German companies, 60 percent of jobs, and over half of Germany's gross domestic product.[5] These companies are ingenious at finding narrow but valuable markets to serve, then using highly skilled labor and advanced automation to produce high-quality products extremely efficiently. My friend Hugh E's employer would be in the Mittelstand, along with 3.3 million others, if it were located in Germany.

Microsoft data indicate that manufacturing is among the fastest-growing segments for AI talent and skills. According to LinkedIn, AI skills increased 190 percent between 2015 and 2017.[6] The idea of creating new, skilled, well-paying manufacturing jobs in rural Brookneal would have been implausible a couple of decades ago. Now it is reality. That's good news. And the better news is that the underlying automation trend will continue to provide ever more powerful, ever cheaper technology that will create even more opportunities for entrepreneurs and workers alike, in both rural and urban America.

In the future, it's likely that some of this automation will be able to do work that humans are doing today. That's a good thing. That's what automation has been doing for centuries.

From the vantage point of the developed world in the early twenty-first century, it means more business and more jobs can be repatriated from overseas, that we can build new businesses with new jobs in the future that would be economically infeasible or technically impossible today, and that we all get higher-quality, cheaper, more innovative goods and services that will improve our quality of life. It's likely that AI can help us equalize some of the inequities that have come as a result of late-twentieth-century global free trade. It's far less likely that we will achieve AI and robotics anytime soon that are capable of completely replacing human workers in arbitrary manufacturing and service jobs. And that's especially true if we choose to place our thumb on the scale and deliberately pursue the former path versus the latter.

In the face of increasingly wild hypothetical scenarios about AI's potential dominance over humans, the reality of what AI is capable of now, and will be capable of in the near future, is more humbling. For example, Daniela Hernandez of the *Wall Street Journal* attended a government-sponsored contest for intelligent robots in 2017. One by one, each robot was stumped by an unlocked door. One was able to wrap its mechanical fingers around the doorknob and open it, but was flummoxed by a slight breeze that kept blowing the door shut. An ongoing "Hundred Year Study on Artificial Intelligence" at Stanford University found in its 2016 report that while computers were becoming more capable at highly specific tasks, a robot takeover is pretty unlikely. "Contrary to the more fantastic predictions for AI in the popular press, the Study Panel found no cause for concern that AI is an imminent threat to humankind. No machines with self-sustaining long-term goals and intent have been developed, nor are they likely to be developed in the near future." If society approaches AI with a more open mind, the authors wrote, technologies emerging from the field could profoundly transform society for the better in the coming decades. Even though AI is progressing incredibly quickly, we still have a way to go before it is able to dramatically transform the world . . . for good or ill.

My visits with the Bass brothers, Sheri, and Hugh E remind me that sharp intellect and attention to detail and optimism, rooted in today's tech reality, remain strong among blue-collar, mid-skilled rural—and I suspect Rust Belt—leaders and entrepreneurs. I firmly believe AI, robotics, drones, and data will continue to augment, not replace, workers in communities like Gladys and Brookneal for generations to come. Every week of every year I sit in product demonstrations and strategy sessions on AI development. Whether it's in my role at Microsoft or as an investor in Silicon Valley, I am increasingly assured that AI will ultimately be about human empowerment, not displacement.

As the autumn darkness descends on Campbell County, I turn the car around and head back to Mom's house, just as I did so many times as a kid. I've been inspired by my old friends. That night, as sleep comes slowly, I imagine what I could do here to create jobs and help rebuild the local economy.

The next morning, I am up early and head an hour south to the little town of Boydton, Virginia, in Mecklenburg County near the North Carolina border. I am going to visit the Microsoft cloud, or at least where part of it is housed in one of the world's largest data centers in the world. The Fourth Industrial Revolution, a term economists have used to describe the coming age of AI, is well underway in rural Virginia. (We've been a hotbed for revolutionaries for centuries.) Not long ago, Microsoft and Facebook completed a joint venture that landed a powerful transatlantic data cable just to the east in Norfolk, Virginia. This cable, coupled with data centers like Boydton, is sparking a new economy in the

Old South. I want to see for myself these building blocks for
the future of data and AI—a massive example of technology
upskilling rural workers and creating jobs for the future.

My drive meanders alongside old nineteenth-century rail-
roads, through farmland, and past nondescript historical land-
marks of revolutions past. Each town center along the way
features the statue of a soldier, head bowed mourning the
losses of tragic conflicts. Unemployment in the area hovers
around 6 percent, but it reached as high as 13 percent just
before Microsoft built its data center.

Once you arrive in Mecklenburg, the data center comes up
quickly on your right. As I write this book, it is Microsoft's
largest data center, with acres of computers organized into
near-endless, neatly aligned aisles. These centers run a big
chunk of the world's digital infrastructure, but they are
largely invisible to anyone driving by. Miss it, like I did, and
you must do a quick U-turn at the "Welcome to Boydton"
sign. I stopped in front to snap a photo, and suddenly out of
nowhere a young Virginia state trooper pulled up behind me,
lights flashing, to offer his help.

I found my way to the data center by turning left on Prison
Road. Had I turned right I would have found a large va-
cant field where Boydton's former largest employer used to
reside—a federal maximum-security prison, closed a few years
ago for obsolescence.

Once I passed through an elaborate security check, the
center's director greeted me in the lobby and escorted me to
a large conference room where a video was already playing,
shot from a drone, to provide an overview of the center's
vastness. He briefed me on the history and operations of the
data center, and then invited a half-dozen employees, all locals, to join us for a lunch delivered by a nearby diner.

The five-hundred-acre data center is surrounded by three
thousand open acres of timberland—lots of space to grow.

And that is the plan. Already, local-based construction workers have built twenty physical data centers that serve Microsoft cloud products like Bing, Azure, and Office 365. Our two power substations (100 megawatts and 128 megawatts) make Microsoft the largest power consumer in the region.

Like Hugh E's company the previous day in Brookneal, Mecklenburg was frantically looking for a relocation opportunity after the 2008 financial crisis. The prison was closing, and times looked very unstable. But the county had plenty of surplus land, nuclear and hydro power, and an aggressive county commissioner. *U.S. News & World Report* came to Boydton as part of its reporting on the Great Recession. Its headline was "A Small Town That Refuses to Die." It was founded in the 1700s.

Ironically, it was money from the settlement of tobacco lawsuits that the Commonwealth of Virginia made available to county commissioners to attract new jobs. When Microsoft expressed interest in Boydton for its data center, the county offered the land for $1 along with tax incentives in exchange for the jobs and taxes Microsoft would pay. Back in 2009 when the company went to the building inspector for a permit, the Mecklenburg county administrator simply took out a piece of stationery and signed it.

Today Microsoft employs 430 people in Boydton. But hiring skilled workers has been a challenge. Trained IT technicians do not want to relocate from the cities. And until just recently the locals have not had the inclination or a place to train.

One of the workers I had lunch with, Nathan Hamm, learned this the hard way. He set up a Microsoft booth at nearby Bluestone High School's job fair. But it was an epic failure. Not one of the soon-to-be graduating seniors stopped by to investigate a career at the data center. Dejected, Nathan packed up his cheerful recruiting materials and headed for the parking lot. A part-time rancher and father of eight, Nathan lived just down the road from the data center and had recently joined Microsoft, first as a vendor and now as an employee. He was asked by his manager—a Chicago transplant—to go out into the community and recruit locals with the qualifications (or a willingness to get them) to join the IT group inside the data center. Demand for the cloud services provided by the data center was growing dramatically. The help-wanted sign was being waved frantically, but applications were scant.

Just as Nathan was about to reach his car, a senior who had not even bothered going to the job fair recognized him and asked how he could apply to work at Microsoft.

"You've got to get qualified," Nathan told him.

"How do I do that?"

"Don't know, but I'll find out."

The student's question led Nathan to Southside Virginia Community College, where he convinced a reluctant administration to add CompTIA technical certifications like A+, Security+, and Cloud+—training that could land the entire graduating class a good job at Microsoft's data center. Unfortunately, it's often harder than just making training available to get people trained for the opportunities that many of us can so easily see. Many students are accustomed to following in the footsteps of their parents, working in the fields and for the businesses that support the farm economy in southern Virginia. High-tech data centers are unfamiliar. Even though the jobs and the training are there to provide full employment for the graduates at Bluestone and Park View, another nearby high school, many students face a difficult job market without tech skills.

To underscore that challenge, the data center's director told me he stopped in a café for lunch one afternoon, and the waitress asked him what Microsoft was doing on that giant property. She told him that prisons provide a lot of jobs for locals, and she seemed perplexed by the very idea of a data center. The director turned to her and said, "Well, a data center is sort of like a prison, only instead of prisoners we protect your data, lots of data." With a healthy dose of skepticism, she flashed a smile and walked away.

The tension between the new jobs that are coming and the old comfortable ones can be felt everywhere. That same year, I overheard the director of a data center in Cheyenne, Wyoming, tell his local team that the region's oil, gas, and coal are dead.

"It's time the kids in this area understand that tech jobs are the future," he lectured.

"Ooh," one of the mid-skilled workers responded, not sure he agreed.

And therein lies a profound tension. If you are a graduating high school student, oil, gas, and coal jobs around Cheyenne will pay upward of $60,000 right out of school, I was told. But they are heavy-labor jobs, like working on an oil rig, that require little additional education and, over time, will pay little more than the initial offer. Jobs built around extracting diminished natural resources also lack the long horizon of other industries. Awakening to this future and preparing for it are essential.

CHAPTER 2

The Career Choice I Made

My mother would smack me for saying it, but we were poor growing up. My brother and I never felt poor, never really wanted for anything, and had parents who worked incredibly hard to make sure that we had what we needed. But the reality was that we lived paycheck to paycheck, had no health insurance most of my childhood, and lived through periods when the only reason we had enough to eat was because of the generosity of our community and my family's ability to hunt and tend the soil in Campbell County, Virginia.

The only thing noteworthy in Gladys proper, at least according to Wikipedia, is Shady Grove, a Federal-style farmhouse built in 1825 that is now listed on the National Register of Historical Places. "Like the interior work, Shady Grove's exterior has an elegance and formality that transcend its provincialism," a historian wrote.

Talk about provincial. Gladys remains a rural, blue-collar place—and it remains one of the most beautiful places on earth to me. The big industries that had been nearby in the middle of the twentieth century were a couple of textile mills, several furniture manufacturers like Thomasville and Lane, and, of course, tobacco farming. My grandmother had worked in those textile mills. My mom and dad both worked at one point or the other in the tobacco fields.

My mom, like her mom, must have been blessed with an overabundance of serotonin because she was just always happy and content, no matter what. She graduated second in her class. After graduating high school, she went to secretarial school in nearby Richmond, the state capital. She started her career as a bank teller in Brookneal, Virginia. After I was born she did part-time work in an accounting office as a tax preparer.

To make ends meet, my dad was a real hustler. He had been a tall, good-looking center for the high school basketball team, had lots of girlfriends, and was superpopular. But like so many others he was drafted into the Vietnam War and returned depressed, a condition that only increased as he grew older. At first, he worked with his father, my grandfather, in the construction business. But working for someone else wasn't for him, so he tried his hand as an entrepreneur—a gas station and convenience store, a trucking company, and later a variety of construction companies. Even though my dad was physically imposing—six feet two, north of three hundred pounds, and incredibly strong from a lifetime playing sports and doing hard labor—he really excelled at the more intellectual side of business. He could bid on a job with shocking speed and accuracy, even before computers were accessible to small-business managers. Even so, those business ventures didn't work out, and we went bankrupt—twice.

To this day, I can remember packing up all our belongings, loading them into the back of a crappy blue Ford Granada, and driving away from the house my father had built with his own hands but could no longer afford. And even now, despite the success I've been fortunate to have in the tech industry, debt makes me anxious; I am loath to take any on, even when financial advisers tell me it would be advantageous to do so.

What I understand now is that the drama surrounding our family went much further and much deeper. We were hardly alone. The town itself was starting to die economically, caught in the crosshairs of technological and political turmoil. I can remember when everyone had jobs, and nearby downtown Brookneal was so busy that there were stoplights, department stores, a local paper full of news. But one by one the textile mills began to close as jobs and factories moved to where labor was cheaper. The big buildings that once bustled with textile workers sat empty. Demand for tobacco dwindled, and the nearby auctions where farmers brought their crop to sell were shuttered. The big furniture plants were the last to close as manufacturing gradually moved overseas. Downtown just disappeared. The local businesses and even the newspaper became shadows of their former selves.

What I remember most, though, and still feel deeply, is the community. People cared about each other. No matter our economic situation, we gave vegetables to others from our garden. My dad stacked firewood for the old church ladies so they would have fuel to heat their homes in the winter. We helped where we could, and folks helped us in return. There was genuine compassion, and I like to think I've carried that with me as an engineer, a manager, and the cofounder with my wife of a family foundation.

Despite the hard times, if you were paying close attention—and I was—there were still a few good jobs around. The industrial engineer who manages the plant and the back-office manager, for example. There were still jobs for those with the education and training to perform the most valuable tasks.

In a small Southern town like Gladys, I was considered kind of weird because I'd rather read the *World Book Encyclopedia* or sit around and contemplate the meaning of infinity. It was a religious town, yet I was always asking in Sunday school about dinosaurs in the Garden of Eden. I was a ball of skepticism and a constant agitator for proof. Most of the answers that I got from the adults to my (undoubtedly irritating) questions were terribly unsatisfying. Even at a young age, I had an abiding faith in the scientific method, in conclusions and theories based on evidence and reproducible experiments. This came naturally to me, but it also was nurtured in a tiny workshop in central Virginia.

Today, when I read about the plight of blue-collar and rural workers, I can't help but think about Shorty Tibbs, my grandfather. It was awesome being the grandson of Shorty Tibbs because everyone in Campbell County seemed to know and care about him, love that improbably extended to me when strangers learned who I was. His real name was Elwood, but his shipmates during World War II nicknamed him for his height, and it stuck. He had a flair for the dramatic. His ship was hit by a Japanese kamikaze fighter plane, which narrowly missed the engine room belowdecks where he was on duty. He returned from the war to work on the family farm and lost his hand in a terrible accident involving a mechanical corn harvester. Despite the setback, Shorty could fix anything, so he decided to start a small appliance repair shop in Brookneal, just down the road from our house in Gladys.

Walking into that dirty, dusty shop as a kid was what I imagined walking into heaven must be like. From the old pinewood floors to the rafters high above were piled old, broken sewing machines, dishwashers, washing machines, and all manner of electronic and mechanical gadgets and widgets in various states of disrepair. One of my favorites among many odd antiques was a foot-powered sewing machine, fully functional but of no practical use by the 1970s, like something from the Island of Misfit Toys. I must have inherited my grandfather's curiosity because his shop was one of the most magical places for me to visit. When we designed our home in California years later, I had the architects reclaim some oak floorboards from a nearby barn to remind me of my grandfather's shop.

I used to watch my grandfather when he worked, not realizing then that his approach was very much that of an engineer or scientist. He would examine a broken piece of consumer technology like a toaster or blender and, through a process of elimination, begin to diagnose what was still functioning and what was broken. Like a computer scientist, he used abstraction to suppress the more complex details that were not relevant to the problem he was addressing. There was no need to work inside the electric motor or heating element, for example, if the problem was one level above that. A broken toaster or blender was just a black box—completely opaque—to the stymied customer who brought it to my grandfather, but for him it was a puzzle to be solved. He could take the problem all the way down through the layers of complexity to bare metal if he had to. For him there was no abstraction boundary. He would just punch through it. There were always new components and functionality to be discovered. He was using the scientific method, an empirical approach, and that inspired me. If he were alive today, I have no doubt that he would fix the advanced hardware and software that now comes in gadgets of every kind. If he didn't understand something, he'd soon master it after watching a few YouTube videos, and employ his dogged persistence.

As inspiring as his engineering feats were, today I am equally enthralled by the larger lessons he taught me. At one level, he showed me the value of making things work, converting something that had been useless into something that was made useful again. Like everyone in our community, he worked incredibly hard. He was self-reliant, and believed in taking care of people. He made the life he wanted, and always did right by his family and neighbors. To me, this is a very American story. Whether you swing a hammer for a living, repair appliances, or come to this country looking for opportunity, these values are part of our American dream.

Perhaps the biggest lesson I learned from my grandfather, and the greatest gift that he gave me, was his approach to problem solving. He was unflappably confident that he could figure things out, that each exploration of a problem, no matter how frustrating, helped him come to a better understanding of himself and his relationship with the world around him, and that human need itself is what makes a problem worth solving. It's this understanding of problem solving and my own humanity that has never once made me wonder what my role is in a world with increasingly capable AI. I'm a human with curiosity about the fascinating canvas of nature and people and our complex creations, with compassion for the problems other humans have, and with a desire to help solve them. To varying extents, this is something we all share. AI is a useful tool for exploring that curiosity and for solving human problems. Neither it, nor anything else, will ever take away that curiosity and compassion.

There are a lot more people with hidden and untapped technical skills like Shorty Tibbs out there in job-deprived rural America and the Rust Belt. My friends Hugh E at the plastics fabrication shop and the Bass brothers on their farm were all tinkerers growing up. Hugh E loved cars and W.B. loved his farm. They tinkered on the things that mattered to them, and today they are sophisticated techs in their own industries. The problem is that our education system treats math, science, and engineering as abstract, intellectual pursuits, not knowledge and skills that can increasingly be applied to almost any passion.

While my friends tinkered with trucks and tractors, I wanted to build video games. It was the early 1980s and video arcade games were beginning to reach even places like Campbell County. I was mystified, and suddenly driven to understand how they worked. I wanted to write a video game, but how? I figured out how to use the computers at school to play games with our attendance and approved-absence systems, which made it possible for me to skip classes for more days than I care to admit. Eventually I got caught, and had to find a more appropriate avenue for my computing ambitions. So I did what a lot of young people in those days were doing. I worked odd jobs, and asked everyone to just give me money for Christmas and birthdays instead of normal gifts, so I could save enough to buy the cheapest computer I could afford, a RadioShack Color Computer II. The CoCo 2—the abbreviated name for this machine—had a tan box with a clunky keyboard, a microprocessor that was kind of slow even by 1983 standards, and a built-in interpreter for the BASIC programming language. It used a television for a monitor, and could be connected to a cassette tape recorder to save and load programs and data. A floppy disk drive was too expensive, and hard disk drives of the era, even if available for the CoCo 2, would have been exorbitantly costly. I had wanted a Commodore 64, but that was simply out of reach. To learn how to program my new computer, I'd go to the Campbell County Public Library hoping to find any books they might have about computer programming, and would pore over magazines for professional programmers like *Dr. Dobb's Journal*. Before I hit adolescence, I somehow had managed to figure out how to code in BASIC and assembly language.

The first serious program I wrote was for the fantasy game

Dungeons and Dragons, which had captivated nerds like me everywhere in the seventies and eighties. I essentially encoded the rule book so that if I were dungeon master, I would have help with the complex task of generating characters, rolling the dice, querying the rules if I had a question, and running an entire campaign. I was quite proud of myself. I must have been eleven or twelve years old.

When it came time for high school, my nerdiness must have caught someone's attention because I was encouraged to apply to central Virginia's Magnet School for Science and Technology, which later became the Governor's School, in nearby Lynchburg. They took two kids from each of the surrounding secondary schools. I applied as a junior and was accepted, but they had only one spot, and I wanted to go with my buddy Eric Holland. I was shy and decided not to accept if it meant going alone. Eric, who is now an exec at Google, very smart, was braver than me. He took the one spot offered to our school. The following year, my senior year, I was accepted again and joined Eric. They should have taken us both to begin with. Hell, our education system should offer a lot more kids the schools they need and deserve. Another friend of ours was equally gifted but bored to death at school. He had problems at home— what sociologists today would call extreme adverse conditions. He dropped out of school but was so smart he found his way into a good job in the IT industry anyway. He committed suicide. On reflection, our entire education system needs to bend to meet the passions of its students, and the opportunity to find the right school should not be arbitrary.

The magnet school gave me the autonomy to pursue my own interests, and I discovered that computer coding was beyond satisfying, almost addictive. I started playing around with both PCs and the Macintoshes in the school's computer lab. For the most part I was just hacking around, but my computer science teacher, Dr. Tom Morgan, saw something else. He encouraged me to participate in Virginia's Junior Engineering Society CS competition. Suddenly it was like someone strapped a jet engine to me, massively accelerating my learning. I began reading every software magazine, programming book, and computer science text I could find, and filling every free moment of my time with coding.

By the time I was a senior in high school I knew I had to go somewhere else. My mom and dad were insistent that I had to go to college, but as the first person in my family to pursue a bachelor's degree, I had a lot to figure out on my own. I was unsure where I should go, how to get in, and, most important, how I was going to pay for tuition. But there was one thing certain—I wouldn't go into significant debt with student loans. So I became a townie at Lynchburg College, the nearest postsecondary option. I lived at home and saved on room and board, although I was so busy that I rarely saw my parents. As a freshman in college I enrolled in junior- and senior-level computer science classes. The college library subscribed to research publications like the *Journal of the Association for Computing Machinery* and *Transactions on Programming Languages and Systems*, in which I immersed myself for long hours even though at first I couldn't imagine a version of myself that would ever understand their research articles. Looking back, it's hard to believe that only a few short years later, while working on my PhD at the University of Virginia, I would submit papers to similar peer-reviewed publications. Lynchburg College gave me a great start. I received my degree in computer science, and I also received a National Science Foundation research opportunity at the National Center for Supercomputing Applications (NCSA), housed on the campus of the University of Illinois Urbana-Champaign, between my junior and senior year.

I had never left the Commonwealth of Virginia before, but there I was, somewhere between Chicago and St. Louis in 1993 with lots of other eager, smart computer science students, including one named Marc Andreessen who had just became familiar with Tim Berners-Lee's open standards for the World Wide Web. That year he released the Mosaic web browser, the forerunner of Netscape. The world was changing, literally, all around me. I was working in NCSA's computational biology research group, writing programs on massively parallel supercomputers like the Thinking Machines CM-5 to help the biophysicists and biochemists in my group better understand how sequences of amino acids folded into the complex three-dimensional structures of proteins.

I had fallen in love with programming, and returned home to Virginia with a lot of energy and a vague plan to become a computer science professor. Though strapped for cash, my parents and I continued to scrape together new computer equipment. I also worked part-time at a start-up, Electronic Design and Manufacturing (EDM), that was entering the highly competitive printed circuit board assembly business. The founder, Robert Roberts, was a brilliant electrical engineer who had gotten his master's degree from MIT, a fact that impressed me to no end. Not only did he seem to know everything from the physics to the engineering, he also was able to teach me. So while I was getting a computer science degree, I was also getting this free degree in electrical engineering at work. Not only that, but I got to participate in building a business from the ground up. I went from assembling shelves for the inventory to writing software for commercial products like Englander woodburning stoves. A woodstove doesn't sound very sophisticated but, in fact, it had an electronics system that fed wood pellets into a combustion chamber using an auger, a fan, and a thermostatic feedback loop. I wrote the software and Robert designed the control board. I played a minor role in EDM's work building the lighting control system for Jerry Falwell's Living Christmas Tree, an enormous six-layer wedding-cake-like platform that supported an entire carol-singing choir. Every year, Falwell's Thomas Road Baptist Church installed something like half a million twinkle lights that followed an astonishing set of patterns that required software instructions and rack upon rack of computer equipment. Talk about Southern engineering!

The last project that I did at EDM was designing the digital controls and software for an electric surgical drill, which was intended for use in outpatient orthopedic surgeries in facilities that didn't have the pneumatics infrastructure that powered most surgical drills at the time. I can still recall the nerve-racking feeling that I was going to get something wrong—a mistake in the code, or too few hardware safety mechanisms—that would result in someone getting hurt.

I managed to save six or seven thousand dollars while working and finishing my undergraduate degree in Lynchburg. A vague sense of wanting to become a computer science professor sent me shopping for a place to study for a master's degree, something Lynchburg didn't offer. Just like when I was confronted with leaving Gladys to attend Governor's School, I still didn't want to leave my family in central Virginia. But curiosity and ambition eventually led me to choose to attend Wake Forest, 120 miles south in Winston-Salem, North Carolina. Wake Forest waived my tuition and offered me a job in the IT department. It was 1996 and Wake Forest was one of the first schools to require every undergraduate in that year's entering class to have a laptop connected to the Internet, something unthinkable even a year earlier. The school wanted students to register for classes, see their schedules, and do research and assignments over an intranet. It was a great idea, but no one knew exactly how to make it happen. The school ran all of its campus information services on an old

Hewlett-Packard minicomputer—registrar information, student records, class schedules—so I needed to write the code for what became their first data warehouse, including what's known as an extract, transfer, and load (ETL) system that would suck all of the data out of the mainframe and make it presentable for students and faculty. My stipend that first year was $800 a month. My rent and car payment cost more than that. Channeling the hustle that I had learned watching my dad, I convinced my bosses in the IT department to give me more hours, and more money so that I wasn't drawing down on my savings quite so fast. I wound up writing a ton of code that powered a bunch of the brand-new campus intranet, and more or less learned as much on the job as I did in the graduate program.

Meanwhile, back home, my dad was struggling to keep his small construction company above water. He'd gotten a contract from the highway department to build a place to store salt for the roads during winter weather. One day his crew was framing the roof for this facility, setting fifty-foot trusses weighing a ton or more. One of these trusses slipped out of the bracket into which it was supposed to be fastened and fell, grazing the side of my dad's head and slamming into his shoulder. A fraction of a millimeter more toward his head and the falling truss would have killed him on the spot. Instead it completely crushed his shoulder and caused a severe concussion. The immediate effect of the brain trauma was badly impaired vision and speech dysfunction. He was a large man who now had to wear thick glasses to correct his sight, and much to the chagrin of the God-fearing nurses and his friends from church, for the most part he could speak only in curse words. He eventually regained both normal vision and speech, but for a time it was something to behold. My parents were living paycheck to paycheck, and I was barely able to meet my own financial commitments. And the deadline to defend my master's thesis was fast approaching. In fact, I had managed to allow myself just a week and half to finish running a bunch of experiments and to write my entire thesis document. This is, unfortunately, a pattern with me, and I managed to pound everything out, no problem. The defense went very well. I had also received news that I'd been given a generous stipend to attend the University of Virginia for my PhD. Right after my thesis defense, my adviser and I headed out to lunch for sushi at Sakura, a nearby restaurant in Winston-Salem. It was May 8, 1998, and the dream of becoming a computer science professor was beginning to materialize. After lunch I drove to my little apartment, walked in the door, and the phone rang. On the other end, back home in Gladys, my mom told me that Dad had died that morning in a car accident. He had just turned fifty. I remember almost nothing about the summer that followed.

By the spring of 2000, Silicon Valley and its red-hot dotcom companies were competing for the attention of every computer science student on every campus in America. The valuations of online pet stores and pharmacies were going through the roof. Within a few months the Internet bubble would burst, and the company that had been at the center of everything, Microsoft, was at risk of being broken in two by a federal court that had heard years of testimony in an acrimonious antitrust lawsuit with the US Justice Department and numerous states' attorneys general. That summer, while still a PhD candidate at UVA, I hopped in my well-used Volkswagen GTI and drove west for the first time to join my adviser, Jack Davidson, for an internship at Microsoft Research in the Programming Language Systems group. Jack is one of the leading researchers in compilers and programming systems. While on sabbatical at Microsoft Research,

Jack helped me land the internship and welcomed me into his group of colleagues.

Once settled in on the corporate campus, I quickly felt like an impostor in every way. My Southern accent and colloquial speech were immediately noticed. It was clear to me that my colleagues had rarely, if ever, had a rural, Southern person in their midst. On TV, yes, but not in person. And the body language, if not the actual language, made me feel like the stereotype that so many people have of Southerners. I thought, *This is a place full of really smart, serious, worldly people, and I don't want them to think I'm a hick.* So I deliberately tried to bury my accent, something I subconsciously do even to this day, though it comes back comfortably in full force when I am with my friends and family back home.

Nevertheless, I had a great time at Microsoft Research, and learned a ton. I also discovered that solving problems on a large scale and having real global impact was intoxicating. I saw my colleagues at Microsoft shipping products that would have an impact on hundreds of millions of people. Yet as a PhD student I might write a paper that, while intellectually very interesting to me, might be read by a few hundred people, and actively used by even fewer. I returned to Virginia after the summer internship with the idea for the first time that maybe a career in academia was not for me.

The road back to the West Coast, however, would take a circuitous route. And that's what love does. In the spring of 2002 I met my future wife, Shannon, through a personal ad on The Onion, the humor website. It only makes sense that the Internet would be involved in some way. After a long series of private messages—hundreds of pages of e-mail that I later bound into a book for her as an anniversary present—we began to date, and realized very quickly that we were right for each other. Shannon was working on her PhD in early modern German history. Not long after we started dating, she told me she had won a prestigious fellowship, which meant she would be returning soon to Germany to do research for her dissertation. Just my luck. I had been alone for so long. Determined not to let her get away, I made a cold call to a professor in Germany who was starting a new computer science program at the University of Göttingen, the city where Shannon would be living. Göttingen is one of the most important math and science universities in the world, with alumni that include Nobel laureates Max Planck and Werner Heisenberg, mathematician David Hilbert, and one of my mathematics heroes, Carl Friedrich Gauss, who was both student and professor there in the late eighteenth and early nineteenth centuries.

"Hey, I'm coming to Göttingen with my girlfriend, who, you know, is a historian," I started. "I just won an Intel PhD fellowship, I have some publications, I've got a recognition of service award from the Association for Computing Machinery. Is there anything I could do in your department?" I quickly had a job offer. My (now) wife to this day still admonishes me that I don't appreciate how truly extraordinary and lucky it was for me to get that job offer.

And just like that, we were a couple living in historic Göttingen, Germany—Shannon cloistered in dank European libraries reading ancient documents and me lecturing on topics like the theory of computation, trying to finish my dissertation and taking German language lessons at the local community college. We led a quiet, spare academic life, partially a reflection of very limited earnings. It was a storybook beginning, and we were very happy, but we were also isolated. Like any young couple, it was also a time of self-discovery. Shannon is an extrovert energized by interacting with people, something she rarely did doing research in near-silent libraries and remote archives. Reflecting on my time at Microsoft, I recalled a colleague who jokingly coined a spoof of Moore's Law, the notion that computing power doubles every eighteen months. Proebsting's Law, named for my colleague Todd Proebsting, was that the best compiler optimization technology basically doubled performance of computer programs once every twenty-four years. Slow. Slow. Slow. I thought, I can either spend the next six months doing something intellectually stimulating—building a bunch of complex optimization software that would improve a synthetic performance benchmark by 5 percent if I were extremely lucky—or I can try to produce something with much more impact in the world.

Google, unbeknownst to me then, would become the perfect resolution to my career crisis. It was 2003, a year before the Internet colossus would go public, and I applied to Google on a lark along with a smattering of other promising but still small web companies. Google seemed completely uncomplicated to me: a simple web page with a box you type questions into. No big deal. I couldn't fathom how these guys would make a nickel, but they flew us from Germany to California for an interview. Shannon dropped me off at the old Google headquarters on Charleston Road and I proceeded to have the time of my life—six fascinating interviews and a gourmet lunch prepared by chef Charlie Ayers, who started with the Grateful Dead and went on to culinary fame as executive chef at Google after the original forty employees handed him the victory in a cook-off.

I climbed back in our rental car at the end of the day, and Shannon just looked at me.

"I haven't seen you this happy in months," she said, beaming.

Google offered me a job. In those days, they had a philosophy of hiring folks without a particular job in mind, and then exposing them to projects to see what interested them. I joined as a software engineer, and we were given the choice of moving to either Silicon Valley or New York City. We had enjoyed living in a walkable European city, so we elected to move from Germany to New York. I had promised myself to find work that had impact, so I frequently raised my hand whenever there was a new project. One such project involved machine learning and the emerging field of online advertising. One week I traveled back to Silicon Valley to shadow some of the engineers within AdWords, predecessor of the company's $100 billion Google Ads business. The idea then was to make AdWords a self-service platform so that anyone could use it to buy online ads. But human involvement was a big constraint to growth. We had a variety of contractual obligations and policy guidelines governing what ads we could run where. Even though some of these obligations and policies were sometimes relatively simple, we had armies of summa cum laude college graduates doing mind-numbing review work. And in some cases, asking them to review inappropriate content. You can easily imagine how some of this inappropriate content might be difficult for humans to review. Google powered the advertising on AOL, then a highly popular service, and AOL had a zero-tolerance policy on adult content. At some points we had $50 million or more in ad inventory just sitting in a queue waiting to be reviewed and approved. These were early days for commercial machine learning, a subset of artificial intelligence, but it was the perfect solution for this problem. I built a bunch of machine learning systems for adult content detection as well as software for identifying the regulated space of pharmacological ads. The new, automated ads review system that included my content classifiers helped unlock our ads inventory and saved the company an enormous amount of money. Our team won a Google Founders' Award for this project.

A reader might be wondering, *You won a prestigious honor for AI that replaces humans, yet you are writing a book about how AI will help human workers.* Indeed! In fact, this is an excellent exemplar of how artificial intelligence can augment human capabilities and result in better, more productive work. You see, humans could not efficiently keep up with the workload and became a constraint to productivity and growth. In addition, they were miserable doing mundane, repetitive, and in some cases objectionable work. With the new machine learning applications doing this work instead, Google was able to move these employees onto work that required human talents like creativity and empathy rather than monotonous, soul-destroying tasks.

I had unintentionally gotten on a rocket ship. Within a year Google had its initial public stock offering, which would lead to the company reaching hundreds of billions in market capitalization. I rose in the ranks of management, switching back and forth between the ad business and the search business. But after four years at Google, I began looking around at what it would take to become head of engineering somewhere, and decided that helping a small company get big was the best avenue. One afternoon, Google's CEO, Eric Schmidt, whose office was located near mine, walked by and asked if I'd like to see one of Apple's announced but not yet released iPhones. "Hell, yeah!" It was clear to me that mobile was going to take off, and soon a little company called AdMob that was building an advertising platform for mobile devices invited me to take over its engineering department. I got off one rocket and onto another. Over the next couple of years, AdMob became the largest mobile advertising platform in the world, an important tool in the mobile ecosystem, allowing developers to monetize their work and to market their applications to sign up new customers. The work was challenging and exhilarating. We were doubling our traffic and other business metrics once every five months, in an all-out sprint to build technology that could keep up with exploding demand.

As things so often go in Silicon Valley, a year later Google bought AdMob for $750 million after another company made a quiet, but ultimately unsuccessful, bid to acquire us. Suddenly I was back at Google. In the ever-revolving door of high tech, my old friend from Google with whom I'd worked on ads automation, Deep Nishar, had left to become head of product at LinkedIn, where they needed a new head of engineering to help scale what had become by 2011 the world's largest professional network. A new rocket was launching.

Over the years, through a variety of positions, I always kept my story, my CV, up-to-date. After anything that happened to me, right away I would go in and meticulously document it so that I understood my career in relationship to other people I admired. *Okay, well, that's the sort of teacher I would like to be when I become a computer science professor,* I'd tell myself when inspecting an academic's resume. Or, *Oh no, I'm so far away from this person's achievements.* I would use my CV as a chart of my progress.

When I joined LinkedIn in 2011, my wife said, "You know, this is the most ironic thing. You're working for a company that's all about people telling their employment stories to the outside world. Your career and your fixation on careers have converged."

At LinkedIn, the news feed is important, but more important is the professional identity that you establish for yourself, and the story that you're telling the outside world about who you are, your interests, and what you're good at. Our shared stories are the maps to both present and future, and the bedrock of how we can function from teams to communities to sprawling societies. Our shared stories are such a fundamental part of being *Homo sapiens* that it can be easy for us to forget their importance. The momentum of our day-to-day lives can cause us to move on, forgetting shared wisdom or accepting discredited old stories.

One of the most important narratives is the one you use to inspire a large group of folks to accomplish a common objective. In the 1990s, anthropologist Robin Dunbar suggested that humans have a cognitive limit, known now as Dunbar's number, on the number of people any individual can know and understand the relationships between in a group. If you've ever tried to lead a group of humans larger than 120 to 150 people, you may have noticed that something is different about these bigger groups. In groups up to this size, a manager might be able to know each member of the team, what they are doing, the boundaries of their capabilities and trustworthiness, their personality quirks, etc. Moreover, every member of the team can have this knowledge about every other member of the team. This trust radius allows leaders to set goals and objectives, assign accountability, and develop reasonable expectations about how work will proceed. It also allows individuals who are accountable for a task whose completion depends on others to have reasonable expectations about how others will collaborate with them.

Storytelling allowed our ancestors to share a vision for the future and to organize themselves around that vision in a way that other human species were not able to replicate. This ability to work toward a common objective with large numbers of other individuals, most of whom our ancestors did not or could not know, is what allowed *Homo sapiens* to succeed in ways that other species of humans could not and laid the foundation for modern societies.

Modern corporations themselves are works of fiction, if you will, brought to life because their employees, investors, business partners, governing jurisdictions, and customers all share a belief that they are real. This pattern of shared belief in the reality of corporations has been around for long enough, is so ubiquitous, and is governed by so many precedents and covenants that talking about corporations as stories seems a bit silly and philosophical. Nonetheless, corporations would not exist were it not for a complex set of stories that large numbers of people choose to believe are true. I'm not suggesting corporations are people, too, but I am suggesting they reflect the stories of their leaders, employees, and customers.

Less philosophically, developing a story about a future that you would like to see realized is at the heart of leading a large team. Telling an inspiring story allows every member of the team to make the story their own. A good story helps the entire team invest in a set of actions that in aggregate allow the story to be realized over long periods of time, involving the efforts of large numbers of individuals. The absence of a clear narrative about what you're trying to accomplish, and why doing so requires a large group of individuals, is a recipe for disaster.

What was true for prehistoric *Homo sapiens*, and is true for corporations and modern organizations of all flavors, is equally true for even larger groups of human beings. Industries are based on stories about how a common set of efforts can produce benefits for companies, their customers, and the societies in which they operate. Stable economic and political systems are based on stories that we've told and refined over time about how we can fairly trade with one another, how we collectively solve the problems of community, and how we react to and resolve conflicts.

For industries to work, and for economic and political systems to remain stable, a preponderance of people must believe in and accept the stories of their existence. This requires that individuals understand how the stories of these large structures intersect and impact their own story, and that they choose to believe and accept them. If these large structures are to thrive, individuals must feel inspired by their stories. Moreover, individuals must also be empowered to ask questions about the nature of the story—who wrote it, what assumptions the story is based on, and how new characters and new voices might contribute to the narrative. Stories are always unfolding; being rewritten, redirected, and, yes, reprogrammed when new information becomes available.

One of the most important and suspenseful stories in each of our lives is the one of our careers. Whether these stories are prospective works of fiction, aspirations of where we want to go and what should be our preparations for the journey; or retrospective memoirs trying to make sense of where we are and how we got there, our career stories are indispensable. I've always been fascinated with these stories in particular, both the aspirational and the retrospective. Enabling folks to tell their stories at scale, and then using the manifestation of those stories—a professional profile—to help folks connect to opportunity is one valuable use of social media. LinkedIn, for example, has brokered countless connections between professionals and workers in every industry—high tech and low tech—over the past decade.

Ironically, the very technology that LinkedIn uses to connect people with opportunity is the same technology about which there is so much anxiety today: AI, and in particular a set of technologies called machine learning, algorithms and statistical models that accomplish certain tasks on their own based on pattern recognition and inference.

I knew nothing about machine learning in 2003 when I left the academy to join Google and started working on systems that could review ads with human-equivalent accuracy. I had spent my time in graduate school becoming an expert in programming languages and compiler optimization, or programs that efficiently and effectively translate the source computer language into the target language. But my first project at my new job required me to become familiar with a new bag of computer science tricks. I worked on a number of projects at Google that incorporated varying degrees of machine learning. Eventually, I led a team at Google that at the time was most likely operating the largest machine learning system in the world, a system that allowed us to estimate the likelihood that someone would click on a search ad so that we could accurately run the search ads auction.

Over the past fourteen years, machine learning has played a part in every technology system that I've built at every company I've worked for. At LinkedIn, it helps show you the right job if you're a job seeker, to render a high-quality feed for you when you visit the homepage or mobile apps, to detect when LinkedIn profiles are fraudulent, and in many other ways to optimize how members experience the site. AI, in the form of machine learning algorithms, played a role in each of those many jobs LinkedIn helped members get. AI at LinkedIn, employed by other job sites and by search engines, helps millions of people find jobs in non-AI fields.

AI's story is so compelling at the moment because of scale, and what that scale is allowing machine learning algorithms to do. We have never had more data and more computing power than we have now, which is allowing breakthroughs in AI and machine learning that researchers have been waiting decades to see. These huge data sets are side effects of the ubiquity of Internet services and mobile devices. And the huge increase in computing power is being driven by cloud computing, and for a certain type of machine learning, by specialized CPUs, first intended to make video games better, called GPUs—graphics processing units. Because of growing data volumes, GPUs, and large-scale cloud computing, our AI systems can now perform a variety of tasks—game playing, translating between human languages, converting spoken language to text, labeling the objects in images or videos, question answering, planning, diagnosing medical conditions, etc.—at levels approaching or exceeding human ability.

LinkedIn's business mission and its hundreds of millions of users also built a great deal of value in the marketplace. By the spring of 2016, its professional network had attracted some of the best-funded suitors on the planet. As a member of LinkedIn's senior leadership team, I was part of the deliberations on a potential merger. We had a responsibility to shareholders to get the highest bid, but we also needed to find the best fit for our customers, many of whom had built their livelihoods on the LinkedIn platform since Reid Hoffman had founded the company in 2003. Our CEO, Jeff Weiner, had been there almost ten years, and I was approaching six years. We had poured heart and soul into the company, which meant the merger and acquisition process for us was emotional and scary. This was our baby. We looked carefully at all offers, but one company emerged as the best fit—Microsoft. Our mission statements, "Connect the world's professionals to make them more productive and successful" and "Empower every person and organization on the planet to achieve more," were entirely compatible, and Microsoft's CEO, Satya Nadella, really impressed us. Ultimately, our board decided to go with the Microsoft offer. Next came the difficult task of communicating the deal to unsuspecting employees, who were unavoidably caught by surprise. Our job as leaders then became one of allaying anxiety about a new trajectory for the company and staying focused on building new features for our customers. By then we were all exhausted, and next came a whole new round of stress: awaiting regulatory approval for the deal to close.

After we had signed the definitive agreement to be acquired by Microsoft, but before the deal closed, I decided to take time off in June 2016 to recharge and look ahead. Alas, I discovered I will never be a good vacationer or retired person. Instead of kicking up my feet, I decided to set up a new organization called Behind the Tech, an online resource to tell the stories of the people who design and engineer the hardware and software in today's world. At the time, as head of engineering and operations at LinkedIn, I had more than three thousand people reporting to me. I got to see all of the amazing work being done by relatively unsung heroes, and I was eager to start telling their stories to help inspire a new generation of engineers and computer scientists. The project was also a creative channel for my storytelling—my writing and photography. The project's singular purpose is to acknowledge the makers of technology and what they do. My hope was to remove some of the mystery surrounding the creation of technology and ensure that history doesn't forget key details about who was doing what at a time of pivotal and rapid change in our industry and society. In 2018 I expanded Behind the Tech to include podcasts, which has been a wonderful way to have conversations with people I admire and to share their stories and points of view with others.

One of the interesting things about doing Behind the Tech, both the website and the podcast, is that just by talking to some of the folks working behind the scenes on technology, you discover that everyone's journey and story is just a little bit different. My colleagues Diane Tang and Carrie Grimes Bostock, with whom I worked at Google, both played foundational roles in helping Google build its machine learning prowess in search and ads. Diane grew up in North Carolina, the daughter of a biochemist and a computer engineer. She was exposed to computers as a child, but her parents didn't push her to choose a career in computing. As an undergrad at Harvard, she started as an applied math major, but became increasingly interested in computers and changed her major in her junior year to computer science, and went on to get a computer science PhD at Stanford. After earning an archaeology degree at Harvard, Carrie went to Stanford to get a PhD in statistics. Both wound up at Google, and because both did their doctoral work on mathematical modeling and data analysis, albeit in different fields, both wound up doing work on the early, large-scale machine learning systems at Google.

My brief June 2016 sabbatical was the first time I had taken off work, ostensibly with no plan, since I joined Google in November 2003. I had spent twelve and half years focusing near maniacally on work, and hadn't taken more than a weekend for a breather in my transitions from Google to AdMob, AdMob to Google, and Google to LinkedIn. I was now the senior vice president of engineering and operations at a midsize company with hundreds of millions of users that had just been acquired for $26 billion by an enormous company I had last been at as an intern. On reflection, I had experienced the American dream. Why?

I had been plenty lucky, sure. But despite my long odds, I'm male. I'm white. I was born in the United States and hit adolescence at a moment in time when the whole world was excited about computers and technology. Even though I was born in the rural South at a time when much of the agricultural and manufacturing economy was on the decline, far, far away from the urban innovation centers where the economies of the future were emerging and thriving, I was a member of a close-knit community where folks cared about the well-being of one another, and where I always felt welcome and valued. I had a stable, loving family. Neither of my parents was technical, or understood exactly what my fascination with computers was all about. But they were supportive and made a bunch of sacrifices to try to help me pursue my interest. Moreover they were always supportive to the extent of their abilities in whatever crazy direction my curiosity turned. We were never so poor that I was existentially distracted by food scarcity or housing security. We didn't have health insurance for most of my childhood, and I didn't have consistent health insurance as an adult until I joined Google in 2003. But I was lucky never to have suffered a serious illness.

I went to small, rural, underequipped public schools that often didn't know how to handle precocious kids like me in the same class as students who were struggling. But I was incredibly fortunate to have a few champions in these schools who cared about me, who did their best to handle a kid who struggled to find scholastic challenges. And in my senior year of high school, I was lucky enough to get into a science and technology school that really showed me that I could pursue a career in computer science. Without these experiences, my career and life may have followed an entirely different path, and I might not be sitting here in Redmond, Washington, writing this book.

My dad had died young, but I was already an adult when he passed away; I had the ability to take care of myself and some limited capacity to take care of my mom and brother. My dad had many failed attempts at starting businesses, and when his businesses failed, it was really tough. But no matter how bad the fall, he always got back up, and he worked harder than anyone I've ever known to provide for his family. I was incredibly lucky to be able to learn from his resilience, determination, and love for his family.

Even though much of the success I've had is due to luck that others did not and do not have, a bunch of the luck that I experienced can be manufactured for more people if we as a society choose to invest. The nonprofit family foundation that my wife runs invests in programs that holistically address the conditions that tend to trap people in poverty cycles. Some of the entirely fixable conditions that can prevent children and adults alike from achieving their full potential are food scarcity, housing insecurity, lack of health insurance and access to high-quality health care, access to high-quality education, and the absence of mentors and role models who can help you make better choices and help you navigate through hardship. Many, perhaps all, of these are things where AI can eventually help. On the policy front, we could use a lot more direct government investment in eliminating these success blockers, and new government investments and regulatory incentives in AI technologies could reduce the cost of eliminating these success blockers for everyone. Dollars invested in these things could go a very long way in creating a lot more luck for a lot of individuals, and more of the conditions that we need so that more folks can create economic prosperity for themselves, their families, and their communities.

All that said, many had the same luck that I did, and still had a different journey. I've always looked at my dad's story and wondered how someone smarter than me, harder-working than me, struggled so much harder than I did to find financial security. Every time that someone suggests I might in some way deserve what I have, I immediately think about my dad, and wonder how anyone could think I'm worthy of wealth when my dad literally worked himself to death, living job to job, paycheck to paycheck. I've always prided myself on working as hard as I can to provide for my family, to do things that fulfill my curiosity, and that make a difference in the lives of others. But I've always struggled with the fact that the value assigned by society to my hard work is somehow different from the value assigned to my father's.

Even though some of that difference in the value assigned to our respective work is characteristic of our economy, a discussion of whose justness and defensibility could easily fill another book, some of the difference, practically speaking, might come down to some choices that the two of us made differently.

My dad, like many young folks, including me, was bored with school and anxious to start his life after graduating high school. He had applied and been accepted to Lynchburg College, my alma mater. He chose, however, not to go to college, and was shortly thereafter drafted to go to Vietnam. My dad was completely determined that I was going to go to college, no matter what. When I worked for him on construction jobs as a teenager, he gave me the hardest jobs he could find—running a jackhammer in a dank basement to break up a floor that we were replacing, or carrying shingles up a ladder all day long in the hot and humid Virginia summer. Even though I was proud of my father and the work he did, and saw great dignity in building things for others, he wanted to make sure that I understood how hard that path could be.

While college is becoming increasingly expensive, with student debt ballooning, and clear evidence is showing that college alone isn't a guarantee of economic prosperity particularly for those coming from low-income backgrounds,[7] research shows that on average there is a million-dollar difference in lifetime earnings between high school and college graduates.[8] I wish my dad could have attended college. I'm very grateful that he pushed me as hard as he did, and that despite my fear of debt, I found a combination of scholarships, grants, student loans, and part-time jobs that allowed me to pursue a college degree.

Not surprisingly, research also shows that choice of major

has a bigger economic impact than the choice to attend college. There is a $3.4 million difference in lifetime earnings between the highest-paying majors and the lowest. It sometimes surprises folks when I tell them that I wasn't always sure that I wanted to be a computer scientist. As a teenager, I was very, very seriously into comic books and wanted to be an illustrator. I had more brochures for design schools than I did for engineering schools. I loved both programming and drawing, but wound up choosing programming because it was easier for me as a young person to visualize a predictable career path with a computer science degree. When I was an undergraduate, I was in love with English literature, and took as many courses as I could in writing and literature as a computer science major. When it came time to think about graduate school, I had a moment when I thought that I might pursue a PhD in English literature. Again, I loved both literature and computer science and could have been happy on either path. I ultimately chose computer science because I could more clearly imagine a career path for myself with that degree.

The moral of this story is not "always choose STEM over the humanities." I join with others who've argued that the humanities will become increasingly important in the AI era—that humanities will be in demand for building AI, and humanities will be valuable outside of AI since they embody human skills so difficult for machines to replace. The moral also is not to always make decisions about what to do with your life based solely on maximizing economic returns. In fact, it would be a sad, sad thing for humanity if we all made our choices this way. That said, I do think that everyone should consider the economics of the choices that they're making. There is plenty of conflicting advice out there ranging from "choose your passion and everything will work out in the end" to "you should choose a nice, safe degree like nursing, medicine, law, science, engineering, or business; everything else is too risky." Real choices for real individuals tend to be a lot more complicated and nuanced. Everyone should try to get as much data and good advice as possible and spend some quality time reflecting before making expensive life choices with very large consequences.

When my dad got back from Vietnam, the impulse to get his life started was perhaps even stronger than when he chose to forgo college. He got a job in construction, his father's profession. He got married, borrowed money to build a house and buy a car, and then shortly after, he and my mom had their first child, me. He still wasn't entirely sure what he wanted his career to be, nor what his financial destiny was going to look like, but because a job, a house, a car, a wife, and a kid were what he thought defined a good life, that's what he pursued as quickly as he could. On the one hand, all these things are great, and I'm very grateful that my dad found and married my mom, and that they had me and my brother. On the other hand, in a very short period of time he took on a very large of amount of permanent responsibility that demanded all his attention before he really understood his own path to contentment and how he would financially support all the responsibility that he had assumed. If he had waited to figure out not just what life he wanted, but how he would be able to sustainably support that life in a way that would leave him content and fulfilled, he might have had a very different experience.

I had a moment as a young adult where I struggled with the same thing. As I was preparing to graduate from Lynchburg College, I was tired and sick of struggling to pay for things. Even though I had scholarships, grants, and student loans, I still spent most of my hours outside of school working a part-time job to make ends meet, to pay for food, my car, clothes, and books while living in my parents' basement rent-free. From that vantage point, graduate school looked like a painful grind. I wanted a nicer car, a nicer computer, and the freedom to do more of the things I thought I cared about. So instead of going straight to graduate school, I took a job with a company in Lynchburg as an engineer as soon as I graduated with my bachelor's degree in computer science.

I will be forever grateful for that job at EDM. I learned how to be a real engineer there, and how a small business really works. Perhaps more important, I learned that the things that the job allowed me to do, like buying a sweet little 1995 Volkswagen GTI VR6, were not enough to make me forget my dream of going to graduate school and doing "real" computer science. So after four years of working at EDM part-time and two years working there full-time, I left to go to grad school with a few thousand bucks in the bank, a new car payment, and an $800/month graduate student stipend. I spent the next five years making almost nothing, living in cruddy apartments, avoiding getting health insurance coverage I couldn't afford, and stressing out about unpredictable expenses because I had no safety net.

But I was happy. Even though it might have seemed to many of the folks around me that I didn't have the things that make for a good life—the regular job, the house, the wife, the kids—I felt like I was working to make myself more capable of doing the job that I wanted to do, and making myself more credible to the types of places where I wanted to work. To me that seemed like a perfectly reasonable trade-off.

My favorite among many memorable Warren Buffett quotes is "Ultimately, there's one investment that supersedes all others: Invest in yourself." If anything, the different choices that my dad and I made were mostly about the extent to which we were investing our time and money (or opportunity cost) in ourselves. Without having ever heard Warren Buffett's advice, my dad believed that he hadn't invested enough in himself, and he was going to make sure I did. Without self-investments, without the time spent acquiring skills, getting an education, and seeking out learning experiences, many of the opportunities I was lucky enough to be present for would have been beyond my grasp.

My wife got similar self-investment advice from her undergraduate adviser. She was graduating from a small liberal arts school with a degree in history and was trying to figure out how to get admitted to the PhD program at Harvard. Her adviser told her, "Go do something to make yourself interesting," after which she moved to Germany for five and half years, mastered the language, worked as a book and museum document translator (among many other jobs), and earned her master's in history from the University of Münster. After completing her degree she returned to the States, where she did indeed get accepted to the history PhD program at Harvard, although for my own selfish reasons, I'm very glad she chose to go to the University of Virginia, where we met.

Which brings me to the final different choice that my dad and I made. My dad was born, raised, and lived his life in Campbell County, Virginia. At some point I knew that if I wanted to have the career I desired I would have to go where the jobs were. That was a bitter decision for me, and it took a long time to make. I love my home in Virginia, and I miss the proximity of my extended family and old friends. I've lived in Gladys, Virginia; Champaign-Urbana, Illinois; Winston-Salem, North Carolina; Eagan, Minnesota; Charlottesville, Virginia; Redmond, Washington; Göttingen, Germany; New York City; and Silicon Valley for work. The opportunity to visit all those places, to meet new folks and learn new things about different parts of the country and world, and to have the ability to learn from the work that I did in each of those places has been incredibly rewarding. But, ironically, I don't really like change. If I had had an opportunity to stay in any of these places and still have the career I wanted, I never would have left.

One of the things that I'm most hopeful about with the future of AI and automation is that technology will create more opportunities in more places, like those at my friend Hugh E's workplace in Brookneal, Virginia, that didn't exist when I was early in my career trying to figure out what to do next.

Back to work, by the end of 2016, we completed our regulatory review and, suddenly, LinkedIn was part of Microsoft. The $196 per share, $26.2 billion acquisition was enormous. A new era for both companies had begun. Naturally, I started wondering what would be next. As Coach K, Duke's legendary basketball coach, is fond of saying, "Next play." What was my next play going to be? A legend at Microsoft, Qi Lu, had just announced he was leaving the company for China's AI giant, Baidu, and Satya Nadella was looking for someone to help look across Microsoft's many products and services in order to think about the company's overall technology vision. The role he had in mind for me was chief technology officer (CTO), which is an interesting-sounding role but, in fact, it has very little operational responsibility. Unlike all of my previous roles, I would not be running engineering, but instead would have the luxury of time and resources to study hard engineering problems and offer fresh ideas and support to my colleagues. I see the CTO job as helping my colleagues advance the company's tech agenda. I have a different vantage point because I look across the entire company, not just one product or service. Where do we need to fill gaps or build something that doesn't exist? How do we harness all of our assets to shape a future that is good for business and society?

Answering those questions would mean spending time both inside and outside of Microsoft. It would mean listening to others' stories.

CHAPTER 3

Stories of Revival

Every May, Microsoft hosts its annual Build conference, a gathering of thousands and thousands of software developers. Google, Apple, everyone does the same thing for their community of developers, usually around the same time of year. The goal is to excite some of our most important business partners by demonstrating our latest and greatest new devices and platforms for which we want them to go home and start building applications that will attract more and more users to our ecosystem.

For as long as I can remember, the Microsoft Build conference was mostly about building products on top of Windows. But not 2018. AI was becoming an increasingly important part of the services we offered and how our customers were doing business. We worked together as a senior leadership team with CEO Satya Nadella to reshape the year's conference into a sort of "All AI, All the Time" funfest. "There is no shortage of data- and AI-related announcements and demonstrations," ZDNet wrote. "If you needed proof that both are crucial to Microsoft's success, even eclipsing Windows in importance, this year's show is it."

Sure enough, we showed off some trailblazing new cloud-based Azure Machine Learning tools that significantly accelerated the algorithms used in AI models. We demonstrated a dizzying array of breakthrough AI technologies that, when fully understood, move us further, faster, and deeper into that AI future so dreamed of by some or so dreaded by others.

One announcement that stood out that week was AI for Accessibility, a $25 million, five-year program to put AI tools in the hands of developers to accelerate the development of accessible and intelligent AI solutions to benefit the one-billion-plus people with disabilities around the world. AI can be a game changer for people with disabilities as we watch the AI community expand its use of computers to hear, see, and reason with impressive accuracy. The previous year we had announced AI for Earth, a comprehensive program to apply artificial intelligence toward unlocking solutions to climate, water, agriculture, and the biodiversity issues facing our planet.

That same week, Microsoft researchers gathered in Building 99, the nondescript offices on campus in Redmond that house thousands of AI and Research experts, to hear a lecture by Tess Posner. Tess runs AI4ALL, a nonprofit focused on developing diverse talent in the AI field. With AI investment from companies like Microsoft, Google, IBM, and others expected to reach $3 trillion over the next decade, her organization is working to attract students into universities to pursue AI degrees.

"It will be embedded in our daily life," she says, preaching to the choir. She notes that 85 percent of Americans are already using some form of AI.

It's her intent this day to elevate the AI discussion beyond business applications, and to call into question the purpose of and ethical considerations for AI development. She describes the need for "moon shots" to solve a wide range of pressing problems from water to agriculture to climate change and bio-diversity. She also describes the need for addressing big risks, including bias in algorithms, diversity in the talent that makes AI, and access as well as understanding of the AI. She reports embarrassingly low numbers of women, African Americans, and Latinos in AI and machine learning. As a result of under-representation, AI does a poor job in facial recognition and other algorithms.

The investigative news unit, ProPublica, reported in 2016 that software used across the country to predict future crim-inals is, in fact, biased against African Americans. "In fore-casting who would reoffend, the algorithm made mistakes with black and white defendants at roughly the same rate but in very different ways. The formula was particularly likely to falsely flag black defendants as future criminals, wrongly labeling them this way at almost twice the rate as white de-fendants. White defendants were mislabeled as low risk more often than black defendants."

To help remedy this, AI4ALL offers a range of education and training programs designed to recruit women and mi-norities into AI fields. One example is Stephanie Tena-Meza, a daughter of a Mexican-American farmworker who in tenth grade founded an AI club in her school and attended an AI education program offered at Stanford. Tess Posner's program is doing good and important work, but given the enormous spread of AI into every sector of society, I fear it is not enough to reach all the communities that must be represented in AI development. To make it truly representative will require a robust public sector commitment. Tess and AI4ALL are help-ing to show the way.

———

I arrived in Memphis, Tennessee, late on a Monday night. As I stepped off the airplane, I could smell freshly cut grass. In water-starved Northern California where I now live, big lawns are rare. Not so in the South, where the warmth and rain of spring and summer bring with them the chore of taming unruly fescue into neat and tidy lawns. That smell of freshly cut grass for me was the essence of summer and, odd as it might sound, makes me all kinds of nostalgic.

Even though this was an especially busy week—earlier in the day on that Monday, I had been behind stage helping with Microsoft's Build conference—I had been invited to Memphis by J.D. Vance to participate in an event called Rise of the Rest. J.D., the author of *Hillbilly Elegy*, is also the managing partner of the Rise of the Rest Fund, which he cofounded with AOL's Steve Case. Rise of the Rest's mission is to help support entrepreneurs in all the places that they may choose to build their businesses, not just those in big urban innovation centers like Silicon Valley and New York City. I jumped at the chance to participate.

Why? Start-ups are the engine of job growth for the United States economy. Over the past three decades, start-ups have created forty million jobs. Moreover, those forty million jobs were the only net new jobs created in the US economy.[9] Other segments of the economy employ large numbers of folks, but businesses in these segments are constantly turning over. Half of the Fortune 500 churns out every twenty-five years, and for every new restaurant that pops up, there's another going out of business. Start-ups play an important role in our economy, not just through the innovations that they bring to market, but through the jobs that they create. Doing what we can to support entrepreneurs is a worthy goal.

But it's not good enough just to support start-ups in the geographies where the innovation economy is already working well, like Silicon Valley. If we want the economy to be uniformly strong across the United States, and for opportunity to be available throughout the country, we must do a better job supporting entrepreneurs around the country, particularly in regions not already equipped for high-tech entrepreneurship through an abundance of access to the resources that help start-ups thrive. In 2016, 75 percent of venture funding went to Silicon Valley, New York City, and Boston, with 50 percent going just to Silicon Valley. Venture funding in Tennessee that same year was less than 1 percent of the total pool invested. And start-up success roughly mirrors this funding distribution as measured by new start-ups created, public offerings, start-ups acquired by bigger companies, etc.

This concentration of start-ups in a handful of regions is problematic for a bunch of different reasons. In his excellent book *The New Geography of Jobs*, Enrico Moretti observed that the economy in the US is bifurcating into two parts. One of these economies is the urban innovation center, typified by places like Silicon Valley (tech), New York City (media and finance), and San Diego (biotech). These urban innovation centers have booming economies, significant job creation for both skilled and unskilled workers, and network effects that serve to reinforce what's already working, thereby creating continued growth into the foreseeable future. The other economy is everything else, typified by cities and towns whose economies and job marketplaces are stagnant or on the decline, and with their own set of network effects including failing schools, obsolete or soon-to-be-obsolete industries, and dilapidated infrastructure that make it increasingly difficult over time to support the types of activities that can create growth.

My friend Reid Hoffman's book *Blitzscaling* goes into

greater depth describing the network effects of Silicon Valley (and of Beijing and Shenzhen in China). Silicon Valley's network effects for tech companies and workers are so strong that it is one of the very few places in the world that can support very rapid scaling, or *blitzscaling*, the type of growth that you see some companies pursue as they work to move from start-up with tiny impact to enterprise with global, or even planetary, impact.

As someone with experience in both Silicon Valley and the rural South, I want to figure out how to prevent these network effects from ripping our country in two. I want to figure out how we can build an economy that supports a rapid pace of innovation *and* access to opportunity for everyone. I would have loved a vibrant tech scene near my childhood home in central Virginia. I tried over and over again not to leave. But by 2003 I had been supporting my mom on a grad student's stipend for five years, and I had asked my girlfriend to marry me, and we were planning to start a family of our own. At that point, hoping that one of the limited opportunities available in Virginia would work seemed like a bad strategy, given the mounting responsibility. So when the opportunity to go to work at Google arrived, we moved to New York, and then a few years later to Silicon Valley. Trading off proximity to family, friends, and a familiar way of life for a dream job and hope for a fulfilling career was one of the hardest decisions I've ever made.

So I found myself dog-tired, early in the morning in Memphis, getting on a tour bus with Steve Case, today's organizer of Rise of the Rest through his investment firm Revolution, J.D., and a bunch of energetic locals for a day of meetings with entrepreneurs in Memphis to learn about their journeys and their businesses, and to try to figure out how I could help.

Our first stop was breakfast with elected officials, business leaders, community builders, and members of the Memphis start-up community at The Kitchen restaurant at Shelby Farms Park. Sitting at the table next to mine was Fred Smith, founder, chairman, and CEO of FedEx, one of the great entrepreneurial successes of the twentieth century and 100 percent the product of Memphis. FedEx is yet another great example of why it is advantageous for the conditions enabling entrepreneurship to exist more uniformly throughout the country.

Memphis has a long history as a transportation and logistics hub. Sitting on the Mississippi River, above the river's floodplain, at the nexus of several rail lines and interstate highways, and hosting a major international airport, Memphis has been an important hub for moving goods domestically and internationally since the early nineteenth century. Today, Memphis has the second-busiest port on the Mississippi River; sits at the nexus of I-40, I-55, and a number of north–south and east–west rail routes; and has the world's largest cargo airport. This history of transportation and logistics, existing infrastructure and expertise, and geographic location were all factors that made Memphis a great place to start FedEx. These factors also led to a set of small-scale network effects that have allowed FedEx to flourish alongside the talent and infrastructure necessary to allow Memphis to continue to be an important logistics hub into the future.

The Kitchen restaurant where we had breakfast is owned by Kimbal Musk, Elon Musk's younger brother, one of a growing number of folks with careers in tech who have made a reverse migration. Kimbal was born in South Africa and had a successful career as an entrepreneur and investor living in Silicon Valley and New York City. He moved to Boulder, Colorado, where he founded a tech company (LiveWire) and opened his first Kitchen restaurant. In addition to restaurants, Kimbal created the Kitchen Community, which has built over five hundred learning gardens throughout the country to help children better understand food, and to give them access to fresh, nutritious produce.

In a way Kimbal's move to Memphis is a logical waypoint on his journey as an entrepreneur and philanthropist. Memphis sits at the center of fifteen million acres of fertile soil and an agricultural industry that is being transformed by tech and entrepreneurs. When he arrived in Memphis, Kimbal found that only a fraction of the fifteen million acres was planted in crops that yielded "real food." Most of the land at that time was planted in soy, grains, and cotton; in other words, crops that had to be processed before being used. For a restaurateur, particularly one with a deep commitment to local, organic food, this wasn't great. How would he get the fresh, organic produce that was the cornerstone of The Kitchen's menu? These bulk crops aren't necessarily great for farmers, either, given that soy, grains, and cotton have a low margin and must compete for customers in a tough global commodities market. But planting different crops is risky: growing a more diverse set of crops is more challenging to manage, and getting those crops harvested and to market before they perish is also difficult.

That's where technology and modern precision agriculture come in. After breakfast our next stop was Agricenter International,[10] a nonprofit institution dedicated to agriculture research, education, and conservation. There we met a couple of entrepreneurs who were working on precision agriculture ideas that exemplified a much larger pattern that I'm seeing across the country and around the world, where technology, particularly technology incorporating modern AI, is making credible strides toward transforming how our food is produced and consumed. One of the entrepreneurs at the Agricenter demo was building an autonomous robot for irrigation. Rather than plumbing a field, pumping water from source to destination, and mechanically and imprecisely spraying crops with no tight feedback loop determining whether crops are being properly hydrated, these entrepreneurs were building a truly twenty-first-century farm machine. Their machine is compact, can bring water exactly where it is needed, can assess how much is needed and dispense precisely that amount, and can do it all with a combination of sophisticated robotics, artificial intelligence, and human supervision. The net benefits could be great: Higher crop yields. Less water consumed as water becomes a more precious commodity due to global warming. The ability to support different types of crops with different hydration needs on the same land. And less runoff, which is better for the environment.

The next entrepreneur we met was building drone technology to distribute fertilizers, pesticides, and other agricultural chemicals to crops as an alternative to bulk spraying. The need for innovation here is significant. Agricultural chemicals are an important part of the Green Revolution,[11] which in recent decades has allowed us to support an ever-growing world population while avoiding the famines and nutrition crises that had been forecast through the late 1960s. That said, these chemicals, sometimes toxic in their undiluted form, are typically significantly diluted with water and mechanically sprayed on crops. This results in many of the same problems as classic irrigation: wasted water, harmful runoff, wasted chemicals when overdispensed, and lowered crop yields when underdispensed. Spraying crops with drones is a nonstarter if the chemicals being sprayed must be diluted. Diluting the chemicals with water would make the spraying payload too heavy for drones to carry. The entrepreneur's innovative solution to this problem was a novel way of atomizing the chemicals into very tiny, electrostatically charged spheres as they leave the spray nozzle. Because of the fine atomization and electric charge, the undiluted chemicals stick to the crops in minuscule amounts, but at sufficient concentration to do their job. When coupled with computer vision and other artificial intelligence techniques to identify crops, how much to spray, and how to navigate the drone, this technology could allow farmers unprecedented ability to deploy these chemicals in an environmentally friendly way.

At the end of these demos I was thoroughly impressed. Their work is every bit as technically innovative as what I have seen as a Silicon Valley veteran, as an investor, and as CTO of Microsoft. We asked them, "Why Memphis?" Their answers give me hope. Perhaps the most important factor is that the problems they are trying to solve are most amenable to being solved in an agricultural region like Memphis. There is a critical mass of agricultural expertise in Memphis. The arable land and agriculture businesses that could incorporate these technologies are in Memphis. One of the entrepreneurs, from Chicago, asserted that the warmer climate in Memphis meant longer growing seasons and more months in the year when his team could test iterations of their technology in the field. In this way, rural America might offer some regional advantages for research and development in fields like agriculture and manufacturing as well as computer design and development.

But perhaps the most interesting answer to "Why Memphis?" is that the technology they're using has become dramatically more accessible over the past ten to fifteen years. Whether it's open source software and AI toolkits, cloud computing infrastructure, drone development platforms, and widely available, affordable robotics components, these folks have access to the tools they need to build their high-tech businesses without the need to physically locate themselves in an urban technology center.

With so few obvious obstacles to innovation in a place like Memphis, it seems like it's on us to figure out how to establish a set of incentives that encourages more investment there and other places like it. The Rise of the Rest Seed Fund is concrete action in this direction. Steve Case, J.D. Vance, and their general and limited partners have invested tens of millions of dollars in dozens of promising entrepreneurs and the companies they've started in places like Memphis. Steve and J.D. aren't investing in these entrepreneurs for charity; they believe that these investments are good business. It's time for other investors to follow suit. In an ideal venture investment portfolio, you have one or two companies that make the fund, whose success is significant enough to produce a good return for investors even if most of the individual investments produce mediocre or negative returns. When a company has breakout success outside of our urban innovation centers, it can make a region.

Breakout companies can have a huge positive impact on a region in terms of direct and indirect job creation, as catalysts for high-ROI infrastructure investment like schools, and through secondary investments in the region from wealth created from a company's success. Making public policy that helps to identify, fund, and nurture companies with breakout potential is a good bet. For instance, the tax cuts for investments in opportunity zones passed as part of the 2017 Tax Cuts and Jobs Act is a step in the right direction. Tax cuts to incent investment outside of urban innovation centers need to be constructed carefully to ensure that the public is getting a good deal. They should, as a general rule, be conditioned on job creation and economic value creation for a region over long periods of time, with clear milestones and metrics for assessing performance and triggering the incentives.

Another potentially useful policy incentive to encourage more geographically diverse development is to raise the capital gains rate—which the government should do regardless—but maintain a low capital gains rate on investments made in small- and medium-size businesses located entirely within opportunity zones, or to investments made in large businesses that have a nontrivial percentage of their high-value, high-pay jobs located within opportunity zones. The resulting investor pressure, in conjunction with the high cost of living and high income taxes in the big urban innovation centers, could actually result in companies making more serious efforts to make their workforces more geographically diverse.

There may be other, better ideas for using tax policy to encourage the types of investments that would more equitably benefit Americans. Whatever those ideas are, we should think about changes to the tax code as ways to get businesses and individuals to change their behavior for some public benefit, not simply as new sources of revenue for the government. Raising that revenue and using it to support programs for the public good is . . . well . . . good. But getting folks to change behavior is the more scalable way to achieve lasting change.

Tax incentives alone are probably insufficient. Direct government investment in tech job creation in communities that are falling behind is probably also warranted. Policy makers are not automatically going to be good venture capitalists, and choosing what to invest in and how much is neither obvious nor risk free. My friend Reid Hoffman, entrepreneur, investor, and master strategist, believes that there are opportunities for venture capitalists and government to collaborate. Consider the government investing as a limited partner, in the same manner that university endowments and pension funds already invest in venture, where the funds must invest in entrepreneurs building great businesses in rural and middle America. The investing partners would be allocated a percentage of the total returns of the fund, known in the industry as *carry*. The partners would be incented to seek out great entrepreneurs and businesses, to fund them, and to help them be successful in order to earn their carry. The government, as a limited partner, would also get a return on their invested dollars directly from the fund, and in the form of economic stimulus in the communities hosting these new businesses. So the government wins twice. And the entrepreneurs, their employees, and their communities are the biggest winners of all as the flywheel of entrepreneurial success begins to spin.

You could also imagine a similar plan to better leverage philanthropic 501(c)(3) dollars. Even though dollars invested and distributed through 501(c)(3) philanthropies are tax-exempt, the government could do things to encourage those philanthropic investments to flow to specific causes. For instance, the government could choose to match private philanthropic investments into approved charities in opportunity zones, even allowing private philanthropic foundations and individual donors a way to amplify their charitable giving, potentially providing yet another routing signal to the government to ensure that dollars are flowing to good charitable investments. You could even consider allowing 501(c)(3) philanthropies the ability to invest in for-profit companies in opportunity zones that are credibly delivering on job creation and other economic stimulus goals.

One of America's most inspired (and inspiring) initiatives, one that galvanized public support for science and technology, was the NASA space program, which started just south of Memphis in Huntsville, Alabama, at the Marshall Space Flight Center. Anyone who has seen *The Right Stuff* or *First Man* knows that it grew out of the Cold War's arms race with the Soviet Union, leading to President Kennedy's "moon shot." *Foreign Affairs* magazine in the summer of 2019 published an essay, "Killer Apps," about a new AI arms race. In 2018 dollars, the Apollo program cost slightly more than $200 billion. As much as for defense purposes, an Apollo program for AI spread out over ten years could be massively beneficial for the United States and would consume less than

0.1 percent of GDP. Any such program should have provisions that the work of the program should be geographically distributed across the United States, with some fixed percentage of the work having to happen outside of California, Washington, New York, and Massachusetts. Any such program should also have as a primary goal that the work it produces—its beneficial AI technologies—should improve the lives and livelihoods of all Americans.

We closed our day in Memphis at the Clayborn Temple.[12] The Clayborn Temple is an awe-inspiring structure, and the site of many important events in the 1960s civil rights movement. Most famously it was the gathering place for striking sanitation workers who were fighting for dignity and equality, and the starting point for a peaceful march led by Dr. Martin Luther King Jr. less than a week prior to his assassination. Clayborn Temple had been in a state of disuse and disrepair for decades until a group of Memphians began the process of rehabilitation in 2015.

On this particular Tuesday night the Clayborn Temple was host to eight start-ups whose founders were pitching a panel of judges on their business. The best of these start-ups would win a $100,000 investment from the Rise of the Rest fund. I was one of the judges.

The companies presenting were diverse in several ways. Their businesses and innovations were in real estate marketplaces, auto safety, eldercare, medical membranes, cyber security and fraud prevention, logistics marketplaces, sound recording, and home services. The best three would have easily been able to raise significant seed-stage investments if they had had access to Silicon Valley investment networks. I believe that the best of the group, on the day of the competition, could have earned an A-round term sheet from several credible investors if his company were in Silicon Valley rather than Memphis. That company, Soundways,[13] builds software to help sound recording engineers manage their workflows, and that helps artists and recording companies manage metadata and rights in a world where music distribution and consumption is becoming ever more complex. In their pitch they demonstrated a differentiated technology and product with a sizable addressable market; a credible, expert team; $1.5 million in annual recurring revenue growing at a very healthy pace after being in business for a very short period of time; and bonuses like earned media through interviews in industry publications like *Billboard* magazine with a charismatic young founder.

The other element of diversity, aside from the businesses and technologies being pitched, were the founders. Half were women. Half were African American or other underrepresented minorities. Some were native Memphians. And some were in Memphis because of its proximity to customers, marketplaces, or expertise that they believe their businesses need more than geographic proximity to folks making capital investment decisions. On many different levels, this is exactly what you want to see for the sake of tech, for the sake of entrepreneurship, and for the sake of equitable access to opportunity.

I walked away from this experience more convinced than ever that we must get out of the echo chamber that dominates our current public dialogue on the future of technology. The stories used to optimize clicks and comments full of outrage are too often trivial, inane, and irrelevant. I vowed to help focus on how we can reinforce what is happening right before our eyes in order to make a better future for everyone. The untold story of the tech industry over the past fifteen years is the extent to which we've put incredibly powerful technology—in the form of open source and open Internet, cloud platforms, and AI frameworks—into the hands of a broader group of developers, builders, and entrepreneurs than ever before in human history. These folks are using this empowerment to build bigger, more ambitious, and more innovative businesses than I could ever have imagined, and are doing so not just from Silicon Valley, Seattle, New York City, and Boston—the capitals of several previous generations of tech innovation—but also in places as varied as Brookneal and Memphis.

The drive early this morning, far from my piedmont home in rural Virginia, is from Seattle to the northern tip of Oregon along the Columbia River. The city slips away slowly, and then suddenly the spring leaves and early green grasses of the rural Pacific Northwest countryside unfurl before me. Country musicians Blake Shelton and Trace Adkins write about their discovery that hillbillies come from everywhere in the US when a friend of theirs, someone they describe as "never been south of Queens," comes to visit the sticks, and loves it.

My destination is a conference on rural economic development, cleverly named "Regards to Rural," which gets underway at 9:30 a.m. on a Saturday. I arrived just in time for a session on workforce development, attended by forty or so ranchers, rural entrepreneurs, and rural development council leaders.

Patti Norris, a business adviser at the Small Business Development Center in Prineville, Oregon, is sitting at my table. She's driven nearly four hours to be here. She's not unfamiliar with what motivated my visit. She tells me about the rural road into her town—an old timber town—where on one side of the highway is the Apple data center and on the other is the Facebook data center. Apple is pretty secretive, she says, but she can recite Facebook's employment figures—about three hundred people, which includes the techies as well as those who support them, the caterers and construction people.

A few days earlier she had gone to meet with some business people locally who own a wood products business. The lumber industry that once gave Prineville the name Pine Town is rumored to be dead, a victim of globalization and federal regulations. But she said the next generation is harvesting smaller trees and innovating new products like veneer and commercial wood moldings. They can't hire enough people. Years ago they ran twenty-four-hour shifts but now they run just one from 6 a.m. to 2 p.m. Even so, they needed to hire qualified people and were curious if she had ideas about how to recruit young people, interns, and apprentices.

Just as she says this, Heather Stafford, director of adult education in Siskiyou County, California, takes the podium and gets right to the point. In many states with large rural populations, the middle class is made up of truck drivers, and AI-driven trucks are going to put them out of work. She lists the barriers to upward mobility, including drug and alcohol problems, mental health problems, lack of skills, limited expertise, limited broadband, and food deserts.

The conference has four tracks—revitalizing rural economies, rural leadership networks, resources for rural communities, and elevating rural voices. I can't be everywhere so I focus on the first two, diving deep into workforce development, the rebirth of traditional rural industries like farming, timber, and commercial fishing. I end the day with purposeful conversations designed to bridge the divide between rural and urban.

Just as the opening session starts to set a dire tone, Heather takes the conversation in a new direction.

"I believe entrepreneurs will save the world."

Melissa Brandao's precision agriculture company, Herd-Dogg, builds Internet-of-things solutions—Internet-connected devices running complex software—for livestock health and wellness. She says, tongue-in-cheek, "We do bovine romance." She initially moved her company to Denver, but then moved it back to rural Oregon because she wants to develop a rural workforce.

"Our mission is to help plant the seed for rural people to become better at tech," she tells the audience. "Malcom Gladwell wrote that we can't separate who we are from where we're from. You can't hire people for livestock that haven't grown up around it. We have to develop our own developers. I want a kid who grew up on a farm to come work for us, not move to the city. There are start-ups like me in every area."

Wally Corwin, Jeld-Wen's corporate manager of product integrity, is also on the panel. His North Carolina–based company makes windows and doors for the construction industry. He takes issue with some of the language used in digital economies when applied to rural people.

"We are not defining gig economy right," he argues. "In manufacturing we call it subcontracting. We have lots of subcontractors. When I grew up around farms, we baled hay. One guy had a baler and another a rake. They were doing gigs. Rural Oregon is not going to need many Uber drivers. We need private business to get involved with helping to provide infrastructure and capital to help with businesses like teaching high school kids to be drone pilots."

On the Warm Springs Indian reservations, for example, they need drone pilots for fire suppression, fish counts, and forest management.

Tyler Freres runs a lumber company in the Pacific Northwest, and tells the conference he is intensely looking at robotics.

"We have to. We need 480 people but we have 430. Amazon is moving a warehouse near us and they are hiring 1,200 people and they are paying better. We can't compete with them. Robotics are going to help give our people longer careers because some of the work they're doing is a rough and dirty job."

Tyler grew up working in the timber business, went to college, and returned to rural Oregon after he got an MBA. He now works at his family business, founded in 1922, as a manager rather than as a laborer, and can see all the way through the business from top to bottom. After timber went bust in the 1990s, he converted to veneer and plywood products as well as residuals like potting soil and wood chips. Today his product will be used in one of the largest mass timber buildings in the trendy Pearl District of Portland. He's recently invested in a new $35 million robotic manufacturing plant in rural Lions, Oregon. But he bristles at state and federal regulations that are holding him back from growth: a new minimum wage law that may work for urban areas but not for rural; paid sick leave; predictive scheduling; recreational marijuana—all of these new state laws have hurt rural businesses, he claims.

"Oregon is a terrible state to run a manufacturing business. In retrospect we should not have put our manufacturing facility in Oregon."

Sensing the political tension rising, the moderator jumps in.

"Sometimes it's hard to hear business voices," she says. "We need to hear those perspectives."

The next session looks at opportunities to invest in rural areas.

"We're going to crash some myths," the moderator promises.

Cory Carman is one such myth buster. A Stanford grad, she moved home to run the family ranch founded by her great-grandparents.

"My family said, 'Good luck, we think you are going to fail.'"

She studied the market and arrived at a strategy to capture

the regional market for premium meats with a superior product and a great story. Her focus became grass-fed beef, no confinement, no antibiotics. She wanted a local network of suppliers that tapped into the energy and spirit she knew existed from growing up in the area.

"We are not focused on AI, but we need to be looking at data," she reflected. "We believe in people instincts."

Angelina Skowronski is a spunky rural entrepreneur with Fishpeople, a company that is bringing back the fishing industry on the north coast of Oregon. As she puts it, her company is competing with slave labor from some countries and government subsidies in others. She says there is a lot of tech in fish processing, and in the actual fishing-finding—underwater location—at sea. Fishpeople is not investing in tech yet, but has its eye on blockchain technology, the distributed ledger that underlies cryptocurrencies like Bitcoin, since it can pinpoint for consumers where their fish was caught and even which fisherman caught it.

Bruce Nissen is the founder of LDB (Let's Dream Big) Beverage in Washington State. His focus is converting a wide variety of apples into prized, high-value ciders. He had built a cider company in California that was bought by Coors. Restless, he got to thinking: Washington has 70 percent of the apples, and the state offers the cheapest electricity in the US. He started a new venture, this time in the highly remote Columbia River Gorge area of central Washington.

"We have people who make $60,000 per year, but can't find a place to live. Some live in their cars. We wouldn't be in a rural business if we didn't like challenges. We eat challenges for breakfast, but it's hard. I can't find people who can run a spreadsheet. Everything comes from away. Our skill set in the Gorge is just a long way from AI and robotics. The more tech I invest in, the more skills I am going to have to have, so it's hard. In fact, there is an aversion to making it too electronic."

All these stories express a common need: access to high-speed broadband and affordable housing in remote areas; addressing the failure of efforts to combat substance abuse; and demand for rural-friendly public policy, skills development, and a workforce not just willing to work in rural areas but in fact with some experience in traditionally rural industries like agriculture. But what they often miss is how AI will help them with data-fed insights and predictive capabilities, operational excellence, and new job creation.

The day concludes with a session on efforts to bridge both real and perceived divides between rural and urban development interests. The goal reminds me of a phone call I had only a few days before with Sam Ford, a bright Kentuckian who is devoting his time and talent to this very cause. His focus is on "how organizations are listening to, developing relationships with, telling stories to, and putting themselves in the shoes of the audiences they seek to reach." A former journalist, Sam is developing a new Future of Work initiative in his home state along with labs at MIT, USC, and elsewhere. He's helping rural entrepreneurs in his native state with "side hustles"—part-time jobs that augment their income. He helps entrepreneurs envision strategies for growing their ideas, ideas like artisanal agriculture for farm-to-table chefs, and creating cooperative regional tourism marketing. As a journalist, he knows how to listen, communicate the idea, link resources, and present the businesses to a larger market.

I wish Sam were with us for this workshop in Oregon. He's taking such positive action in the face of the occasional pessimism that creeps into even the most enthusiastic people. At my table we're asked to describe urban and rural differences.

What assumptions or misconceptions, positive or negative, impact how those differences show up?

One woman in her fifties, a redhead in a bright summer dress, rejected the framing of the question. She squinted hard at the question and decided she didn't like the word *divide*.

"Why aren't we talking about connections, not divides?"

Another woman decides a joke is in order. "What is rural?" she asks. "It's what you have to drive through to get to the city." No one laughs.

Someone at the table pipes up, echoing an oft-repeated accusation in rural communities everywhere: Salem, Oregon's capital city, and Portland, its business center, get all of the state government benefits. It's not fair.

A confident millennial at the table who seems to work in state government suddenly chimes in that he's letting us in on a little secret. He's seen the numbers; rural people do, in fact, get fair value from state funding. His assertion shuts down the older women at the table because they haven't seen the numbers. They just know how it seems. It got me thinking: Do urban people understand their dependencies on rural people? And do rural people understand their dependencies on urban people? I wonder if urban people understand the value they get from rural people, and vice versa.

To wrap up, moderators go around and ask each table to report the results of their conversations. One table says that rural people were not heard in previous elections, and that's why the election of Trump went the way it did. But, they said, there is new dissatisfaction, and people are more focused now on their local elections. Another table complains about misinformed stereotypes on both sides. Another table hatches the idea that cities should pick brother and sister cities not from other countries but from rural places. The last table puts it bluntly: "There is an assumption of low intelligence among rural people, and that city people are assholes."

Looking at this as someone whose life has spanned the rural-urban divide, none of the disconnected perception seems new to me. The stereotypes that urban and rural folks can have of one another have been there for decades, if not centuries. I've watched Southern friends attempt to erase the traces of their Southernness—their accents, the stories of their childhood, even their food preferences—in order to blend in with their academic or professional or social group of choice. For me, I started to hide my Southernness as a teenager. I didn't see myself at all in the stereotypes of Southerners portrayed in the media, and had a hard time reconciling my home state's past with the future that I hoped we were all headed for. As computers and programming became more and more a part of my identity and aspirations, I struggled to find any Southern role models. So I rejected a big part of my identity for a very long while.

One tragedy of our modern lives is that the technology intended to radically connect us and to make information abundant and free allows us to occupy ideological bubbles that reinforce our own beliefs and preferences, and that isolate us from others with different beliefs and preferences. The isolation resulting from this fragmentation of ideas, information, values, and actual connection to our fellow human beings does more than just reinforce our differences. It actively deprives us of the opportunity to find common ground. The activist Eli Pariser coined a term for this phenomenon: the filter bubble.[14]

As we've come to see from recent political news, AI can be used as a tool to entrench these filter bubble effects. A machine learning algorithm designed to give you the information that you want as measured by how much you engage with it—do you read something, do you like it, do you comment on it, do you share it, do you react in similar ways to similar types of content from similar sources—will hyperefficiently keep you within your bubble. If the only measure of success for the machine learning algorithm is your level of engagement, it's doing nothing to help expose you to diverse perspectives, nothing to filter out false and counterfactual information, and nothing to prevent you from being exposed to overt propaganda and manipulation. In the worst case, there is a feedback loop in these systems that starts with you seeing something sensational, then you reacting to it because of the fear, anger, or anxiety that it provokes, which teaches the system to show you more things to make you fearful, angry, and anxious. As one of my former bosses used to say, *no bueno*.

Ironically, AI may be the very thing that we need to help temper this pernicious feedback loop. In the fall of 2016 I was on the cusp of taking on a new job that was going to place new demands on my time, and I had reached a breaking point with my own media consumption; I found myself reading random bits of content that wasn't delivering long-term value. I decided to do an experiment where I dramatically increased my consumption of high-quality information. I implemented a 70/25/5 rule where 70 percent of my media consumption time needed to be spent on high-standards, editorially and/or peer-reviewed, long-form content related to my work and professional interests. That covers a lot of ground, given my job. Twenty-five percent of my media consumption time was to learn something new and different, not necessarily related to my job, and not necessarily from one of the media sources I tend to favor. And 5 percent is everything else, which is enough to scan through blog headlines a couple of times a day, and maybe spend a few minutes a week checking out what friends and family might have posted to Instagram.

This meant that, once again, I started reading more peer-reviewed computer science papers and textbooks. I started reading one nonfiction book a week. I subscribed to *Nature* and *Science*, two high-quality weekly journals for the natural sciences that contain both rigorously peer-reviewed articles and content authored with high standards of editorial review. I subscribed to the *Economist*, the *Financial Times*, the *New Yorker*, and the *Atlantic*. I curated a high-quality set of podcasts to listen to while commuting. I surrounded myself with high-quality, genuinely informative content. And in my 25 percent bucket I might watch a YouTube video from *This Old Tony* or Jimmy DiResta to learn how to make something, or, make myself read something thoughtful that is outside of my comfort zone.

I started this routine over two years ago, thinking that it might last a month or two. I had taken some brief social media holidays over the prior couple of years because I was letting myself get too worked up over stuff that, in retrospect, wasn't even remotely worth the emotional energy. The surprising thing is that feeding myself healthier information was almost like going on a diet. I felt less anxious, less irritated, and much, much better informed. I had a small, lingering fear that my information diet might make me miss some high-quality bit of knowledge along with all the noise that it was filtering out. But that small fear was nowhere near significant enough for me to go back to my old habits.

AI could help all of us make better information consumption choices. If the machine learning systems scrubbing through mountains of information for me knew the rules of my information diet, and optimized for that instead of emotionally provoked engagement, the benefit to me would be enormous. Not everyone should be on the same information diet as me. But I'm guessing that hundreds of millions, if not billions of folks, are bingeing on unhealthy information right now and should be able to design their own get-healthy diet, which AI could help them adhere to. Perhaps if we had more folks demanding healthy information diets, the world would have few filter bubbles, less outrage, and more opportunity to use the technologies that we've built for their intended purposes, to actually come together and find the common ground we need to be on in order to have a healthy, functioning society.

The last session of the final morning of the rural conference in Portland, Oregon, turns out to be an emotional one about the future of rural farms and ranches. I came here to learn from people working directly within rural economic development. I wanted to hear if and how they are viewing next-generation technologies. But "next generation" takes on a very different meaning here.

Nellie McAdams of Rogue Farm Corps in Yamhill County, Oregon, opens with some sobering statistics. Two numbers she cites stand out. First, 64 percent of her state's agricultural lands will change hands in twenty years, largely reflecting national trends. Second, the average age of a farmer is sixty, near retirement age for most professions. To further the point, Mark Bennett, a sixty-five-year-old farmer and rancher from Unity, Oregon ("We aren't even rural; we're frontier"), recounts the story of his town dying, a serious accident he survived recently, and the conversation it forced with his wife and their kids about the future of the sprawling ranch.

"What do we do with this darn thing that we've poured love into," he asked, his friendly Western voice breaking just slightly. "What are our options?"

One option is to sell to foreign investors. He notes that the next ranch over is owned by these investors, who are described as interested in profits, not land stewardship. Another option is what he calls the Rockefeller approach, a sort of gentleman rancher model in which wealthy owners build an enormous country home but don't work the land.

"We set out to prove that we can protect the land, protect wildlife, and make money running livestock. I could have made a lot of money selling land to a solar company, but I saved it for the sage grouse. I thought, Do those sage grouse really need all of this land? God made us stewards of this land."

Succession planning is something we take very seriously at Microsoft and at the companies where I am an investor. Why had I not thought about it in this context?

Diana Tourney, our next speaker, cannot stop thinking about it. She is an adviser and instructor at Clackamas Small Business Development Center. She can't run a tractor, but she can run a computer, she adds.

"I love numbers and I love working with farmers and ranchers to help the land remain a farm. I do have a prejudice. The farm has to be a viable business."

Diana has seen land lost to poor planning and lawsuits, but the problem she encounters most frequently is family squabbling. The aging parents create succession plans but then the kids cannot agree with the plan because they feel left out or have other ideas. She advises getting the kids involved early, tapping their often complementary skills, and addressing their questions and concerns. She's very astute about the EQ side of things, insisting that families have their first meeting about succession planning outside of the house in neutral territory. Sitting around the old kitchen where the brother used to kick the sister under the table will prolong divisions, while a neutral space will elevate the conversation.

The next morning, the *New York Times* runs a nearly full-page report on Australia: "A Booming Economy with a Tragic Price" for farmers. People living in rural areas take their lives at twice the rate of those in the city. Research shows farmers are among those at the highest risk of suicide.

A few months later, rural economic development leaders

gathered again in Washington, DC, for America's Rural Opportunity at the Aspen Institute. This time their focus was what they describe as "2Gen strategies" targeting two generations of rural families—parents and children. When children and adults together are the focus, the likelihood of parents being able to work, and kids being able to contribute down the road, is much better. Makes sense. 2Gen is a holistic approach to improving conditions in rural America: early childhood development, quality child care, health and well-being, housing, social capital, building economic assets, and creating pathways to postsecondary.

The importance of this approach was underscored in John Seabrook's insightful 2019 article "The Age of Robot Farmers" for the *New Yorker*. "If the future of fruit-and-vegetable farming is automation," he writes, "farmers will not only need the machines, and the funds to afford them, they will also require a new class of skilled farm workers who can debug the harvesters when something goes wrong." Historic extracurricular programs like 4-H and Future Farmers of America are increasingly focused on math and engineering. Turns out that whether you are a parent in rural, urban, or suburban America, everyone wants the same for their kids—opportunity.

These rural-urban differences I've been seeing and listening to are universal, and the implications are much deeper than cultural and political: isolation, substance abuse, inadequate resources to keep up with failing infrastructure, a growing housing crisis, a shrinking and aging workforce, lower-paying jobs, and inadequate child care if you do have a job. The problems are overwhelming, dispiriting. In recent decades the inner city has correctly attracted national and international attention. Urban populations continue to grow, and rural populations diminish. Both deserve our attention.

CHAPTER 4

The Intelligent Farm

In the summer of 2018, wildfires in the forests of British Columbia coupled with winds from the north were driving hazy smoke across the normally crystal-blue skies of Washington State. More than one-third of the nation was experiencing moderate to exceptional drought, yet crops like wheat, corn, and soybeans were beginning to pour into markets at abundant rates, driving down prices for farmers, including the farmer I was driving to visit. Meanwhile, in Washington, DC, a pitiful scrum of white nationalists and a much larger group of antifascists had spent the weekend exchanging heated insults in the streets of the nation's capital. The farm bill—the federal government's primary instrument for agricultural policy—languished over the summer break in a reconciliation committee while a trade war had broken out, prompting the administration to propose giving farmers $12 billion in federal funding as a stopgap measure while international negotiations proceeded.

It was against this backdrop that I was visiting a small farm about fifteen miles east of Microsoft's sprawling campus in Redmond. A group of developers in the company's AI and Research group had invited me to see how they are using low-cost sensors and digital mapping to gather agricultural data like soil temperature and moisture to improve crop outcomes. A smallholder farmer just outside of Carnation, a community named for the evaporated milk company, had allowed the researchers access to his land in exchange for valuable data.

Seattle's rush hour traffic was spilling onto the rural roads just outside the farm. We parked our car beside a big red barn and then had to sprint across the road to avoid being hit by commuters racing home. Not all farmers are at the end of a dirt road in a flyover state. In his thought-provoking book *Hinterland: America's New Landscape of Class and Conflict*, Phil A. Neel divides his observations between a far and a near hinterland—deep rural and just barely. While Richard Florida's work on the creative class explores why economic development is concentrated in cities and metropolitan areas, Neel explains what's happening just beyond. "But beyond the city, where there is little question of inclusion, it becomes clear that these populations are also unified by something else: the commonality that comes from being increasingly surplus to the economy, though also paradoxically integral to it." Rural regions, he concludes pessimistically, are becoming wastelands for global production.

Not if Dr. Ranveer Chandra, a Microsoft researcher, has anything to say about it. Ranveer is a cheerful product of the famed Indian Institutes for Technology and Cornell University's computer science department. He's walking us through endless rows of produce ripening under today's filtered Pacific Northwest sunshine. Ranveer grew up in the Indian state of Bihar, which borders Nepal. He worked a small ten-acre farm with his grandparents, who grew sugarcane, wheat, rice, and mangoes. His passion is to create technologies that both help rural people like his grandparents and the friends he left behind, and that help to increase food production by up to 70 percent to feed the growing population of the world. And while he believes in the power of tech, he believes even more in the human element that is needed to grow food, to cultivate the earth.

"We want to supplement the farmer's knowledge," he tells us while unpacking a small white drone from a case. "Rather than intuition alone, we can use data. Rather than water and pesticide everywhere, we can be more precise so that it's only used where it's needed."

With that he flips open a Surface book and pulls out his mobile phone. He'll need these to monitor the images and data as they flow in. The drone lifts off about one hundred feet in the air. From his notebook we can see the rows of plants from above, and follow its path as it zigs and zags across the entire acreage, collecting the soil's pH levels, moisture, and temperature. With this data it can build a heat map to help the farmer pinpoint problem areas. The data that's collected, as much as 200 megabytes of images per acre, is transported to the cloud's edge back at the farmer's house, where another computer stores and analyzes the information in real time.

There has been a lot of focus in recent years on cloud computing, rightly so, but *edge computing* is also fundamental to the future of AI in precision farming, medicine, and other applications.

With edge computing, data is run and analyzed on a nearby device, close to where it's being generated, rather than flowing to a faraway data center. This way data can be analyzed in real time, rather than being hostage to a rural area's low-latency, slow connectivity to the cloud. With an estimated

25.1 billion devices expected to be connected to the Internet by 2021, edge computing will empower and transform the Internet of things (IoT), like this farm, for years to come.

Take a look around your house, office, or even the next store you visit, and you'll start to notice that Internet-connected devices are bringing us closer than ever before to a world of ubiquitous computing and ambient intelligence. As these Internet-of-things devices become increasingly common-place, people will start to expect computing to be more inte-grated into their lives, to anticipate, understand, and seamlessly meet their needs. They will expect software to respond to spoken natural language, gestures, body language, and emo-tion, and for it to understand the physical world and the rich context surrounding each user as they navigate their personal life, their work, and the world around them.

This trend has more promise than just bringing additional convenience, productivity, and connections to our everyday lives. Smart sensors and devices are breathing new life into industrial equipment from factories to farms, helping us nav-igate and plan for more sustainable urban cities and bringing the power of the cloud to some of the world's most remote destinations. With the power of AI enabling these devices to intelligently respond to the world they are sensing, we will see new breakthroughs in critical areas that benefit humanity like health care, conservation, sustainability, accessibility, di-saster recovery, and more.

We call this next wave of computing the *intelligent edge* and *intelligent cloud*. And these new technologies may be just as transformative for problems rooted in the physical world as AI has been for the consumer Internet. The raw material for building things with modern AI is data. The data that you have dictate what the AI is able to use. If those data are clicks on search results, ads, likes, and shares, then you can build AI systems that can optimize the quality of your search results, that can show you better ads, and that can learn what information to show you in a news feed based on what appear to be your preferences. If those data are soil moisture, pH, temperature, humidity, weather forecasts, and images of crops, then you can build AI systems that can help farmers make better decisions about what to plant and when, how to irrigate more effectively, how to deploy fertilizers and supplements, and when to harvest. The net effects of making better decisions about these things are higher crop yields with less environmental impact.

This extension of the power of modern AI into the physical world is truly exciting. I would argue that AI will ultimately have a far greater positive impact on our lives in the era of the intelligent edge and cloud than it has had through the aperture of the consumer Internet alone. Smart sensors that can collect data and act on physical events as they happen will enable us to build models that have knowledge about, and the ability to interact with, an incredible diversity of things in the physical world. And those models will be able to assist humans in making better, quicker, higher-quality decisions, or used in systems that take autonomous action to supplement humans when environmental conditions and scale merit.

In the world of conservation, the intelligent edge and cloud have special promise. Conservation efforts are often constrained by the cost and scale of the effort (e.g., observing animals over millions of acres of their habitat). Even if you could afford it, you couldn't hire enough humans to do all the animal and habitat conservation work that exists in the world today. Disney's Animal Kingdom is already leveraging the intelligent edge to study the purple martin bird. They worked with Microsoft to develop hundreds of tiny "smart houses" in Disney's Animal Kingdom to learn more about the species and help inspire a new generation of conservationists in the parks. The scientists now have unprecedented insight into the nesting behavior of the purple martins.

At a grander scale, there are efforts underway to deploy sensors—cameras, microphones, motion detectors, and more—at massive scale for several conservation tasks. Smart Parks, a nonprofit wildlife conservation organization that is trying to prevent poaching of endangered or threatened species, has deployed a network of sensing technologies in Rwanda, Tanzania, and India to monitor and alert for potential poaching activity over thousands of square kilometers of habitat. Another conservation organization, Rainforest Connection, is transforming recycled smartphones into smart sensors to detect illegal deforestation in rain forests so that authorities can be alerted and act before these precious ecosystems can be harmed. In the case of both conservation efforts, deploying the sensors and getting the data is the first step in a process where AI will be able to deliver higher-precision detection of harmful activity and better response automation to handle the truly vast scope of the conservation task. Our human resources are too scarce to solve these problems without the help of AI.

Another noteworthy area where the intelligent edge and cloud paradigm can have a huge potential positive impact is climate change and conservation of our natural resources. How do we transition to renewable sources of energy as quickly as possible while immediately mitigating the deleterious effects of consuming carbon-based fuels (oil, gas, coal, wood)? One of the challenges in navigating this transition is economic: it will be extremely expensive, costing tens or hundreds of trillions of dollars, to fully complete; and using abstinence as a strategy for managing the cost of the transition is fraught with political peril, particularly in parts of the world with rapidly expanding economies where higher energy consumption goes part and parcel with a higher standard of living. The costs of not making the transition are catastrophically high, which means that this is not a problem that will just go away. Nor will it get better over time.

As we collect more data about physical phenomena, using AI to optimize power production, transmission, and consumption may allow us to fundamentally alter the economics and speed of the clean energy transition. Already Schneider Electric is using the intelligent edge in oil fields to monitor and configure pump settings and operations remotely, sending personnel on-site only when necessary for repair or maintenance when, for example, intelligent pump monitoring indicates that something will go wrong. This contributes to overall worker safety and improved resource management. But there is also the potential to make our electric power generators more efficient, to more efficiently generate and transmit power to points of consumption when needed, and to make power consumers themselves more efficient. The holy grail here, in my opinion, is using the intelligent edge and cloud, and sophisticated AI, to globally coordinate the production and consumption of power to achieve higher efficiency. We do this now with crude mechanisms like higher prices when demand is high, and in the worst case, rolling brownouts when the grid is oversubscribed. We perhaps already possess the technological capability to make generation and consumption of energy smart, with the networks and cloud infrastructure to do this global coordination.

You may have noticed a pattern emerging from the agriculture, conservation, and energy examples. We as a country, in most cases as a species, face some challenging problems that may at first seem to be zero-sum. In other words, the problem is so much bigger than the resources available to solve it that we are not only forced to solve a small subset of the problem, but we sometimes are confronted with extremely contentious public debates about how to allocate our finite resources to solve even a constrained version of the problem. One of the themes of this book is that AI and advanced automation can be a tool to turn these constrained, zero-sum problems into non-zero-sum ones. In other words, AI can be used to create a new type of abundance that can then be used to break the zero-sum gridlock, whether that's how to feed a growing population, how to conserve our precious natural resources, or how to solve climate change. AI isn't a miracle and can't completely solve these gigantic problems by itself, but it can be an extremely effective tool in helping us make progress that might otherwise be impossible.

We need to give all organizations and developers the tools to build these kinds of increasingly ambitious solutions that span the intelligent edge and intelligent cloud. Moreover, these tools must give developers strong security foundations and help them to place security at the very core of their solutions. Devices on the edge handle some of our most sensitive business and personal data in our homes, workplaces, and sometimes physically remote places.

As we talk about an increasingly connected world with smart sensors and edge computing, we can't avoid thinking about and investing in security. To protect our data and privacy, security needs to be baked in from the silicon to the cloud. This has been one of the central design principles of Microsoft's intelligent edge products and services. Many cloud providers are working hard on this. Azure Sphere is our intelligent edge solution to power and protect connected microcontroller unit (MCU)–powered devices. There are nine billion of these MCU–powered devices shipping every year, which power everything from household stoves and refrigerators to industrial equipment. With more processing power than traditional MCUs and a holistic security approach, Azure Sphere will, we believe, make our increasingly connected world safer. In addition, Azure IoT Edge enables you to run cloud intelligence directly on IoT devices and includes security—from device provisioning and management to hardware and cloud services—that runs on top of the devices. Azure Stack, just one of our many tools to power hybrid scenarios, offers customers the flexibility to securely deploy in the cloud, on-premises or at the intelligent edge.

Every cloud provider should possess all these building blocks, and every developer and solutions architect should have a choice of tools in their arsenal for designing better security in a sensor-rich world of edge computing.

There are several innovations Ranveer and his team are working on to advance precision agriculture in their experimental work on the farm in Carnation. The first is solving the lack of Internet connectivity in rural America. From a primitive shed in the midst of the field, a solar-powered television antenna exploits what's known as TV white space—unused portions of UHF and VHF radio waves that can be used to spread the Internet and Wi-Fi at very low costs. This arrangement has transformed the surrounding field into an agrarian Internet-of-things network. The second innovation is the aerial mapping to feed the data model. Using machine learning techniques like visual similarity and spatial smoothness, the aerial imagery makes studying a field like studying a gene or a cell. It provides the farmer with the pulse of the farm. Finally, the team is working to bring down costs and increase ease of use for farmers, particularly for air, plant, and soil sensors.

I ask Ranveer if these AI tools are going to augment or replace farmers. He smiles and says he gets that question a lot, including from a congressional committee chairman who had just visited the week before.

"We are purposefully not automating. The goal is to augment."

He notes that all of this requires humans. There is setup and assembly required. Human analysis and judgment are required. He said county extension agents are quite enthusiastic because they will be able to offer even better advice and guidance to farmers. And Ranveer's group is working with Future Farmers of America and North Dakota State University to train students.

Not far from North Dakota, in the great agricultural state of Nebraska, former Microsoft executive Jeff Raikes now runs his family's large farm and ranch in a community located between Omaha and Lincoln. I never worked with Jeff, but he is the legendary creator of the Microsoft Office productivity suite and has long used computers to help run the family farm. Not surprisingly, the Raikes farm continues to pioneer the nexus of tech and agriculture. He notes that in the 1940s it took three hundred people to run the family farm. Today it takes far fewer. Wi-Fi–enabled feedlots, for example, provide cattle just the right amount of food and water.

But it's not as simple as that. Farming has become more technical. He points out that he learned to drive a tractor when he was seven years old, but today would be unqualified to run any of the tractors on his farm.

"You have to be technically literate to work on this farm," he said.

Raikes has a theory that a smallholder farmer today is one that is below the "minimum viable economic unit." By his estimation, in the last century that MVE was about 40 acres. In the 1970s it was about 400 acres, and today it's 1,000 to 1,500 acres—depending on the soil and weather conditions of where your farm is located. In addition to great crop productivity and lower environmental impact, AI technologies for agriculture are already becoming accessible to small farmers, and those technologies could significantly change the MVE, giving small farms located practically anywhere the ability to prosper and to create jobs in their local communities. By making small farms easier to start, cheaper to operate, more productive, and more competitive in the marketplace, we will get more small farms in more communities along with the jobs that accompany them.

Granted, this means that the future of farming may look a bit different. Future farmers will need some minimum level of technical skill. But I don't see this as some great obstacle. Training for these technical skills should come from school, in perhaps a twenty-first-century version of the "Ag" classes I took in middle and high school. Farming has never been easy, and good farmers have always been great technicians with a mastery of soil, seed, and the technical equipment that has been making farms more productive at a regular pace for hundreds of years. AI will be just another tool in the farmer's arsenal. Moreover, if we all do our job right building an AI platform that's useful for agriculture—and conservation, energy production, medicine, etc.—it may very well be one of the easiest tools to master. We'll talk more later about how cloud platforms have a variety of economic incentives to make AI more accessible, how open source is a democratizing influence for AI tools, and how new breakthroughs like machine teaching can further lower the barriers to entry for AI.

In addition to the immediate economic stimulus that AI and advanced automation could potentially bring to rural economies by making small businesses easier to start and more competitive, both the AI platforms and the AI businesses that they power are without doubt going to bring with them brand-new jobs that don't exist today, and that even for the futurists among us might be difficult to imagine. According to LinkedIn's 2017 US Emerging Jobs Report, 65 percent of children entering primary school today will ultimately hold jobs that don't yet exist. When I joined Google in 2003, data scientist wasn't yet a role. Today data science is one of the fastest-growing professions in the world, and we have a *shortage* of over 150,000 of them to fill open roles, according to LinkedIn's August 2018 Workforce Report.[15] It is difficult to predict what new jobs AI may soon create, but it's not difficult to believe that the jobs will come based on the history of technology revolutions both recent and further in the past.

Two new types of AI jobs are already beginning to become important. There is a growing number of independent software vendors (ISVs) who specialize in helping customers build their products and run their businesses with AI. Those ISVs are popping up wherever there are businesses needing help on their AI journey, and those customers are increasingly outside of Silicon Valley. And then there are machine teachers.

Machine teaching is exactly what it sounds like. If you would like to train a model to look for aphids, for instance—insects that can harm crops and forests—knowledgeable people need to examine thousands of images and label how many aphids are on a plant, and at what life cycle. There are tens of thousands of teachers employed right now labeling data and in other ways producing the specific type of knowledge that machine learning systems need to digest in order to build accurate models for the tasks in which they are to be employed. If you think about all the uses to which AI is going to be put, and all the little tasks that we are going to want AI to do, we are going to need lots of machine teachers to help train the AIs. Those are real jobs for the future, and they are ones where geographic concentration is neither necessary nor particularly beneficial. Later in the book we'll talk about machine teaching more broadly, which is much more powerful than just data labeling and has the very real potential to create lots of geographically diverse teaching jobs for the millions and millions of AI models that our future economy will be built upon.

This question of what jobs will look like in an age of AI and advanced automation, particularly those jobs that could theoretically be completely automated away, is a question preoccupying a lot of economists. Writing for the journal *Science*, Erik Brynjolfsson and Tom Mitchell examine the workforce implications of machine learning and conclude that for human tasks to be automated, those tasks would need to meet all of these eight criteria:

1.   Have well-defined inputs and outputs
2.   Have lots of training data available
3.   Have clear goals and metrics
4.   Not require the use of logic, planning, or common sense
5.   Not require explanation of how the decision was made
6.   Be tolerant of error
7.   Not change quickly over time
8.   Not require specialized dexterity, physical skills, or mobility

That may sound like some farm chores, but it doesn't sound like the work of a farmer to me.

PricewaterhouseCoopers (PWC), the global accounting firm, published a report in July 2018 that looked at this question in the United Kingdom. They estimate that the countervailing displacement and income effects on employment are likely to broadly balance each other out over the next twenty years, with the share of existing jobs displaced by AI likely to be approximately equal to the additional jobs that are created. PWC identified several policy areas where action could help to maximize the benefits of AI, including mitigation strategies such as job retraining for displaced workers.

Walking back to our cars, I tell Ranveer we need to figure out how to get his team's work to scale. I love that they've started with small farms, because the lessons learned can apply to millions of smallholder farmers around the world who rely on farming for survival. By some estimates, half the people in the world work in agriculture, and many of those are self-employed as farmers. The work Ranveer is doing can help them increase yields and keep costs down with the goal of moving out of poverty.

Curious about the news I was reading from Washington, DC, I spoke by phone that same week with Burton Eller, the national legislative director for the National Grange, an organization that describes itself as working to "bring America's farmers, ranchers and other rural residents the resources they require to stay current and competitive in today's ever-changing global and local economies." In addition to helping to shape farm policy since 1975, Burton is also a farmer in a region of Virginia not too far from Gladys, where I grew up. He runs 150 acres of beef cattle on the Virginia and Tennessee border.

From his office overlooking Lafayette Square and the White House beyond, Burton has seen administrations come and go. He explains that except in rare instances, the farm bill is written by Congress, not the president. An exciting time of bipartisanship was the 1970s when Senator George McGovern of South Dakota, a Democrat, and Senator Robert Dole of Kansas, a Republican, worked together to say the farm bill is needed both to feed people and to help create strong farms. They worked toward a more aligned policy, trying to balance the interests of food and farm. An estimated 80 percent of the bill is focused on food programs for the needy such as the Supplemental Nutrition Assistance Program, or SNAP for short. The remaining 20 percent deals with farm supports. One such program is the Rural Microentrepreneur Assistance Program, which provides low-interest loans and grants to support business creation in small towns and rural areas. But these programs are not backed by mandatory funding. Over the summer of 2018, the Aspen Institute, which has long hosted a rural-issues coalition, noted that even though the Rural Development component (Title VI of the Food, Conservation, and Energy Act of 2008) accounts for less than 1 percent of the farm bill's proposed outlays, "we know first-hand that rural America relies on this funding."

Over the past several decades farm policy has become increasingly market-based. Burton remembers when farm bills were more about paying farmers not to produce in order to manage the nation's supply, demand, and ultimately prices.

"Now it's market-based," he said. "It's up to the farmer and the good Lord if it fails. Now there is disaster insurance. We've changed dramatically."

But little prepared him for the seismic change in tone surrounding his issues since 2016. He said in the days and weeks following the election, members called to ask what he was seeing and hearing. Looking out his window at Lafayette Square, he joked that people seemed to be gathering for a spelling bee.

"They are learning how to spell r-u-r-a-l," he laughed. "I've never seen such sensitivity to rural."

Jonathan Rodden of Stanford, quoted in the *Economist*, reports that nearly half the variance in the county-level vote shares in the presidential election of 2016 could be explained solely by their number of voters per square kilometer.

Federal initiatives are increasingly shaded with a dose of "here's what this can do for rural people." One example is

Federal Communications Commission (FCC) policy, which is prioritizing the spread of broadband Internet into rural communities. It helps, he said, that the FCC commissioner, Ajit Pai, grew up in the rural southwest corner of Kansas. A memorandum of understanding was signed among various federal departments that manage land to bring down barriers that might inhibit the widening of rural broadband. Even health initiatives now carry the noble purpose of telemedicine for rural people.

"The federal government is not going to spend money on taking 5G [fifth-generation wireless systems] to every corner of the country. But it is paying a lot of attention to rural areas."

I wrote earlier that in my hometown, churches played a big role in helping families get through rough times. The tragedy of hunger is often too big, though, for one church or one nonprofit. I was encouraged to see churches band together to end hunger through an advocacy group in Washington, DC, called Bread for the World. As the 2018 farm bill was debated in Congress, Bread issued a revealing report, "The Jobs Challenge." The report faced head-on a dispute between Republicans and Democrats over how much of a work requirement should be included in hunger programs. In it, ministers explored the "dignity of work," and make the case for policies that will help create more job opportunities. One that caught my eye was this: "In rural areas, invest in high-speed Internet to overcome barriers to jobs, education and social services."

Bestselling author John Grisham is known to the world for his *The Pelican Brief, The Firm,* and other legal thrillers, many set in the South. But his relative Vaughn Grisham perhaps surpasses his renown in the world of rural economic development. Vaughn Grisham's *Tupelo: The Evolution of a Community* is something of a classic of its own kind. According to its foreword, "The Tupelo Story does not offer a one-size-fits-all blueprint for community development. . . . And yet, for many of his listeners, whether they live in Maine or Montana, Grisham's narrative does serve as a sort of catalyst, inspiring them to imagine how they might best build upon the one asset that all small communities have in common, regardless of their external circumstances—their people."[16] One of the guiding principles of the Tupelo model is that local people must address local problems. Each person should be treated as a resource. So the community development process begins with the development of people. The goal of community development is to help people help themselves. Community development must be done both locally and regionally if the full benefits are to be achieved. Never turn the community development process over to any agency that does not involve the people of the community. Expenditures for community development are an investment—not a subsidy—and will return gains to the investors. So people with money have both the responsibility and an interest in investing in the development of their own community.

The intersection of AI, agriculture, and rural development is a good case study for the broader set of ideas and issues that will come up repeatedly as we think about AI's benefits and costs on other segments of the workforce. I don't purport to have all the answers, but there are some clear things we must do if we want to realize a democratized version of AI and advanced automation whose benefits will be equitably distributed, and where rural development is a first-order objective, not an afterthought.

First and foremost among these is really ensuring that we build AI as a platform to serve both the needs of big technology companies and the very long list of AI applications that folks will want and need to build to serve their businesses, large and small, local and global. As I've mentioned, companies with cloud platforms have a very clear economic incentive to make AI more accessible: storing data for AI, training AI models, and using AI in applications results in the consumption of cloud services. I've also mentioned that many AI tools are being built as open source software, which means that communities of developers can easily form around the tools and participate in their creation. Having lots of people developing these tools makes it more likely that they will serve a broader set of purposes than if individual companies develop them. Perhaps more important, the *open* part of open source means that the tools are available for anyone to use who can clear what, for professional developers, are modest hurdles.

All of us should be encouraging more of this, and making sure that we don't inadvertently break anything that is already working to democratize access to AI.

Second, we need to ensure that AI development marketplaces are emerging in a way that serves a diverse set of businesses and entrepreneurs. There is a lot to unpack here, and we'll cover this in more detail in chapter 8. But in short, we need the AI platform companies to make it easy for ISVs serving geographically diverse businesses to get started with AI infrastructure and development. We need the AI platform companies to help with the education and onboarding of these businesses, and even to focus on solutions and industry- or market-specific tools to help these businesses get started on their AI journey. We need community colleges, universities, and incubators to put programs in place to help individuals learn and practice the skills that these local businesses will need. And we need communities that are enthusiastically supportive of this type of development and transformation.

Third, we need to make it much, much easier to train models. We'll talk about machine teaching and transfer learning later, but in short, we need new techniques and breakthroughs to reduce the effort required to teach an AI system how to do a new job. Right now, this training task is expensive and requires huge amounts of labeled training data, which has made state-of-the-art AI a thing that's mostly only accessible to large companies with both lots of expertise and resources. There's a lot to be hopeful about here, with both AI platform providers and a whole host of data labeling start-ups racing to solve this problem. And there have been multiple technological breakthroughs in these areas as I've written this book.

There's certainly opportunity to do more: for governments to provide incentives for the creation of machine teaching companies, and for them to fund research on machine teaching, transfer learning, and other techniques that make AI training less costly. In February 2019, the president of the United States signed the "Executive Order on Maintaining American Leadership in Artificial Intelligence,"[17] which in Section 5(a) directs all agency heads to identify sources of data within their agencies that might be useful for AI, and to work to make that data available for nonfederal use. This, and other government investments and incentives to make more data publicly available for training AI models, is a very good thing.

There is also a very real opportunity for the emergence of open source and commercial marketplaces for pretrained models as transfer learning becomes more effective. Transfer learning, as we briefly touched upon, allows someone to use a model trained for one task to more easily build models to accomplish different tasks. Right now, pretrained models are available for very general types of tasks, like recognizing the objects in an image. For the most part, these pretrained models are too general to be useful in the types of highly specific tasks that businesses are going to want to accomplish, which is why the current best practice for most applications is training models from scratch. With transfer learning, this could change, making it possible for a huge number of pre-trained models to be used in a huge number of tasks that the original model trainer could never have anticipated. Such pretrained model marketplaces could dramatically lower the cost that a small, rural business might have to incur to build an AI model to solve a problem.

Fourth, we should pick some very specific problems at the intersection of AI and rural, and bring together stakeholders from AI platform providers, rural businesses and communities, and government to try to solve those problems. The problems could be ones in agriculture, or health care, or transportation, or energy. Basically, whatever matters to the community that will demonstrate how AI can be used to tackle the problem and others like it, and how AI empowering rural businesses can create jobs and local stimulus. Once we have demonstrations that these projects are good business and good policy, then more will happen organically. This would be another great purpose to which a grand AI initiative, on the scale of the Apollo program, could be put.

Fifth, and finally, is that we really do need to invest in rural infrastructure. The intelligent edge and cloud can't enable any AI transformations if our rural communities don't have access to high-speed networks. Microsoft has been developing and deploying high-speed wireless infrastructure for rural communities with its Airband initiative.[18] Airband uses reclaimed television radio frequencies to try to solve the last-mile networking problem in rural communities, where low population density makes wired infrastructure very costly to deploy. Whether it's Airband, fiber, 5G, or something else entirely, it is absolutely critical to get these rural communities connected. In addition to being table stakes for the intelligent edge and cloud, and a foundation for rural businesses to benefit from AI, high-speed Internet is also a necessity for the digital workforce of the future to want to live in an area.

The other critical piece of infrastructure that we must invest in is high-quality technical education and training that is geographically and economically accessible to residents of rural communities. It is crazy to assume that we are going to be able to train and re-skill all of the workers needed to make the rural businesses of the future hum if the cost of that training is tens of thousands of dollars or more, or if you have to uproot your life and move to a new community while you go through that training. Some folks, like me and my wife, will do this. Others cannot or will not. It's not their fault that they want to live in the communities where they were born and raised, near their family and friends and the local institutions that they cherish. That is, in fact, a great thing. And it is on the collective us to find better ways to allow them to live the life they want to live, and to get the training they need, to have economic security for themselves and their families.

These are ideas I can see working back home in central Virginia, and ideas that I hope will guide rural policy in Washington, DC.

PART II

Where We're Headed, and How to Get There

CHAPTER 5

AI: Why It's Needed

The old Cherokee Nation capital in North Carolina, today recognized as that of the Eastern Band of Cherokee Indians, is not too far from my boyhood home in Virginia. In 1815, a Cherokee named Sequoyah developed a syllabary that enabled nearly the entire tribe to become literate. But beginning in 1830, the US government rounded up the Cherokees and forcibly removed them across the Trail of Tears to Indian Territory in what is now northeastern Oklahoma. As many as four thousand Cherokees are believed to have died along the way, and the forced assimilation that resulted nearly killed the Cherokee language.

It's estimated that some 2.4 million Cherokee documents produced before, during, and just after the Trail of Tears hold valuable stories and lessons, but today are not accessible as so few can read the old language. During a recent hackathon at Microsoft, Native Americans working at Microsoft decided to do something about this problem. Using an optical character recognition (OCR) scanner to digitize and transpose the written documents, to build a data set of the orthographical grammar and taxonomy of the Cherokee language, the team began teaching the Microsoft cloud how to translate Cherokee into English. History was brought back to life for researchers, and a powerful AI translation engine was the result.

As this story illustrates, AI can be a force for good, as much as it is a force for change. Increasingly technologists will be forced to grapple with the outcomes created by new developments, not only because they will depend on communities, labor markets, and government to help them create and regulate these advances, but because it's become increasingly clear that new technologies do require more thinking and understanding of their consequences, both good and bad. Some technologists promote the idea that technology is neither good nor bad, that it's neutral and amoral. This may be true, but it doesn't mean the consequences of new developments are without ethical or moral quandaries, that change itself is always good, exciting, and happy.

There are several fundamental reasons, in my view, *why* we need AI. To begin, even if undesired, the AI genie is out of the bottle. And there is no realistic, global way of putting it back, so to speak. We need to continue to develop AI technologies to help defend ourselves from the inevitable bad uses to which folks will put AI (e.g., deep fakes, fake news, and the automation of hacking).

There is also a strong argument that if country X bans or constrains AI development, and country Y invests heavily in it, that country X may find that its global competitiveness and quality of life for its citizens may suffer relative to country Y. At the beginning of the Industrial Revolution in the late eighteenth century, those countries that embraced the new technologies of automation gained economic advantages for their citizens that became so deep and so enduring that we still today talk about the developed world and the developing world, industrialized and nonindustrialized nations. If you believe that AI is the most powerful automation technology that humanity has ever built—as I do—then you should also be thinking about the long-term economic consequences of the decisions being made about AI now.

More important, since the dawn of our species, technology has been our way to a better life. Technology fuels economic growth and prosperity. Some argue the last major technological innovations that provided real increases in individual prosperity happened in the first half of the twentieth century. Whether or not that's true, by most traditional economic measures (e.g., GDP) our growth is slowing in the West. AI-based technologies are one of the biggest bets we have in the pipeline that could potentially stimulate growth on a revolutionary scale, like the steam engine did. The steam engine was the specific technology that kicked off the Industrial Revolution in earnest. Unlike the innovations in textiles production that technically marked the beginning of the Industrial Revolution, the steam engine was a substitute for human labor at a scale that literally powered the explosion of industrialization. I believe that AI most likely will have a similar impact, and as with the various stages of the Industrial Revolution, that these impacts will benefit all of humanity.

Technology is the way to turn zero-sum games into non-zero-sum ones, to transform situations where there is scarcity and contention with winners and losers to situations where there is abundance and opportunity for everyone. AI is going to be the most powerful technology that we've built to date for transforming zero-sum games into non-zero-sum ones. This is one of the most important conceptual things to grasp about AI, because almost all of the good that AI can do, and almost all of the harm it could cause, are because of its ability to remove the constraints of scarcity. As a society, we can apply this property in three ways to make life better for everyone:

1. Creating abundance to support basic human needs
2. Accelerating human creativity and entrepreneurship
3. Helping us to better understand ourselves and the world around us

Many of the most challenging problems we face right now are ones where there is scarcity in the resources we need to exist, and to have a decent quality of life in the modern world. Think about the bottom two layers of Maslow's hierarchy of needs, which we will explore further: food, clothing, shelter, education, health care, and safety. Where there is scarcity, high costs, and constraints over how resources are allocated, we should think about how AI could be used to solve those problems. Your first impulse when you hear that AI can now do X shouldn't be that all of the folks doing X are going to lose their jobs, but how the world could be better if X were to become cheap and abundant.

Some of the zero-sum questions that we are asking with increasing frequency have an existential urgency to them. For instance, how do you feed a growing population in the face of climate change? A recent UN study estimates that we'll need to produce 70 percent more food by 2050 to feed a likely population of nine billion people. Climate change is already transforming the agricultural landscape and challenging crop productivity. And with most of the world's population growth happening in Africa, a part of the world that will most likely have some of the most severe climate change impacts, producing enough food will become all the more challenging. Using AI to help optimize planting times, the nitrogen cycle, and irrigation, and then to automate some aspects of crop production, could be a big part of how we feed ourselves in the future.

Similar questions must be asked about many other subsistence challenges that we are currently or will soon be facing. How do we manage the rising costs of real estate in the urban geographies where job growth is currently happening? How do we provide better, more ubiquitous health care in a world of rising medical costs? Who will do all the work, and who will take care of the elderly, in places like Western Europe, China, Japan, Korea, and parts of the US where over the next few decades the old and retired will outnumber the working young? How do we support the needs of all our citizens, young and old, to learn new, relevant skills when they are faced with rapid workplace change and rising education costs? AI could be an important part of the answers to all these questions. We'll spend more time later in the book talking about how AI, with the right incentives, safeguards, and smart policy, can do just that.

In addition to issues of subsistence, AI and advanced automation are already helping accelerate human creativity and helping entrepreneurs start businesses and create jobs that would have been inconceivable just a decade ago. My friend Hugh E and his employer, American Plastic Fabricators in Brookneal, Virginia, are a prime example of this trend. The reason that small manufacturing businesses like APF can compete in a global economy is because of automation. A CNC machine costs the same to buy and run in Brookneal as one in Shenzhen. As automation improves for these small businesses—from the tools they use to connect and communicate with customers, to the CAD/CAM tools they use to design what their customers need, to the CNC machines and 3-D printers that do the actual manufacturing—their unit cost of building things goes down and the complexity of things they build goes up. That means that they can bid competitively on more work that might have otherwise gone overseas, and repatriate jobs in the process.

It also means that humans are doing less low-value, repetitive work that is most vulnerable to the pressures of industrialization. At the same time, we are spending more of our time doing things that machines can't yet do, and that they may never be able to do as effectively or as cheaply as a human. As mentioned earlier, one of my first jobs after I graduated from high school was at EDM, a small firm in Lynchburg, Virginia, that helped other companies design electronic control systems for their products, and that did small manufacturing runs of printed circuit board assemblies. In my first summer there we had a contract to build circuit boards that controlled the types of commercial dryers sold to laundromats. To get power and control signals into and out of the boards, each had a set of electrical connectors called tabs that had to be physically riveted onto each board. If I recall correctly, there were about a thousand circuit boards and six tabs per board. My job, all day long for days on end, was grabbing a board, putting the six tabs on the board and six rivets through the tabs and circuit boards, and pulling the handle six times on a manual rivet press to crimp the rivets into place. Eight hours a day. Day after day. Until my hands were callused and my arms were sore. On the one hand, no pun intended, as a new high school graduate anxious about paying for college starting in a few months, I was grateful to have a job. On the other, it would be a colossal failure of imagination to believe that if this process had been automated, there wouldn't have been something more valuable for me to do. In fact, I spent a good bit of my time, while doing this mind-numbing task, trying to figure out how to make it go faster. Unless you believe that there is some finite cap on human inventiveness, ingenuity, and creativity, there's always going to be something better for folks to do when a menial task like this is automated away. I for one have faith in all of us.

One of the things that has been most surprising to me over the past several years is how AI is being used to help us better understand both ourselves and the world around us. One of the distinguishing characteristics of modern experimental science is that experiments generate a lot of data, and in many cases sifting through all that data puts an upper boundary on the scale of experimentation, both for the size of individual experiments and for how many experiments can be done in a period of time. AI is very good at sifting through large volumes of data and uncovering patterns that are difficult for humans to see. Over the past few years scientists have been increasingly applying AI—perhaps with best effect the techniques of deep learning—to a variety of problems. Astronomers are using deep learning to find binary stars with stable orbits and the potential of having habitable planets in orbit around them. Particle physicists are using deep learning to discover new exotic particles. Biologists are attempting to use machine learning to discover mappings between immune system profiles and disease, which could have huge implications for drug design and therapies for human illness. And conservationists are using machine learning to sift through huge amounts of data to track and protect threatened wildlife populations. As AI becomes more effective and the access to AI tools more ubiquitous, I expect these trends to continue.

Some folks believe that the study of artificial intelligence may be a way to better understand human intelligence. In his book *Genes, Brains, and Human Potential*, Ken Richardson presents scholarship challenging our definitions of intelligence, and the relationships between these measures and heritability and potential. The brain itself, with approximately a hundred billion neurons and trillions of connections between them, is one of the most complex structures that humans have ever tried to decipher. All this complexity reveals surprisingly little about the nature of intelligence itself. I've begun to think of AI as the moral equivalent of physics for human intelligence. Much as physics provides a framework and mathematical models for understanding the natural world, AI may provide a similar framework and models for better understanding human intelligence. As AI has evolved over the past six decades, we've had to rethink many of our assumptions about human intelligence, frequently learning that things we've accorded high status as great intellectual feats are relatively easy for AI, and that many things we take for granted and have trivialized are, in fact, the foundational qualities unique to human intelligence. Rather than mimicking our behavior and taking our place in the world, AI may prove to be the tool that helps us better understand the very nature of our intelligence and that ennobles us in the process.

Another way to look at the *why* is from the perspective of Abraham Maslow's hierarchy of needs, the triangle that portrays and prioritizes human needs from physiological at the bottom; then safety, love and belonging, and esteem; up to self-actualization at the pointy top. Maslow published his theory in 1943, around the same time that American painter Norman Rockwell debuted his iconic portraits of President Franklin Roosevelt's *four freedoms*—freedom of speech, freedom of worship, freedom from want, and freedom from fear. Like postwar America, we are again revisiting these needs and freedoms in the AI era.

Advanced machine intelligence, with the right focus, could elevate humanity so that we are able to spend our time pursuing the top three levels of Maslow's hierarchy versus struggling for subsistence and the fulfillment of our basic needs. I am an optimist that AI will help society bend the cost curve—that is, lower the cost—of our most pressing and pricey needs such as health care and housing. Although advanced machine intelligence could grant us the ability to achieve these lofty goals, the only way this becomes a reality is if we choose to invest our capital in efforts which can produce these outcomes. Directing capital to machine intelligence, automation, science, and engineering to provide Maslow's bottom two layers to everyone may be the only way to avoid the cataclysmic—and controversial—predictions about extreme inequality put forth by economist Thomas Piketty in his groundbreaking *Capital in the Twenty-First Century.* His central thesis is that the rate of return on capital (r) is greater than the rate of economic growth (g) over the long term. The result is concentration of wealth, and socioeconomic instability.

The artificial intelligence being developed today, and that will be developed for the foreseeable future, is based on a simple concept: learning from large amounts of data generated by humans from repetitive action. When you search the web, click or tap on a device, or use an app and your phone's GPS to navigate home through traffic, you leave behind a trail of data that is then used by AI to improve the services that you are using. The machine learning systems at the heart of modern AI typically improve with more data, making the products and services they power better and better over time. When you have small amounts of data, produced from irregular or sporadic activity, it's hard to achieve high-quality AI results. If you just imagine all of the small, irregular, nonrepetitive tasks that we all do on a daily basis in order to perform our jobs, it's hard to imagine AI systems that could gather sufficient data about all of these tasks in sufficient quantities to learn how to do everything. We already see this as AI rolls out: it can automate individual tasks, but rarely complex jobs. That's unlikely to change anytime in the near future. If your job is about performing one or a small number of highly repetitive tasks, if those tasks can be done less expensively with automation, and your employer can't find a way to leverage your ingenuity and industry to make their business better, then yes, watch out for AI. But that's a lot of ifs. The far more likely path for the foreseeable future is AI enhancing human productivity by doing the gruntiest of grunt work and freeing up humans to do things they are much better suited to do. AI isn't going to replace human intelligence, judgment, and creativity anytime soon.

The other thing that AI will have a very hard time replacing anytime soon, perhaps never, is human empathy and the desire that all humans have to want their creativity, their work, and their identity to be valued by other humans. The difference between good and bad AI, in the limit, may very well be a function of whether AI systems are used to augment these essential human qualities and desires, or to ignore or suppress them.

A good example of how this fork in the road could manifest is with AI and customer service. Many companies are pursuing the use of conversational agents, powered by AI, in their customer service operations. One potential use of this technology seeks only to optimize the cost of delivering customer service and uses conversational agents as substitutes for expensive human agents. This may yield some short-term economic benefits, and in certain scenarios might be the best choice that a business can make given the complicated set of constraints under which it may be operating. In the long term, however this isn't a winning strategy.

A better, more complementary way to use AI in delivering customer service is to look beyond cost. How can a combination of AI and human skills deliver a better experience to those needing customer support? At an industry event I attended in early 2019, I had lunch with the chief operating officer of a well-known consumer Internet brand that has quite a large customer service operation. Without me asking, this exec started to tell me about how his company was using conversational agents to improve customer service.

Rather than using the AI agents to replace humans, they began to use the AI agents to do tier 1 customer support. The job of the AI agents was to answer the simplest questions and to route the less simple questions to humans who were not only able to solve the customers' problems, but to empathize with them, to express a genuine understanding of the customer's frustration, and to let them know that someone cares. The humans are, by far and away, better than the bots right now at problem solving with the customer. And it's unclear if an AI will ever be able to make a connection with a customer the same way that a human is.

The amazing thing about this combination of AI and humans is that it appears every stakeholder won. The human agents were delighted not to be doing tier 1 support, which is menial and repetitive, and were far happier doing things that let them use their brains and their emotions. The customers were measurably happier because they got better overall service. And the company solved a huge problem that it was facing. Every company that does customer support has to figure out what percentage of its revenues it can spend on this function. In this particular case, the company had run into a brick wall. Given the constraints of their budget, and the already very high levels of productivity in their customer support operations, they couldn't figure out a way to drive customer satisfaction with support any higher. With AI in the loop, they were able to deliver record levels of customer support per dollar and were actually able to invest in hiring more human customer support agents.

This is yet another instance of the pattern that we see over and over again where AI can be used to turn a zero-sum situation into a non-zero-sum one. We start with constraints that seem impossible to relax and resulting consternation over how limited resources are going to be split up to find some sort of quasi-satisfactory equilibrium. But with AI as a tool for creating new types of abundance, a better equilibrium can be found.

The ability to use AI to remove constraints and create abundance in pursuit of solutions to our most important problems, and the opportunity to do this in ways where we pair the strengths of AI with the strengths of humans, is the real answer to "Why AI?"

CHAPTER 6

AI: What It Is (and Isn't)

Pity the radiologist. For whatever reason, this highly trained medical professional has been a favorite meme in the debate over AI replacing human jobs. If a machine can take an X-ray, it will soon also read the X-ray results and make highly accurate medical diagnoses, thus replacing radiologists—or so the argument goes. The logic leads to fear that if a doctor can be replaced, surely anyone can be replaced.

But let's examine this argument a little more carefully, only I'm going to use a cardiologist instead of a radiologist. Recently Stanford University published a paper reporting that an AI had been created that can exceed the average cardiologist performance at detecting and predicting human arrhythmias, or irregular heartbeats. The authors were able to collect and annotate a data set of about thirty thousand unique heart patients. Using electrocardiogram data from these patients, the authors trained the data model, a deep neural network, much like we train a human brain to detect patterns and transfer knowledge.

Using off-the-shelf and open source software on specialized computer hardware, they were able to train and test the model through cycle after cycle until the error rate was so low that the system could sufficiently predict arrhythmia as well as, or better than, a human cardiologist.

Such findings outside academic publications would hasten a headline predicting the demise of careers in cardiology, and a further decline in human employment. But, as with many applications of AI, there are several ways to look at this development.

If you believe that cardiology is perfect as it is and incapable of evolving, and that the world has enough cardiology to go around, then an AI that can cheaply perform cardiologic diagnosis equivalent to that of human experts will create disruptive displacement. Machines will take over the task, expensive human labor will lose their jobs, and the folks who make the AI will profit. This is perhaps what folks most fear about a future with AI.

If, however, you believe that cardiology is an evolving field, that there is a benefit to diagnosis being earlier, more accurate, cheaper, and more ubiquitous, and that therapies for cardiac illnesses have room for improvement, then this AI diagnostic system for arrhythmia becomes just another tool at the disposal of the field and the professionals who have trained to treat patients. It is a tool that could result in healthier patients by detecting their illness very early, perhaps by gathering heart data from their smart watch, analyzing it with software running on their smartphone and in their cloud, and referring them to a cardiologist for treatment before they're even exhibiting the traditional symptoms of cardiac illness when treatment can be expensive, disruptive, and potentially too late.

This is, in fact, the mission of a small company in Silicon Valley called Cardiogram (in which I am an investor). There simply aren't enough cardiologists in the world to constantly read the heart data coming from hundreds of millions or billions of smart devices looking for signs of illness. And even if there were, that would be a miserable job. Imagine spending every hour of every day bombarded by signals, notifications, prompts, and warnings. In this case, AI allows us to create abundance that didn't or couldn't exist without it. And it's a meaningful abundance: ubiquitous early diagnostics that can potentially prevent strokes, heart attacks, and other hugely disruptive or fatal illnesses. Rather than taking a cardiologist's job, this AI enhances it, potentially allowing them to spend more time treating and healing the patients they are oath-bound to help. Given the volume of folks who have undiagnosed cardiac illnesses, this AI could even increase the demand for cardiologists and cardiology jobs. And in places with a serious deficit of doctors, particularly in the developing world, technologies like this might be the only reasonable way for individuals to get any health care at all.

Aside from these cardiology jobs, an AI algorithm like the one created by the Stanford researchers or by Cardiogram has the potential to create many other jobs. There are the researchers themselves who devise the algorithm. As AI becomes more accessible, you see not just folks with PhDs in machine learning developing them. Those who created these cardiology AI algorithms come from a variety of fields—AI experts, general computer scientists and software engineers, statisticians, and cardiologists—as barriers to participation and innovation are becoming lower. Many of the most impactful AI algorithms are based on an approach called supervised machine learning and require not just large amounts of data, but data whose meaningful patterns have been identified by human beings with what AI practitioners call "labels." Over just the past several years many, many companies have arisen to do data labeling for supervised machine learning, from start-ups like Scale that specialize in data labeling for autonomous driving to an entire industry of labelers in China.[19] Preparing data, selecting the right machine learning algorithm, and then tending the experimental process required to train and refine a machine learning system is similar, in many ways, to laboratory science. It is a hugely important part of how modern AI is done, and it's a rapidly growing source of high-paid jobs. And all the infrastructure that everyone uses to build these AI systems, from open source AI tools and frameworks to hyperscale clouds, requires lots of people, from expert infrastructure engineers to the operations professionals who keep all of the data centers humming.

The current state of AI and how we, the public, are attempting to wrap our heads around it reminds me a lot of my grandfather's appliance repair business. His customers depended on technology—their appliances—for the smooth functioning of their lives. They treated these bits of technology as black boxes: not thinking too much about their inner workings when they were functioning as expected, and at a loss to do anything other than call Shorty when they were broken. Shorty would know what to do.

Even though for some folks the inner workings of a consumer appliance might seem just as dauntingly incomprehensible as the inner workings of an AI algorithm, AI is a bit more complicated. Wikipedia's definition of artificial intelligence (AI) sounds deceptively simple: intelligence demonstrated by machines. AI is the name for a broad category of technologies whose purpose is to automate work that, until the mid-1950s, was the exclusive dominion of human minds. Even though the idea of machines mimicking human behavior has its origins in antiquity, and even though we've actually been building human-mimicking machines in earnest since the beginning of the Industrial Revolution, artificial intelligence as a formal discipline was given its name and came into being in the summer of 1956 at a workshop held in Dartmouth, organized by John McCarthy and attended by other pioneers including Marvin Minsky, Claude Shannon, and Herb Simon. In their proposal for the workshop, they asserted:

> *We propose that a 2 month, 10 man study of artificial intelligence be carried out. . . . The study is to proceed on the basis of the conjecture that every aspect of learning or any other feature of intelligence can in principle be so precisely described that a machine can be made to simulate it. An attempt will be made to find how to make machines use language, form abstractions and concepts, solve kinds of problems now reserved for humans, and improve themselves. We think that a significant advance can be made in one or more of these problems if a carefully selected group of scientists work on it together for a summer.*[20]

Despite an already fuzzy, ill-defined name, the use of the word *intelligence* in the name for this collection of technologies further lends to the confusion, particularly because we still don't have a crisp, universally accepted definition of the human intelligence AI seeks to mimic. Moreover, the technologies underlying modern AI are changing at an incredible rate.

Consequently, most of us may not really understand what to expect out of AI, much less know whether it's functioning as it should. Even though we have reached the point where almost everyone has daily interactions with technologies that incorporate varying degrees of AI, and we are heading into a future where AI will have a bigger and bigger role to play in our lives, there is no Shorty Tibbs to help us figure things out.

The good news is that we understand enough about AI

and the forces behind its recent, rapid advances to articulate a handful of high-level AI concepts that are easy enough for everyone to understand. These concepts can help you better reason about what AI is and isn't, what it is likely to be able to do in the future, and to have rational opinions about what AI should or shouldn't be doing for you, your business, your community, your country, and the world at large.

There is danger in reasoning about AI at a high level of abstraction. Not fully understanding what's going on in the black boxes of AI makes it easy to veer off into very speculative territory. Moreover, the nature of AI itself—the notion that machines are emulating aspects of human intelligence—can sometimes make speculation sound rather convincing even when it has only the slightest of connections to technical reality. So, in addition to concepts for reasoning about AI, we will also give you some tips and techniques for detecting AI bullshit. Developing some rationally informed intuitions about AI will be very helpful, whether it's for figuring out which, if any, of the mutually conflicting opinions about AI you should believe, or checking your own wild optimism or pessimism about the future of AI.

Artificial intelligence may prove to be the most powerful tool that humans have ever built. Even so, it's just a tool. Building and using tools are cornerstones of our humanity. Most of the empirical evidence for behavioral modernity— the point in history where *Homo sapiens* differentiates itself from other hominids and primates[21]—is based on construction and use of tools. For tens of thousands of years we have built and used tools to adapt to the conditions of our environment; to build safer, more predictable means of subsistence; to fulfill our creative ambitions; to communicate and better coordinate our efforts with one another; to better understand the world around us; to extend our life-spans; and in many, many subjective ways, to make our lives better.

Whether you're a scientist, an engineer, a politician or policy maker, a journalist, an entrepreneur, a teacher, a student, or a worker, you have a role to play in determining what the future of AI looks like. You get to choose whether you use this tool to help you make your life, and the lives of those around you, better, or whether this tool uses you to fulfill someone else's goals.

THE LIFE AND TIMES OF
TECHNOLOGICAL BREAKTHROUGHS

Before we dive headfirst into an explanation of artificial intelligence, there are a few conceptual things about technology that are going to be worth keeping in mind as you start more deeply understanding AI.

From stone arrowheads and fire, all the way to spaceships and quantum computing, technological change over the millennia has come in fits and spurts, not as one smooth, continuous, predictable, and well-planned process. We've had long passages of time with relatively little progress, punctuated by moments of technological breakthrough and breathtaking progress that can challenge our ability to cope.

It's very hard to predict when meaningful breakthroughs are going to happen and what form they might take. Just have a look at early- and mid-twentieth-century popular science and science fiction to get grounded on how many predictions haven't come to pass, and how many that have, but whose impact is so different from what we imagined. I'm still waiting for flying cars! You can even get a feel for how bad we as humans are at predicting breakthroughs by just rewinding your own experience ten or fifteen years and honestly assessing how much of now you would have imagined possible back then.

Certain types of technological breakthroughs, once made, can unfold in relatively predictable ways if you know what patterns to look for. In particular, technologies that serve as foundations or platforms upon which more technology can be built often bring sweeping change with them. There are two types of these platform technologies: ones that are simply building blocks that enable or accelerate the development of other tech; and ones that have direct or indirect, self-improving feedback loops. Both can trigger huge amounts of change. The latter, however, can result in such quick and significant change that the world seems to remake itself as you're watching.

My great-grandmother lived to be ninety-nine years old. She was born at the end of the nineteenth century, in 1898, and passed away a few years before the new millennium in 1997. She lived through several radical changes in the world brought by technological breakthroughs with feedback loops. When Grandma Ischer was born, there were no mass-produced cars, no airplanes, and no electricity in the rural parts of the United States. Antibiotics had not yet been invented. You cooled perishable food in ice chests, chilled with literal ice. There were no computers, no television, not even radio. The world was almost unrecognizably different ninety years later. I was always amazed that someone could have experienced and adapted to so much change in a single lifetime.

Let's take three of the big technological changes that Grandma Ischer experienced in her lifetime: ubiquitous electricity, ubiquitous refrigeration, and television. One is a platform technology with self-reinforcing feedback loops; simply put, it is used to make other technology possible, and it can be used to make itself better. One is a platform technology that powers a huge variety of other technologies, but is missing the feedback loops. And the other is not a platform technology at all.

Of the three changes, ubiquitous electricity has been the most transformative. It is without question a platform technology. An enormous chunk of what we think of as technology in the modern world is literally powered by electricity. But electricity is also used indirectly to improve its own means of production. For instance, electricity powers the machines that are used to build better electric power capabilities, where better might mean more efficiency, larger scale, or completely new ways to generate and deliver power. More recently electricity has been used to power computers that have further enhanced how power is produced, delivered, stored, and consumed. Computers are used for everything from generator design to power grid management to the design of completely new forms of power generation and storage like batteries and renewable energy sources. This feedback cycle has been operating for close to 150 years and continues to result in a cheaper, more ubiquitous energy platform for the rest of technology. Interestingly, although it is in their very early days, AI and machine learning are already being used to further enhance electric power production, transmission, and consumption. When I imagine the planetary-scale challenges that we're facing in the coming years, like how to control climate change while still leaving open the opportunity for the developing world to raise standards of living, AI optimization of our power systems stands to play an enormously important role.

Ubiquitous refrigeration, although less impactful than electricity, is still one of the most important technology platforms of the past 175 years. The vapor compression refrigeration cycle that powers most modern refrigerators was discovered in the nineteenth century. The first commercially viable refrigeration systems started showing up in the 1850s. The earliest popular, commercially viable application of the technology was supplying ice to breweries and home iceboxes. During much of the early part of her life, ice made in town by one of these big commercial refrigerators was how Grandma Ischer's family kept their perishable food cold in their icebox.

In the early twentieth century, refrigeration technology made its way into the home, with the first electric refrigerator brought to market in 1914. The refrigerants used in these early home refrigerators prior to the invention of freon were quite dangerous, not just to the ozone layer! Since then, vapor compression refrigeration technology has become crucial for modern society. It not only allows us to keep foods and medicines in our homes with less risk of spoilage and foodborne illness, but also has shaped our landscape, allowing humans to live in otherwise inhospitable places and to move perishable food safely from where it is produced to where it is consumed. Refrigeration is a key platform technology not just for consumer and commercial refrigeration units, air conditioners, and chilled transport, but is also used to liquefy industrial gases like helium, nitrogen, and oxygen, for metallurgy and in dozens of other industrial and scientific applications. It doesn't have the same feedback loop that electricity has: vapor compression refrigeration doesn't help make vapor compression refrigeration better. But it's still hard to imagine what the world must have been like before the ubiquity of refrigeration technology.

Television is another of the big technological changes that Grandma Ischer witnessed during her long life. Every year her entire extended family would gather in her little home in Bedford County, Virginia, for Thanksgiving. Her four daughters and their extended families would come bearing their favorite dishes and eat the meal of the year in the company of loved ones we had waited a year to see, all while a tiny little color television sat in the corner with the Macy's Thanksgiving Day Parade humming in the background. Despite the television's role as a cultural anchor in many of our lives, it isn't a platform technology. It informs us, entertains us, and connects us in very different ways than the newspapers, books, and radio that preceded it. But TV technology can't in any meaningful way help improve itself, nor does it serve as a platform for building other forms of technology. It consumes tech versus empowering other technology. And if Grandma Ischer were still alive today, she might get a chance to witness another shift as people's consumption of this technology is replaced by newer tech like streaming.

I would argue that platform technologies—like electricity and refrigeration—tend to have bigger and more durable impacts on society than nonplatform technologies. If nothing else, they get embedded in and become commingled with many other things above and beyond our patterns of consumption. This means that they not only can endure as patterns of consumption shift, because of the variety of ways in which they are used and the other technologies which depend upon them, but that they potentially can thrive and serve as platforms for new technologies that continue to emerge. Moreover, platform technologies with feedback loops—like electricity, the PC, the Internet, the cloud, and AI—can have huge amounts of impact in very short periods of time because their feedback loops mean not just that they get better over time, but that they *get better faster over time* until they reach some plateau.

One of the things that made American industry so successful in the twentieth century, and that continues to drive success today, is investment in platform technologies, on infrastructure that supports our ability to create and build. Even some of our biggest investments whose end goal hasn't been platform technology—for example, our space and defense programs—have produced many important platform technologies that have been essential building blocks for other technologies that touch and influence our daily lives. These technologies include things as grand as the Internet, and as tiny as the silicon image sensors that power billions of digital and smartphone cameras around the world.

As we explore what exactly artificial intelligence is, you will hopefully see how and why it too is an important platform technology, perhaps the most important in a series of digital platforms that we have created over the past seven decades. AI has very powerful self-improving feedback loops that will continue to result in AI becoming more and more capable very quickly. Like all platform technologies with feedback loops, AI will have plateaus where its rate of change will flatten out and slow down. When and where those plateaus will come is very hard to predict. Even though we are in a period of intense change right now, no one knows for sure when progress will slow, nor how much we will have achieved when we arrive at the next plateau.

What isn't hard to predict is that as a technology platform, AI will put more and more power into the hands of those who choose to use it as a tool for their creativity, ingenuity, and ambitions. Without that creativity, ingenuity, and ambition, AI is a bit like electricity. It sits there with great potential, waiting to be used. And the more of us who choose to put AI to good uses—equitable, fair, and ennobling uses— the richer the world will become.

A LETTER TO SHORTY

I'd like to think that if my grandfather had been born fifty years later he would be just as fascinated by AI and advanced automation as I am, and more likely than not, he would be working to make it part of his repertoire of tools and techniques to help him build and fix things. If he were still alive, I know he would have been curious about how this technology is developing and what it can be used for. And I would have done my best to explain it to him. In that spirit, let me try to explain it to you.

Artificial intelligence is an attempt to get machines to do intelligent things. Since that Dartmouth workshop in 1956 when the founders of AI named the field and set its early ambitions and goals, there have been three distinct phases of AI. The first I call *systems of reasoning*, when researchers attempted to emulate intelligence by explicitly modeling the world's knowledge and articulating a set of logical rules by which that knowledge could be manipulated. The second phase I call *systems of learning*, when instead of explicitly modeling knowledge and the rules for manipulating it, researchers designed algorithms that could learn to emulate intelligence from large volumes of data. This second phase of AI has driven much of the growth of the consumer Internet. The third phase of AI development I call *systems of simulation*, where in addition to learning from human-generated data, researchers are teaching AI agents to emulate intelligence through simulations of the real and synthetic worlds. We are just entering this phase and have already seen it producing some of the most spectacular accomplishments in the history of AI, from beating humans at complex games like Dota and Go to automobiles and delivery drones that can autonomously navigate the real world.

Our poor understanding of human intelligence itself notwithstanding, what constitutes an "intelligent thing" for a machine to do has changed a lot over the years. I took my first AI class as an undergraduate in the early 1990s. The first AI programs that I wrote in this course solved logic problems. One of them went like this:

You have a cabbage, a goat, and a wolf that you must get from one side of a river to the other. You have a boat, but the boat can

only carry you and one other item in a single trip across the river.
If that's not enough of a pain, you have an unstable situation on
your hands with the cabbage, goat, and wolf. If left unattended,
the goat will eat the cabbage, and the wolf will eat the goat. Circle
of life, I guess. You can, however, make as many trips back and
forth across the river as you like. Is there a way to get all three
items to the other side of the river without losing one? If so, how?

You may have seen this brainteaser before. Turns out there is a solution.

TRIP 1: Carry the goat with you from side A to side B.

TRIP 2: Move back to side A.

TRIP 3: Carry the wolf with you from side A to side B.

TRIP 4: Carry the goat back with you from side B to side A.

TRIP 5: Carry the cabbage with you from side A to side B.

TRIP 6: Move back to side A.

TRIP 7: Carry the goat with you from side A to side B.

In this sequence of trips, the cabbage and the goat are never alone together, and neither are the goat and the wolf.

Whether human or machine, is being able to solve this problem a sign of intelligence? Hard to say. There are thousands and thousands of books, games, physical puzzles, and apps containing logic puzzles and brainteasers designed to stimulate your brain and entertain you. These sorts of things show up on our standardized tests as measures of our ability to reason. And mastery of the big brothers of these small puzzles—games of strategy like chess and Go—has historically been viewed as an indicator of high human intelligence.

The point of turning this particular puzzle into an AI programming exercise was to teach us how to encode a common type of logical reasoning into rules that a computer could understand.

As a programmer, you do this by creating a representation of the problem state. For this puzzle, the problem state records which side of the river you and each of the three items are on. You define what moves you can make from one state to the other. In this case, on every turn you can move from one side of the river to the other and take one item with you. You define what the winning and losing states are. Here you win when all three items are on side B of the river, and you lose if either the cabbage and goat or goat and wolf are on one side of the river and you are on the other. And once you have these three things, you use a search algorithm to explore which moves get you closer to a winning state, and which moves get you to a losing state. You want to explore the former and avoid the latter.

The search algorithm that you would use for a problem like the cabbage, goat, and wolf brainteaser isn't as fancy as you might expect. If you think about the problem a bit, we're trying to explore the moves that you can make from the beginning state, where everyone is on side A of the river, to the winning state. You can write all these states down and organize them as something that looks like an upside-down tree. You start with the beginning state at the root of the tree. From this state, you add a branch for each possible move, and you attach the new state to that branch. You fill out the tree by repeating this process for every new state that you add to the tree until you reach either a winning or a losing state.

The search algorithm walks through this tree to find the winning states. Simple versions of the search algorithm explore the whole tree, making very simple choices about how to choose the next step in a path. The problem with this is that for most problems, the tree can be very large. For the game of chess, for instance, a tree has 10^{120} branches. That's more than the number of atoms in the entire universe. A lot more, in fact. Which is why in practice, you want to be clever about how to choose the paths you explore in these trees. With a clever search algorithm and lots and lots of computing power to run the search, this approach can pull off some impressive feats, like beating the world champion at chess, which is exactly what IBM's Deep Blue did in the now famous match with Gary Kasparov in 1997.

My first AI program is a microcosm, a trivially simple microcosm, granted, of the first phase of AI, what I have called systems of reasoning. For many years scientists and engineers tried to build intelligent systems by encoding human notions of logic—symbolic reasoning like solving algebraic equations and proving theorems, and our explicit knowledge of certain domains like medicine—into software. The big idea was that as you encode more things in this way, you will have machines that are capable of increasingly intelligent behavior. It's not a bad approach, and honestly, I believe that there is a huge amount of opportunity ahead of us in extending these classical techniques and combining them with some of the contemporary approaches that are showing so much promise. But building systems of reasoning is a lot of work. And, as practiced in the 1990s while I was an undergraduate and graduate student, it's a lot of work that had to be done by specialists and experts. That made for slow, expensive progress.

What comes next, and the part of the story that Shorty would have been especially fascinated by, is the world of machine learning that has been on fire for the past two decades or so.

CHAPTER 7

How Models Learn

Around the time that I dropped out of my PhD program in 2003 to take a job in industry, there were two trends that were about to change the nature of AI. One was rapid adoption of the Internet, and the flood of data generated directly and indirectly by users as more and more of their daily lives moved online. The second trend was the emergence of the cloud, a new massively scalable distributed computing platform that was emerging to handle the growth of the Internet. With these two trends, the subdiscipline of AI called machine learning was about to kick into high gear, and the second phase of AI—what I have called systems of learning— was born.

Unlike my early experiences with AI that emphasized logic, symbolic reasoning, and encoding and manipulating expert knowledge, machine learning uses *data* to build *models* and then uses those models to do intelligent things. The first machine learning program I wrote in preparation for a bigger machine learning project I had been tasked with at work was a spam classifier for e-mail.

Classifiers use machine-learned models to determine what class something belongs to. In the case of e-mail, you might want to take everything that comes into your in-box and determine whether it's spam or not. To do that you need a bunch of e-mail messages—your training data—with each message labeled *spam* or *not spam*. The more data, and the more representative that data is of typical in-boxes, the better. You then take this *labeled training data* set and train a model using the machine learning algorithm of your choice.

For my classifier, I used Naive Bayes. What that is and how it works aren't super important. The important thing is the idea: if you have enough labeled data, you can train a model that is able to make *inferences* about things it has never encountered before—in the case of my classifier, determining whether brand-new e-mails that show up in an in-box are spam or not. When you write a machine-learned spam classifier, you don't have to know beforehand all the words and phrases that spammers use in their messages to trick you into doing something you shouldn't. You just need to have examples of spam so that the system itself can learn the patterns that make a message spam or not. Rather than having to encode rules and relationships and logic and explicit knowledge, the algorithm learns what it needs to learn from the data. The more training data you have, the better your learned model will be. And the more frequently you can gather labeled training data and retrain, the easier it will be for your model to adapt to new patterns that might emerge.

It sounds complicated, but the pattern is simple. You have some data you want to be able to reason over. You make a bunch of examples of what you want the machine learning algorithm to learn by labeling your data, whether that's *this e-mail is spam* or *this image contains a cat*. You then use these examples, the labeled training data, to train a model. If you do your job right, when you pass new data through the model, it has learned what to do with that data, whether that's inferring a previously unread message is spam or tagging a cat in a previously unseen image.

Perhaps the most exciting thing about machine learning, and one of the reasons that this second phase of AI and its systems of learning have made such rapid progress compared with the first phase of AI and its systems of reasoning, is that machine learning progress is driven by how much data you have and how much computing power you have available to train models using all of this data. With the Internet and the cloud, both data and *compute power* have been growing at astronomical rates over the past two decades, which has helped us to make stunning progress in machine learning. One way to think about this is that instead of having thousands or tens of thousands of experts building systems of reasoning during the first phase of AI, we now have tens of thousands of experts building systems of learning that are in turn being trained by the data being produced by a few billion people as they use the Internet, their smartphones, and the increasing number of smart devices that permeate our lives.

HOW MODELS LEARN

The machine learning approach I just described is an example of *supervised learning*. With supervised learning, a human being labels all the data required to train a model. You can think of this labeling process as a way to teach a model how to recognize patterns in data. To borrow an analogy from Sean Gerrish's book *How Smart Machines Think*, it's a bit like teaching a young child about the world through flash cards. The cards are the labeled training data, and the training process is repeatedly showing the cards to the child until they grasp the pattern. Any child is a far more advanced learning machine than a machine learning algorithm, so you don't want to carry this analogy too far. But at a high level, this is the essence of supervised machine learning.

Your model is only as good as your data. If you are teaching it to recognize a bucket, you must figure out what readily definable features of your data are going to help your model learn. For e-mail that might be easy because e-mails have lots of easily discernible structure. It's a lot tougher to say what the features might be for recognizing buckets. A human, when asked to describe useful features of buckets, might say things like "they sometimes have handles" or "they're kind of cylindrical and have holes in the top" or "they're usually made from plastic or metal." But for a computer, those aren't readily definable features. They are difficult to describe directly to a machine that knows nothing at all about many things we take for granted like handles, holes, and materials. In fact, the difficulty of describing such complex features to machines is one of the reasons machine learning was invented in the first place!

Once you've figured out features, you might have to label a hundred thousand different buckets of all different shapes, sizes, and color, from different perspectives and under different lighting conditions. If you don't provide enough variety and quantity of training examples, the model won't be able to generalize, to recognize buckets that it's never seen before, or to say that a picture of a dog is not a bucket. If you have biased data, you will likely train a biased model. If, for instance, you mostly used pictures of red buckets in training, your model might not recognize blue buckets as buckets at all, which is problematic in a world with both red and blue buckets.

Some of the biggest challenges in modern supervised machine learning arise from the need to make your training data representative enough of the domain you want the AI to learn. A tremendous amount of human effort goes into feature engineering and labeling data. You must make sure that the features you choose are predictive, that the labels are accurate, and that the training data is representative. Human developers, data scientists, machine teachers, and data workers also must manage bias in the data they are feeding the AI. Machine-learned models learn what we teach them. It is far too easy for harmful human biases, naturally present in human-generated data, to make their way into models where those biases can be amplified at AI scale. For example, if all the labeled data identifies doctors as men, your model is going to learn that all doctors are men and blithely propagate this bias and inaccuracy.

All this machine teaching and data manipulation is time-consuming and extremely expensive. Even for large technology companies with hundreds of millions of customers with whom they interact daily, data is the biggest thing that limits what you can accomplish with AI. You might have a perfectly good idea for a problem that you think could be solved with machine learning, but find yourself in a spot where you don't have the right data: too little, too expensive, the wrong type, too biased, etc. There are several techniques that can help when confronted with these sorts of data problems, chief among them *deep learning, machine teaching, transfer learning, reinforcement learning*, and *unsupervised learning*.

DEEP LEARNING

Supervised machine learning can accomplish an unbelievable number of things using a relatively simple pattern: engineer your features, label your data, train your model, deploy your model, and use it to make your product "better," resulting in more user engagement and more direct and indirect data to use to make your model better; wash-rinse-repeat. This cycle has driven much of the growth of the consumer Internet over the past fifteen or so years.

The first step in this cycle, feature engineering, isn't something that folks talk about a lot, but it is a necessary step and one of the most important parts of doing machine learning. In every machine learning system, you have data and something that you want to learn from these data. In order to learn from the data, you must tell the machine learning algorithm what features of your data you believe will help it to learn. For some types of data and machine learning problems, like e-mail and spam detection, figuring out the features can be easy. With e-mail you already have some structure: whom it's from; whom it's to; a subject; a date and time sent; a body with words and sentences and paragraphs; attachments; links to web pages; etc. All of those, or combinations of them, might be useful features to use in your model.

For images you're using to train a bucket detector, the only structure you may have is a list of numbers telling you what color each pixel is. Are those pixels the right features to help your model recognize buckets? If not, what features do you use? Your guess is as good as mine.

Deep neural networks, DNNs for short, can be a very effective way to build models when you have lots of labeled training data but you're not too sure what the right features are for your data. DNNs are based loosely on the biological neural networks in our brains. DNNs are much smaller than a human brain. As of this writing, the largest of the largest DNNs have fewer than ten billion synapses or parameters, although that number has been increasing in recent years by as much as a factor of ten every year, given massive increases in available compute power. Still, our largest DNNs are many orders of magnitude smaller than a human brain, which has approximately a hundred trillion synapses. It also bears mentioning that even though our largest artificial DNNs are much smaller and much dumber than a human brain, the computing infrastructure and power required to run them might consume a hundred thousand times the space and power of a human brain.[22]

Structurally, deep neural networks are also quite different from a human brain. AI scientists and engineers design DNNs to solve categories of problems. DNNs for recognizing images tend to be structurally different from those that translate text from one language to another. The structure of these DNNs are far more regular and much less complex than our biological neural networks, and typically only good at the narrow range of tasks for which they were designed. We are still at the very early stages of research into techniques like transfer learning that allow DNN models designed and trained for one task to be combined with other models to solve different tasks.

With DNNs, you determine some very high-level structure of your data and problem, and then select a DNN category. If you're trying to do some sort of inference on images or data with two-dimensional structure, you will probably use a convolutional neural network (CNN). If you're trying to build a model that can predict the next word in a sequence or the next action to take after a sequence of prior actions, you might use some sort of long short-term memory network (LSTM). If you're trying to build models that are operating over recorded speech or on handwriting, you might use a more general recurrent neural network (RNN). Once you've picked a DNN architecture for your problem, you're then mostly off the hook for specifying features.

The idea of neural networks has been around for a long time, and technically predates the field of artificial intelligence. The first neural network models were created in 1943 by Warren McCulloch and Walter Pitts, and there was significant progress in neural network research over the next couple of decades. Things stalled out by the late 1960s, primarily because the ambition of research had exceeded the ability of computers to keep up. Progress slowed because there simply wasn't enough compute power to do the next set of interesting things with this flavor of AI.

In 2006, Geoffrey Hinton, Simon Osindero, and Yee-Whye Teh published a seminal paper, "A Fast Learning Algorithm for Deep Belief Nets," describing techniques for effectively training deep neural networks. In 2009, Andrew Ng pioneered the use of graphics processing units (GPUs) for training deep neural networks, achieving improvement by a factor of 100 in training performance. Since then, DNNs and deep learning have, in many ways, dominated the field of machine learning, allowing AI experts to make stunning breakthroughs, most noticeably on perception tasks like labeling the objects in images and recognizing the words in spoken language. Part of this is because DNNs solve a very hard problem in feature engineering. Part of this is because of an explosion of this perception data. And part of this is because the algorithms used to train deep neural networks are amenable to running on GPUs, processors originally designed to accelerate computer graphics, which has allowed us to train DNNs in reasonable amounts of time where, prior, their training compute requirements were impractically large.

DNNs are a hugely useful technique currently being used in all the major flavors of machine learning: supervised, reinforcement, and unsupervised. They make feature engineering easier, but still require lots of labeled training data to perform well. Lots and lots of labeled training data. The good thing is that DNNs can be used in conjunction with other techniques to help reduce the burden imposed by their thirst for data. When using DNNs in supervised learning applications, combining them with machine teaching or transfer learning may provide a way to bootstrap the training process from smaller training data sizes. Reinforcement learning and unsupervised learning use DNNs, but in these applications, the data that fuels the DNNs are generated in massively scalable simulation loops.

One of the weaknesses of DNNs is that we don't yet have a precise science governing their design. A deep neural network is composed of layers of artificial neurons, each of which is connected to neurons in other layers. How many neurons are in each layer, how many layers, and how the neurons interconnect is known as the architecture of the DNN. Each of the connections between neurons has a weight, and this weight determines how much signal flows from neuron A to neuron B when A is activated. As with biological neurons, activation is typically a nonlinear function of the neuron's inputs. The rectified linear unit, or relu, is the most popular of these nonlinear activation functions in 2019, but as with anything in AI, this could change very quickly with dramatic, unpredictable effect. And you don't need to worry about what relu is or even what a nonlinear function does. The important thing to understand is that a neuron is either off or on. It takes a bunch of signals from neurons in other layers, and if those signals surpass some threshold, the neuron turns on and passes a signal to all the neurons to which it is connected in proportion to the weights on those connections.

The job of the learning algorithm is to flow training data from the input layer to the output layer, learning the weights on all the connections in a way that maximizes the likelihood that the output layer outputs the right thing. For example, if we are training a DNN to recognize buckets, we would likely use a convolutional neural network architecture. We would take labeled training data consisting of images with and without buckets and flow those data through the DNN, learning a set of weights that maximizes the likelihood that the output layer emits a *bucket* signal when the training data contains a bucket, or a *no bucket* signal when there is no bucket.

One other trick that DNNs use in training is a technique called dropout that prevents the DNN from overfitting the model to the training data.

Imagine the following exchange:

"Every CEO is old and gray."

"But my boss is a CEO, and she is neither old nor gray."

"Well, that's the exception that proves the rule!"

"I still think you're overgeneralizing!"

"Really? I don't think so. Just because your boss is a CEO doesn't mean that we can't say that all CEOs are either old and gray or else look like your boss . . ."

Overfitting is a problem that any machine learning system can have, not just DNNs, that results from the model learning from the training data so well that it has trouble generalizing to any data that wasn't in the training data set. Since generalizing to previously unseen data is the point of building machine learning systems, overfitting is a bad thing, and having techniques at your disposal for dealing with it is very important.

To see the point with just a little bit more technical depth, one could use a confusion matrix to depict a group of people—our training samples—according to age and grayness, and whether or not they are CEOs.

We can use machine learning to learn a rule, or function, that predicts if a person is likely (or unlikely) to be a CEO. The blue line represents one such function. The function that it represents is a simple one—linear regression, to be specific—that despite its simplicity seems to do a pretty good job determining if someone is likely to be old and gray enough to be a CEO.

A more complicated function might be depicted by a green

line. On the surface, having more complexity seems to give us more accuracy. The green function better separates the group of real CEOs from the non-CEOs. In fact, imagine that one little red dot near the bottom might represent someone just like my boss, who is a CEO, but neither gray nor old. It might even be my boss!

But the problem here is what happens when we use these machine-learned functions to analyze data we've never seen before. For example, my friend is about as young as my boss. But he is not a CEO, nor would one normally think of someone as nongray and young as him to be CEO material. In this case, what we see is that the green function is not really a good one—it is guilty of overfitting.

Neural networks today are capable of learning extremely complex functions—in fact, the most complex functions ever built by humankind (with machine assistance, of course). If left unchecked, given enough data and the right DNN architecture, the functions/rules they learn would essentially account precisely for every single "exceptional" case in their training sets. Simply put: Neural nets today can learn too much from their training data. This capability needs to be tamed. So a big part of the research on neural nets has centered around how to control this overfitting problem.

Dropout turns out to be one of the most effective approaches to preventing overfitting in DNNs. A simple way to think about dropout is that it's like selective forgetting. If the network remembers everything that it has seen, then it may never learn to generalize beyond its memory, which is a bad thing. The goal of any machine learning system is to be able to generalize beyond the data on which it has been trained, to be able to respond with good answers when it is asked a question about data that it has never seen before. It's the same as wanting your child to be able to eventually do arithmetic more complicated than what they've memorized from flash cards.

Dropout forces a DNN to forget some of what it learns in each stage of training in order to force it to learn how to generalize. With dropout, during each stage of the training process, some neurons within each layer are chosen randomly to be removed—or "dropped out"—and consequently don't propagate signals to other neurons in other layers. The probability of dropping a neuron out is a configurable parameter of the training process. If you forget too little, you may fail to learn to generalize. If you forget too much, your model may never learn anything. So choosing the correct value for this parameter is important.

When the training stage is complete, the dropped-out nodes are reinserted. This process is repeated in every stage until training is complete. Why dropout works as well as it does is not entirely understood, which is a common refrain with deep neural networks. The most plausible theories that folks currently have is that randomly dropping out nodes is like changing a little bit of the DNN architecture during each training stage, which makes it harder for model weights to co-adapt, which can lead to overfitting.

As a side benefit, doing dropout also reduces the amount of time and power required during training since we're only training a fraction of the nodes at each stage. Whether the dropout is a fifty-fifty thing (as in a coin flip) or some other probability, and whether every stage is handled the same way, and lots and lots of other tweaks and variations, is a subject unto itself. But the bottom line is that what people generally want out of a machine learning system is a fairly "smooth" function. Dropout has the effect of smoothing things out, so that weird spikes—like having someone as young and dashing as my boss in your training set—won't lead us to conclude that all such people are CEO material.

Many of the choices that we make about the configuration of a DNN to make it work well are determined through experimentation. Researchers and AI developers have been exploring ways to automate this experimentation to quickly and automatically determine what configurations work best for a particular problem or class of problems. These efforts are colloquially known as AutoML, and the most sophisticated ones use machine learning to determine DNN parameters, like how much dropout and what activation function to use, and even DNN architecture. Doing this experimentation manually is time-consuming, expensive, and error-prone, in many cases resulting in a suboptimal model. Sometimes that means training a DNN with poorer than ideal performance, which may result in people giving up on deep learning prematurely. And sometimes it means that an individual or team doesn't try deep learning at all, because the whole process seems too daunting.

Microsoft's AutoML system has been applied in dozens of machine learning systems in active use across Microsoft's portfolio of products and services. In our own uses of AutoML, it is often able to build better models than the best hand-tuned ones that data scientists and AI experts were able to achieve on their own. In some cases, AutoML makes machine learning accessible for the first time for teams without AI expertise. Given how successful AutoML has been internally, we've made it available for other developers as a service in Azure Machine Learning, and for nondevelopers in tools like Power BI, where it is truly making the power of machine learning accessible to whole new audiences. Due to its promise and demonstrated utility, AutoML is a very active area of research and development in industry and academia.

MACHINE TEACHING

Just as flash cards are limited tools for teaching children, our current best practices for data labeling and data engineering are very limited ways to teach a supervised machine learning system to make inferences about data. Patrice Simard, the originator of machine teaching, writes, "While machine learning focuses on creating new algorithms and improving the accuracy of 'learners,' the machine teaching discipline focuses on the efficacy of the 'teachers.'"[23]

If I wanted to build an AI system to recognize all the pages on the web that contain food recipes, using typical supervised machine learning techniques, I would need to find perhaps hundreds of thousands of examples of recipes among the tens of billions of pages on the web—because I would want all my training examples to be accurate; i.e., actual recipes and not unrelated things like instructions for grooming your cat or lists of facts about an actor. A human who knows how to distinguish recipes from these other things would have to look at each page and label it. Because I potentially need so many labeled training examples, I would need lots of humans, and it would take a very long time. And even after I spent the time and money to gather all these labeled examples, I might get a model that doesn't work well and need to gather different data for subsequent rounds of training.

Machine teaching seeks to make it easier for humans, who can quite easily discriminate between recipes and nonrecipes, to convey their knowledge of a domain like this to a machine learning system. For instance, one of the things that a human might easily grasp about a recipe is that each one typically contains a list of ingredients. Things without lists of ingredients are unlikely to be recipes, and things with them have a much higher probability of being recipes. So, instead of just simply labeling things as *recipe* or *not a recipe* and hoping that the machine learning system figures out ingredients lists, why not teach the system to recognize ingredients lists as part of teaching it to recognize recipes?

Machine teaching is an incredibly promising new direction in machine learning. It has the potential to dramatically reduce the amount of data and data engineering required to train a model, and consequently to lower the expense of training. This could make machine learning significantly more accessible, making it just as possible for a small business as for a giant tech company to build bespoke models for problems that they are trying to solve, and for both large and small organizations to solve problems where data scales and/or budgets would never be big enough to solve the problem at hand. It also makes bias an easier problem to grapple with. It's far easier to train a small group of folks how to recognize and deal with bias than it is to get very large groups of data labelers or the whole Internet to confront and deal with conscious and unconscious biases. Author Ted Chiang, best known for his short story that inspired the film *Arrival*, explores this idea of machine teaching combined with systems of simulation in his novella *The Lifecycle of Software Objects*. Picking up on the great Alan Turing's suggestion that an alternative to programming intelligence would be to teach an agent to speak English and then have it learn like a child over time, Chiang explores each stage in the agents' development, tracing their progress from one step to another.[24] His approach is not far off—machine learning whether supervised or unsupervised ultimately requires a lot of human nurturing, teaching, care, and feeding before it's able to do anything useful.

BOOM AND BUST

Even in our ancient stories, humans imagined machines that could mimic life. When my daughter learned about Greek mythology, she declared that Hephaestus must have been the god of engineers because he built robots in his workshop. Over the centuries, humans have gone from telling stories about automata to building them. It seems that every time we have made the jump from imagination to reality, we go through a cycle of surprise and incredulity, followed by amazement and wild optimism, then fear and anxiety, and, ultimately, to understanding and acceptance of the limitations of the leap that was made.

With artificial intelligence, the cycle starts with folks making claims that we are either very far away from, or very close to, the point where a machine could do some tasks as well as a human. When the machine subsequently bests humans at one of these tasks, we enter a period of hype where we question our understanding of what is hard and easy, imagine the many other things that machines might be able to do if they can do *this*, and then start making attention-grabbing predictions about the future in either utopic or dystopic directions. Since the Dartmouth workshop in 1956 made many bold predictions about what cognitive feats machines would soon be able to do, we have been frequently so awful at predicting the future of AI, leading to so much disappointment when bold claims fail to materialize, that the busts that typically follow the periods of hype have a name: the AI winter.

We've had several periods of AI hype followed by AI winters. We are almost certainly in a period of hype right now, which means that, to borrow a phrase from George R. R. Martin, winter is coming. AI is not the only human pursuit that exhibits this pattern, and this boom and bust cycle might be unavoidable. But it is unfortunate because the hyperbole of the boom, and the pessimism of the bust, are distractions from steady progress on a tool that is becoming more and more useful by the day.

I fear that the next AI winter will have disproportionate impact on the parts of AI that have the most promise for broad, beneficial impact on society, mostly because we are underinvesting in those things right now. The big institutions funding AI right now—big tech companies and the Chinese government—have a deep understanding of the value that AI can create, and will almost certainly continue to fund it at high levels even when the public hype bubble bursts. AI winters of the past, however, have resulted in dried-up funding for public research, fewer folks pursuing advanced degrees in AI, and small companies going out of business. If we believe that democratization of AI—making it a tool that almost anyone can use to achieve their goals—is important, and that encouraging the use of AI for the public good is necessary, then an AI winter would be bad, and we should try to avoid the next one.

FALSE EQUIVALENCE AND MYSTICISM

The causes for boom and bust cycles are as complicated as humans themselves. I do, however, believe that with artificial intelligence, there are a handful of things contributing to the ups and downs of the field. The first is the false equivalence that folks may assume between the mechanism of artificial, and that of human, intelligence. A brain and a piece of software attempting to mimic some aspect of human behavior are two very different things. A human brain contains about 100 billion neurons, 100–500 trillion connections between them, and runs on about 25 watts of power. The largest neural networks, as of 2018, are ten thousand times smaller than a brain and require many orders of magnitude more energy. Moreover, these networks, which are much smaller and much less energy efficient than brains, perform computations that are mere fragments of full human intelligence.

Perhaps more vexing even than the temptation to conflate the brain with the digital hardware and software that powers AI, the very notion of human intelligence is so ill-defined that analogizing it with artificial intelligence can be tricky. Ken Richardson writes in *Genes, Brains, and Human Potential*:

> *Intelligence is viewed as the most important ingredient of human potential. But there is no generally accepted theoretical model of what it is (in the way that we have such models of other organic functions). Instead psychologists have adopted physical metaphors: mental speed, energy, power, strength, and so on, together with simple genetic models of how it is distributed in society.*

Richardson, and a growing number of scholars, believe that standard measures of intelligence, e.g., IQ tests, are poor indicators of human potential. Indeed, many of the things that we have traditionally believed to be indicators of high human intelligence, e.g., mastering strategy games like chess or Go, reading passages of text and being able to answer questions about them, translating between human languages, etc., are things that machines are readily able to do. Contrariwise, there are tasks that nearly any human toddler can do that are formidable, unresolved challenges for machines. In one famous behavioral experiment, with a toddler watching, a person with an armful of stuff walks toward a cabinet with closed doors, and feigns frustration at not being able to put the items away because they don't have a free hand to open the door. The toddler watches, gets up, and opens the door for the adult. This simple act of commonsense reasoning that is within the capabilities of a human child too young to even speak would be challenging for existing machine learning systems to do.

Unfortunately, making a false equivalence between human and artificial intelligence is an easy thing for us to do. I catch myself doing it all the time. Whenever I see a surprising new AI achievement, I tend to immediately start asking, *If it can do that, then what else might be possible?* And depending on whether I'm in an optimistic or pessimistic mood, I can go down the path of *Damn, that's really exciting,* or *Oh no, that's pretty scary.* Both paths are usually fruitless and tend to lead to bad predictions, which at best is a waste of time, and at worst can be a distraction from better, more practical paths that deserve to be explored.

When I'm gripped by excitement with AI, whether positive or negative, I try very hard to calm down and ask myself what is it that I'm excited about. If it's about the implications of what I'm seeing, then the very next question I ask is whether I really understand what's going on beneath the surface of the new thing. I've been excited so often about so many things that led nowhere that I try my best to assume nothing.

Renowned futurist and science fiction author Arthur C. Clarke once said that any sufficiently advanced technology is indistinguishable from magic. Even though I love Clarke's work, and I understand that humans have a long history of ascribing magical or mystical qualities to complex things they don't understand, I'm not a big fan of this way of thinking. AI is advanced, and indeed complex. I spend most of my time every day working with some of the most accomplished AI experts in the world, and have been building machine learning systems for over fifteen years. And I can say without any shame that I'm nowhere close to understanding all there is to understand about AI. (Many of my colleagues will happily attest to that fact!)

But AI is a human work of science and engineering. Despite its complexity, it is within our ability to understand it. We should not ascribe magical or mystical properties to AI technology just because the complexity is daunting. AI is like any other technical discipline, with a bunch of folks focused on the theory of how to build intelligent machines, a bunch of folks working on experiments to refine theory, and a bunch of folks trying to build things of practical use based on our theoretical understanding of what is and isn't possible. In the science of the natural world, you might observe an apple falling from a tree. You may wonder what caused the apple to fall. Your first impulse as a scientist would be to observe apples falling as carefully as you are able, to do some experiments, and to discern patterns in your observations. You then formulate a theory of why the apple falls. Like all good scientists you want your theory to be as general as possible, i.e., to work for things other than apples being pulled toward the surface of the Earth. You then do some more experiments to try to prove or disprove your theory. When you're confident that your theory is a good model of some aspect of the natural world, you share it with others who poke it at, run their own experiments, and refine it in ways large and small. As we get more and more confident that the theory is a good model, we start using it to build things, from brand-new theories to technology that is powered by or dependent upon the theory.

This is exactly how the development of AI works. Researchers and practitioners in the field have ideas about how to imbue software with intelligence. Like Newton's gravity, we don't at first know what mechanism is behind the aspect of intelligence that we're trying to model. We postulate some theories about what's going on that we can then model with math and computation. Some of our theories prove to be good models of certain types of intelligent behavior, good enough at least for us to have been building useful AI software for decades, with increasing utility in recent years. Nothing magical at all is going on.

Approaching AI with scientific rigor is the only real way to have agency over such a complex system. Ascribing magical properties to AI, appealing to its metaphysical qualities, or otherwise surrendering to its complexity not only puts you a bit further away from conversations that can influence the development of AI, but it's selling yourself short. None of this stuff is impossible to understand.

That doesn't mean that you need to make yourself an AI expert. It just means that when you see someone making claims about AI, you should have faith in your ability to challenge those assertions, and to dig in deeper to understand.

BEWARE SNAKE OIL SALESFOLK

All the way at the bottom of the many layers of abstraction upon which modern AI is built are a set of very complex principles and technologies. There are tens of thousands of researchers and engineers around the world attempting to push the frontiers of AI forward, and the body of work that they are creating is so vast; requires such a deep degree of expertise across so many disciplines of computer science, mathematics, and neuroscience; and is changing so rapidly that it's a challenge even for the folks in the trenches to stay fully up-to-date.

Case in point: as I am writing this in December 2018 one of the most prestigious AI conferences, the Neural Information Processing Symposium, known more commonly as NeurIPS, has just been held in Montreal. The best paper at the conference, authored by a talented group of researchers from the University of Toronto, was "Neural Ordinary Differential Equations," and its abstract reads:

We introduce a new family of deep neural network models. Instead of specifying a discrete sequence of hidden layers, we parameterize the derivative of the hidden state using a neural network. The output of the network is computed using a black-box differential equation solver. These continuous-depth models have constant memory cost, adapt their evaluation strategy to each input, and can explicitly trade numerical precision for speed. We demonstrate these properties in continuous-depth residual networks and continuous-time latent variable models. We also construct continuous normalizing flows, a generative model that can train by maximum likelihood, without partitioning or ordering the data dimensions. For training, we show how to scalably backpropagate through any ODE solver, without access to its internal operations. This allows end-to-end training of ODEs within larger models.

This was an unexpected result, a brilliant connection of the area of AI called deep learning with the much more mature discipline of numerical methods, and it may have a big impact on the way that we think about training certain types of deep neural networks.

This level of detail is necessary if you are one of the scientists or researchers trying to push the frontier of AI fundamentals forward. It's also the case, at this level of detail, that bullshit is no match for scientific scrutiny, well-designed experiments, and mathematical rigor. In the labs and offices, we are trying to build an intellectual fortress to support very precise ideas that will either become the next breakthrough like "Neural Ordinary Differential Equations" or send us back to the drawing board. Unverifiable opinions and untestable speculation, regardless of the reputation of the speculator and the degree of their conviction, are irrelevant.

I interact with a lot of folks at many different levels of AI knowledge and expertise, and my own AI knowledge and expertise has gone up and down over time as the field has advanced. When trying to wrap your head around all the information coming at you about AI, it's essential to know your level of expertise, and the level of expertise of the person who is espousing an opinion or asserting a point of view.

The most confident I've ever been about machine learning

systems was when I was directly involved in building them on a day-to-day basis. On those systems I knew exactly what they could and couldn't do, was surrounded by other experts, and spent a considerable amount of time tracking the state of the art in the areas of AI related to my project. I was deep, but narrow. If I was telling you something about how my system or a system like it worked, it would have been a good bet to pay attention.

Even when I was that deep and narrow, there were many folks more technically expert than I was. These folks were actively working to advance the state of the art in some aspect of artificial intelligence. These folks typically had a PhD in computer science or mathematics, or an equivalent degree of intense, focused experience. The field is complex and moving fast, so becoming a technically expert specialist is partially about getting to a high degree of accomplishment in all the scientific, mathematical, and engineering methods and tools one needs to practice the craft at the very highest level. And it's partially about staying on top of the incredible volume of work that other specialists in your area are producing.

Specifically, at the very frontier of a discipline, abstractions tend to form, then break, and then be re-formed at a rapid pace. You must understand not just the torrent of new abstractions that your colleagues are producing, but also the tools by which these new abstractions are formed. Obviously you must have a high degree of facility with these tools so that you can produce your own innovations, but also so you can help to scrutinize the work that others are producing.

The "Neural Ordinary Differential Equations" paper is a very good example of work produced by technically expert specialists. The new idea that they produced, the new abstraction, so to speak, was modeling the interior of deep neural networks as a system of ordinary differential equations. If you don't understand what that means, don't worry. It's something that had not appeared in the literature for deep neural networks before, and required a group of researchers who were not just immersed in the current state of the art in their own area of AI, but also had the necessary sophistication in mathematics and in the adjacent field of numerical methods to make a new connection and apply a set of classic techniques in a new and interesting way.

Being a technically expert specialist in one area of AI does not necessarily mean that you are able to keep up with everything going on across the entire field. That's an impossibly difficult task for any individual, given the volume of work happening in AI now. Jumping sideways into another area of AI may require a technically expert specialist to spend significant amounts of time ramping up on the current research in that new area, and potentially to invest in learning a new set of tools being used by the specialists in that area.

Even though I've built and overseen many big machine learning projects that have operated at massive scale, I've had periods over the past six years where I have gotten embarrassingly out-of-date as my work became less about day-to-day AI execution, with the field heedlessly moving forward at a blistering pace. For instance, I failed to stay current on deep learning as I was growing LinkedIn's engineering team from 250 engineers to 3,100 engineers from 2011 to 2016. When I jumped back in where AI again became a day-to-day part of my work, it was shocking how much I had to catch up on.

When I'm trying to make sense of someone's AI pontifications, I typically look at a person's breadth of AI focus, the fraction of their time they're spending on AI, and the specificity of the point of view that they're expressing. If the person is narrowly focused, spending most of their time on AI, and is expressing specific points of view related to their work, then it's far more likely that what they're saying is going to be trustworthy and insightful rather than some super-broad generalization from a person who is very far away from hands-on and spends only a tiny chunk of their time doing AI.

This might seem obvious, particularly given that it is also true for things other than AI. If you have a heart condition, you would probably trust your cardiologist for advice over your general practitioner, and your general practitioner for sure over someone who watches a lot of medical dramas. It's worth saying, though, because the frequently assumed similarities between natural and artificial intelligence invite some very broad, very confident assertions that are so out there that there's not even a way to put them into a proper scientific framework where a reasonable conversation can be had.

This is not to say that if you're not in the trenches, there's no way for you to connect to the AI conversation. Even folks in the trenches need the ability to connect to the broader conversation about AI. The field is advancing so quickly on multiple fronts, and not everyone in AI is in the same trench. It's nearly impossible to stay on top of everything. Fortunately, you don't need to operate at the lowest levels of detail in order to use modern AI. It's a near certainty that anyone reading this book interacts daily with technology that incorporates varying degrees of AI. An increasing number of software developers at all levels can use higher-level abstractions to incorporate AI into the technology that they're building. And as we've already observed, some of the most promising developments in AI may put the capability to build and create with AI into the hands of folks with no prior programming experience.

FOLLOW THE MONEY

Perhaps the best practical advice I have for anyone trying to understand what impacts AI is having on their lives is to try to understand who is profiting from it. Who is getting paid? Since the boom that thrust the consumer Internet into all our lives, the deal that we've had with most Internet companies is that we get to use their services for free in exchange for their gathering data about us that is subsequently used to create more engaging products and services, to grow those services more quickly, and to target ads to us to which we are more likely to respond. These companies make more money as they gain more users, as users use their products more, and as they are able to show you more and more compelling ads. I've worked for and helped build two companies that make most of their revenue this way.

This is not necessarily a bad bargain. We just all need to be aware that there are machine learning systems at the core of most of the ad-supported applications. As we've seen, machine learning systems are very good at optimizing exactly what you teach them to optimize. If the machine learning systems only optimize for more users, more engagement, and making more money, that is exactly what you get, along with whatever side effects that they bring.

The next time you are navigating the web or using your favorite application, ask yourself why you are doing the things that you are doing. Why are you clicking on that link, taking your time to read a piece of content, liking that friend's post, or sharing that article? Why were you shown what you were shown, and who profits from your interacting with it? Are you getting fair value in return? These are perfectly reasonable questions for you to ask, ones that you wouldn't hesitate to ask in other parts of your life where you are transacting business. When the party on the other end of a transaction is a machine learning algorithm, it's probably even more important that you demand to understand what's going on than you would when a salesperson is pitching you on a purchase, or a telemarketer is trying to talk you into something.

This isn't to suggest that anything sinister is going on. Without this business model many of the great things that enrich all of our lives, like search, for instance, would not exist. I use "free" Internet services all the time, fully understanding that the price I pay for using them is my data. Most of the time that's fine. And when it isn't, I try to pay for the service, tune my settings to provide some acceptable degree of privacy, or find an alternative to the service. Mostly I try to be constantly aware of what I am consuming or acting upon, and ask myself whether I'm getting fair value in return and whether I'm in control or being manipulated. When I believe that the value exchange is off, or that I'm being deliberately or inadvertently manipulated, I change my behavior.

Judy Estrin and Sam Gill have introduced the notion of digital pollution[25] as a mechanism for understanding and dealing with side effects of algorithmic and machine learning systems that try to extract business value from human attention. They write:

> *Digital pollution is more complicated than industrial pollution. Industrial pollution is the by-product of a value-producing process, not the product itself. On the Internet, value and harm are often one and the same. . . . The complex task of identifying where we might sacrifice some individual value to prevent collective harm will be crucial to curbing digital pollution. Science and data inform our decisions, but our collective priorities should ultimately determine what we do and how we do it.*

There may be other constructs for reasoning about and addressing the side effects of attention-oriented, ML-powered business models, but this is a good start. We have clearly arrived at a moment where we can no longer pretend that there are no side effects and accept inaction as an appropriate response. Some people fear the specter of an AI that develops superhuman intelligence, and that poses an existential threat to humanity like Terminator's Skynet. I'm far less worried about this than I am by the unintended side effects of completely explicable machine learning algorithms innocently pointed at perfectly reasonable business objectives, like making a product as engaging as possible.

ARTIFICIAL GENERAL INTELLIGENCE

One late summer morning, Dario Amodei addressed a small gathering of AI scientists at our Redmond labs in Building 99. Dario leads AI safety research at OpenAI, then a nonprofit AI research company that described itself as "discovering and enacting the path to safe AI." It was originally funded by individuals like Elon Musk and Reid Hoffman as well as by tech companies. In the summer of 2019, I helped to lead a multiyear, $1 billion investment in OpenAI to build a platform to create new AI technologies and deliver on the promise of artificial general intelligence. The title of Dario's presentation caught my eye: "AI Safety through Integrating Humans in the Training Loop."

"Reinforcement learning systems have made great advances in optimizing fixed, well-defined reward functions (as in games like Dota or Go), but are less well-equipped to pursue complex goals that embody human values or judgments," he wrote. This inability to translate human intentions into behavior (or the very slow loop of doing so through mathematical specification of reward functions) can lead to unintended consequences and practical safety problems. His research focuses on learning from human preferences, or human-in-the-loop training.

Amodei points out that failures in AI can generally be pegged to one of three problems—a problem with the algorithm; a problem somewhere in the software stack; or the AI was trained for the wrong objective function, the wrong reward. He demonstrated by showing a video game his team had programmed in which a speedboat was rewarded for making laps around a water course. The failure was immediately obvious. The boat veered this way and that, crashing into things and even catching on fire, but it was racking up points—rewards—because that's what the developer had mistakenly prioritized in his or her reinforcement learning model. The AI boat had learned how to get a turbo boost and create fires, which accrued lots of points. It was going around the course racking up points in any way it could. He later showed a robot arm that was trained to move a puck from one end of a table to a target on the other end. As the puck approached the target, the robot arm would nudge the table slightly to achieve the goal. Not optimal, but it worked.

The rewards didn't correspond with what was really wanted. Therefore, a human was really needed in the loop.

The type of AI that OpenAI is pursuing is called artificial general intelligence (AGI), sometimes known as strong AI. It is the type of AI that the founders of artificial intelligence sought to create at the birth of AI at the Dartmouth workshop in 1956, AI that would be indiscernible from human intelligence for arbitrary cognitive tasks. Even though the dream of AGI has existed since at least 1956, probably earlier, perhaps even back to antiquity, progress has been extremely slow and frustrating. We've had more instances of thinking we were close, only to have those hopes dashed, than we have had major breakthroughs. But with reinforcement learning and unsupervised learning, a good chunk of the world's knowledge represented in some form or the other on the Internet, and computing power increasing at a blistering clip, folks are more hopeful about the feasibility of AGI in the near future than perhaps they have been since the fifties and sixties.

Getting to AGI is no sure bet, though, and opinions about when or if we're likely to achieve AGI are widely varied even among experts. The most optimistic credible estimates are five to ten years, and the most pessimistic are never. Anyone who tells you with absolute certainty when AGI will be here is most likely wrong.

Why is making this prediction so hard? One reason is that AGI's goal of emulating human intelligence is one of the most complex problems that humans have ever attempted. Unfortunately, our definitions of intelligence itself are imperfect and not terribly helpful when trying to define what AGI should or could be. Perhaps more important, our understanding of how the brain works, how it manifests human intelligence, is still poorly understood. We do understand some of the microscopic structures of the brain. We know what a neuron is and what axons, dendrites, and synapses are. We know what a neuroreceptor is. We understand how these microscopic structures function in isolation and some of how they interact in proximity with one another. We understand some of the neurochemistry of the brain. We know how neurons use these structures and chemistry to transmit signals from themselves to other connected neurons. We've understood some of this for a while and, in fact, that understanding informed the development of artificial neural networks back in the 1940s.

The thing we don't understand as well is how all these microscopic structures of the brain come together in a way that results in human intelligence. With approximately a hundred billion neurons in a human brain and an average neuron connecting to a thousand other neurons, it may be a long time before we've fully characterized brain function and worked our way to an understanding of human intelligence from a neurobiological perspective.

Even if you were to believe that artificial neural networks are the precise digital equivalents to biological ones—which you shouldn't—and that if you had the ability to train a hundred-trillion-synapse (parameter) DNN—which we don't, yet—AGI is almost certainly not as simple as training such a large DNN using the world's knowledge. This large DNN still would not possess an equivalent neural structure to a human's, a structure evolved over very long time horizons that we don't fully understand.

This doesn't mean that the pursuit of AGI is pointless. Quite the contrary, the problem itself is so fascinating that we continue to make attempts at solving it even after six decades of slow progress. The two big organizations attempting to achieve AGI, OpenAI, and DeepMind, are making incredibly useful discoveries as they pursue their longer-term goal. Many of these discoveries are being shared with the rest of the AI community in terms of open source software and research papers, which is helping to accelerate other AI efforts unrelated to AGI. Some of these discoveries will have commercial utility and could show up in products and services that benefit us. The quest for AGI itself might also prove to be an incredibly useful way for scientists to better understand the mechanisms of human intelligence.

As a platform company, Microsoft is interested in providing the best possible tools and infrastructure to AI researchers and practitioners, no matter how ambitious their goals. As I am writing in 2019, we are not actively attempting to build our own artificial general intelligence systems. But we are proud to partner with folks who are working on AGI, and I am intensely curious about the process of discovery they are on. Their ambition helps us to invest in more and better AI platform capabilities that we can then make available to everyone.

Many have expressed concern about AGI, although the nadir of that worry, at least for the time being, seems to have occurred in 2018. Elon Musk and Stephen Hawking, for instance, have believed that AGI is an existential threat to humanity, and Musk has been publicly calling for strict regulation for several years now. What exactly that strict regulation would be like is unclear. But the fear and anxiety that the very thought of AGI provokes in some is crystal clear.

Despite these concerns, I do believe that we need to think about any potential regulation of AGI very carefully. No one knows exactly what steps would be required to achieve AGI, much less a malevolent or destructively indifferent one. If, for instance, we wanted to regulate AGI like we do weapons, then given the current state of things and our present knowledge of how AGI might work, we could very quickly create a regulatory regime that would not only make it more difficult to reap the many positive benefits of AGI for fear of the bad, but the regulatory blast radius could make it harder to do ordinary AI and even normal software development.

Why? Sticking with the weapons analogy, we regulate the development and use of arms, like nuclear weapons, by making it illegal to possess them, and by tightly controlling the key ingredients for making them. That's not the easiest thing to do, but arms are physical things, and it's reasonably well understood how to construct them. That means that we can write careful regulation, set up monitoring processes, enter into treaties, etc., where detection and enforcement are well-understood and narrowly scoped to preventing the specific bad things we want to prevent.

AGI, on the other hand, isn't a physical thing, and the ingredients for making one are human ideas turned into code. Moreover, we don't even know which ideas are going to be the ones that lead to AGI, much less the full scope of what bad stuff an AGI could do that we would want to prevent. Once you begin to think about how to regulate the wrong ideas and our ability to write those ideas down as code, a whole bunch of things that today look like free expression could become illegal. That's not to say there should be no regulation. We should simply be very, very thoughtful about what it would look like.

So how concerned about AGI should we be? And how do we place those concerns into the broader context of immediate things that we should be worried about with mainstream AI, about the things that are happening and that we have very high confidence will be happening soon?

I do think that it's prudent and reasonable for us to guard against the creation of an AGI that would harm humans or, more strongly, would do anything other than serve the best interests of our species. Codifying what exactly that means would be tough. Isaac Asimov, the futurist and science fiction author, is famous for his three laws of robotics:

1. A robot may not injure a human being or, through inaction, allow a human being to come to harm.
2. A robot must obey orders given it by human beings except where such orders would conflict with the First Law.
3. A robot must protect its own existence as long as such protection does not conflict with the First or Second Laws.

Even though it might be an oversimplification, I believe that we need the equivalent of Asimov's Laws for AGI. I also believe that OpenAI may currently have the best, simplest articulation of what good AGI governance could look like. If you look at the OpenAI Charter,[26] the research lab's board commits to specific actions to ensure that the group's work on AGI has broadly distributed benefits, a specific focus on long-term safety, investment in technical excellence, and a cooperative orientation. At the time of this writing, they have taken several actions that are consistent with this charter. They have a new financial structure called a public benefit corporation that allows them to fund their charter at high levels, but that caps investor and employee returns at a fixed level, and transfers returns above and beyond those levels to a nonprofit organization with public governance to ensure that most of the value of a realized AGI would go to the public. Their safety review committee has also recently elected not to publicly distribute a new language model given its potentially dangerous uses, including its potential to be used to create fake news.

CHAPTER 8

AI: A Threat or Boon to Jobs?

Recalling that night back home when I tossed and turned in bed trying to visualize what I might do to help restart jobs and economic opportunity in Campbell County, I remember taking an inventory of the computer science experience I'd accumulated over the years, and then worked to link that understanding with the workforce available in rural communities like Gladys, Rustburg, Brookneal, and other little towns that dot the region. Too often, the conversation about AI and human employment ends just as the fretting starts. What will the grocery clerk, the filling station attendant, the bank teller, the tobacco farmer do for work when advanced technologies take over these tasks? What is the future of work for these workers? That's what kept me up that night.

Since then, I've met with a lot of experts and done plenty of reading about labor trends, especially in the manufacturing and agricultural sectors. The truth is that software and computer control have already had a huge impact on these job sectors. Most experts focus on the negative impacts that robotic assembly lines have on blue-collar jobs: the mindless, repetitive, error-prone, low-skill work that industry has been trying to make more efficient for decades. Automation and globalization are just two of the ways that we've increased economic productivity. But according to the FRED blog, published by the Federal Reserve Bank of St. Louis, manufacturing jobs as a percentage of the total US workforce have been on a very steady decline for decades, starting long before either globalization or automation were big factors driving efficiency. Even without AI, this trend would continue down to an equilibrium point where a very tiny fraction of the population can meet the needs of the whole.

We've seen the same trend in agriculture since the Industrial Revolution began. Depending on which data source you look at, in the eighteenth century somewhere around 75 percent of the working population made a living from agriculture. In the US, after World War II, we were at 13.5 percent of the population, and we've steadily declined to 1.5 percent since. A Federal Reserve Economic Data chart shows the percentage of agriculture jobs in the US as a percentage of the civilian workforce since early 1948. It's the same degree of decline until right around the new millennium, where we seem to have hit an equilibrium point where approximately 1.5 percent of the population can serve the agricultural needs of the whole. No AI. And we're not pining away for a world where we go back to our subsistence farming roots.

Once I eliminated all the noise about a human employment apocalypse brought about by AI robots, I began to think more clearly. There are actually many reasons to be optimistic—but it's going to take work. We know that demand will continue to grow for software engineers, researchers, data scientists, and machine learning experts. We also know that AI will need talented writers, lawyers, teachers, and other professionals to train AI and its intelligent bots. Sure, highly educated people will continue to prosper, but what about lower-skilled and mid-skilled workers?

Elisabeth Mason at Stanford's Poverty and Technology Lab reminds me of something Reid Hoffman, founder of LinkedIn, knows so well. "Even as AI threatens to put people out of work, it can simultaneously be used to match them to good middle-class jobs that are going unfilled. This is precisely the kind of matching problem at which AI excels." It can even predict where the job openings will be.

This is where I began to think harder. Researchers at McKinsey & Company looked at the limitations inherent in AI getting to scale. Limitations for AI are opportunities for humans. Limitation number one is data labeling. AI models must be trained, and humans must be employed to obtain, organize, and label ever-increasing, massive amounts of data sets. For the most part, humans are needed to explain the data, to make sense of it and stand guard against bias in the data and algorithms. These are jobs for the very farm and factory workers we worry about.

In agriculture, I've been inspired to watch innovators like Plenty, a fully autonomous farm in San Carlos, California, backed by venture capital. They are doing the equivalent of thirty acres of farming within a fraction of an acre indoors within a robotic farm. All of that production happens with less than one-eighth of an acre footprint for the grow room, and about two times that if you include the seedling room and thermal systems for climate creation. Not only is it more efficient, but AI helps to ensure they don't lose a single plant. Furthermore, so-called fresh produce that is actually shipped two thousand miles from farm to market can now be supplied much closer to where the food will be consumed. Similarly, Bowery Farming in New Jersey is creating new jobs growing crops vertically in an industrial park. Algorithms and robots help to ensure the right amount of light and water reach the plants at the optimal temperature. They can grow more, faster, with no pesticides. And again, because the automation makes small-scale, local farming more competitive, it has the potential to help create more jobs in more communities than large-scale agriculture alone.

On the manufacturing side, I began to imagine a new business opportunity. For argument's sake, let's make up a fictional company named Mid-Atlantic AI, Inc., and it might be located in an old abandoned tobacco-curing barn, a furniture plant, or a textile mill in central Virginia. What will be increasingly necessary in the near future are firms like the one I have in mind to label and structure data, and then to train AI technology using that data.

In September 2019, the *Times of India* published a story about how AI is creating jobs, not stealing them. The article reported that poor families were learning to annotate images so that those images could train AI data models. "Now I can get a salary on time, work in an office, and can spend some time with my family as well," one worker proclaimed. Some speculate even data labeling will become obsolete, but experts note that the precision, nuance, and sophistication required to label data will require humans to review, audit, and monitor it.

The company I worked for while attending Lynchburg College, Electronic Design and Manufacturing (EDM), built small runs of electronic circuit boards, and one of the pieces of equipment they used in that manufacturing process was an infrared reflow oven. Infrared reflow ovens resemble commercial pizza ovens, melting lead solder paste that has been screened onto a printed circuit board and onto which small electronic components have been placed, usually by a robot colloquially called a "pick and place" machine. When the solder melts, the electronic components form mechanical connections to the circuit board. This technology is widespread, used to manufacture the hundreds of circuit boards that are in nearly everything that you own.

Suppose a company, a future Mid-Atlantic customer that makes infrared reflow ovens for circuit board manufacturing, calls and wants to build a new version of its oven that uses cameras and AI to automatically inspect and flag boards coming out of the oven with soldering defects. Infrared reflow soldering can have many types of defects, most of them detectable by visual inspection. If solder were improperly masked onto the circuit boards, the manufacturer may have incomplete solder joints. If the reflow conditions are not just right, the result is "tombstoning": small surface-mount components that raise up on one end like little tombstones because one side solders correctly and the other does not. These defects, when caught, must be identified by human visual inspection under a magnifying glass or microscope. It's a time-consuming and error-prone process, and one that infrared reflow oven manufacturers think customers would pay a premium for to have automated. But the reflow oven manufacturer has no AI expertise, just a suspicion that such a thing should be possible. So Mid-Atlantic AI in Campbell County, Virginia, to the rescue.

Mid-Atlantic AI consults with the oven manufacturer to get cameras installed on a bunch of customer ovens to take pictures of circuit boards coming out of ovens, all of them, whether or not they have defects. They also get a library of circuit board defect images from the oven manufacturer and identify some web repositories of images of the types of circuit boards that are produced by reflow soldering. They send a couple of AI trainers to the oven manufacturer's customers and have them shadow their quality assurance (QA) people for a couple days so that the AI trainers can learn what the QA people look for in terms of defects.

The AI trainers back at the office begin to label images they have gathered and are receiving from the customer as defective or not, based on what they've learned about circuit board quality assurance. A team of ten trainers labels images for two weeks and produces 24,000 circuit board images, and with a 3 percent actual defect rate, they discover 720 images of defects. They supplement this with images provided by the manufacturer, from their Internet searches, and with machine teaching tools that allow them to more accurately describe the nature of defects to the machine learning system. They send the training data to a data scientist who builds a relatively straightforward model using PyTorch and cloud GPUs. The model is tuned to be very conservative, rarely giving an "all good" judgment to boards with actual defects at the cost of judging more boards to be defective when they really aren't.

Let's suppose that human inspectors who examine boards coming off of a reflow oven are right 95 percent of the time. If the real defect rate is 3 percent and they examine 10,000 boards, 300 should have defects, and they will say that 5 percent of those 300 defective boards, or 15 of them, are fine when they aren't. Those then go off to customers who will eventually have to deal with the defective product. Not a great experience for those small number of unlucky folks, and a waste of time and money for everyone.

The conservative AI system that Mid-Atlantic trained is able to achieve a 1 percent false negative rate, and a 10 percent false positive rate. In other words, it will allow 3 of the 300 defective boards to pass inspection, at the cost of flagging 1,000 boards as defective. Those 1,000 flagged boards will then be sent to human inspectors, who again with 5 percent accuracy and a 3 percent actual defect rate will only allow 1 or 2 defective boards of those 1,000 to make it into the hands of the customer.

With no AI assistance in the inspection process, the inspectors must examine 10,000 boards and send 15 defective pieces of work to customers. Afterward they must inspect only 1,000 of the 10,000 boards, and only 4 or 5 defective pieces of work slip out to the customer. For one-tenth the effort, customers are getting three times fewer defective boards. The oven manufacturer quickly determines that is a better result, that their customers will be thrilled at the prospect of being able to make a higher-quality product at lower cost for their customers, and that this new automation technology will allow them to sell more ovens at a higher price. The cost of this model development was less than $75,000, which was easily within their R&D budget and far less expensive than hiring their own AI experts to complete the project in-house. And it's not a foregone conclusion that they would be able to hire an in-house AI expert at all, given the likely short supply of these folks that will persist well into the future.

As part of the contract, Mid-Atlantic AI for $10,000 per month has agreed to retrain and provide quality assurance for a new reflow defect model based on labeled images of defective and nondefective boards supplied by the manufacturer from actual usage. This in turn allows the manufacturer to sell a subscription service to their customers to provide new models, which helps their machines to become more personalized to the customer, with higher accuracy the more they are used.

This might sound a bit like science fiction, but as I've already mentioned, companies in both Silicon Valley and China are already doing similar work for the burgeoning AI industry. And we're already seeing that the use of AI and advanced automation in small manufacturing operations allows these businesses to be more price competitive, to bid on and win more work that might otherwise be offshored, and as a consequence to grow and create new jobs.

To be sure, AI and automation technologies more generally pose a threat to a wide range of jobs. Most repeatable, highly regular work, whether low or high skill, will likely be done by machines at some point in the not-too-distant future. It's less a question of if, and more a question of when, the economics make sense: When will the cost of using automation fall below the cost of the equivalent human labor required to perform the task? Although that is probably a bit further off in the future for most tasks than we might think. A 2013 Oxford University study found that 47 percent of US jobs were at risk of being automated in the next two decades. However, Oxford researchers four years later reversed themselves in a study with Pearson and Nesta. Their later conclusion was that tomorrow's jobs will be more technically demanding, but won't disappear.

Along the way, however, there will be disruption. Let's meet one of the eager disruptors.

It was one of those golden California fall days, and I was excited to meet Rob Goldiez, the cofounder of an innovative robots-for-hire company, Hirebotics, at a pizza joint down the mountain from my home in Los Gatos. Rob is based in Nashville, Tennessee, and his customers are manufacturers located in the Midwest. A visit to the Silicon Valley is fairly rare for him. It's refreshing to have the tech entrepreneurs of the West Coast learning from a colleague from the heartland.

We order pizza and dive right into a discussion about the future of manufacturing and automation. Rob got the inspiration for Hirebotics from reading Peter Thiel's *Zero to One*, after which it became crystal clear to him that a new opportunity would result from the confluence of cheaper robots, more powerful cloud computing, and a trend toward manufacturers renting rather than owning. Rob's firm is essentially a high-tech temp agency for robots, and it's growing. Wherever there is a human standing at a machine for hours every day, doing a repetitive task for multiple shifts, a Hirebotics robot can do the job faster and cheaper. Rob admits that the humans get defensive when they see a robot with arms and hands that can twist and turn like their own. But it doesn't take long for them to see the common sense in robots. The ideal tasks for robots are monotonous and sometimes even dangerous. Meanwhile, there are often jobs requiring more skills and imagination that go unfilled. A well-known national pizza chain once used humans to stack trays of pizza dough at a central location in near-freezing temperatures around the clock, but a robot took those jobs. Rob reports the company was able to reassign those workers to more productive jobs. Same thing at a major auto manufacturer, which had people filling bags with bolts to fulfill a parts recall. In my work as a young man at EDM on the manufacturing floor, I did countless repetitive tasks that could have been done by automation, where the automation could have freed me up to do any of the endless things that must be done to make a small business successful.

Rob tells me he has never heard of a customer reducing its workforce, only increasing it. In fact, he says, his partners would turn away a customer that was approaching robots for the purpose of replacing humans. Not for altruistic reason, but because he says those customers are going to be so frugal they won't care about quality. His customers call because they have labor problems—high attrition and turnover. Robots help create labor stability.

Hirebotics is on the leading edge of creating more and more competitive, productive manufacturers. It's also saving people from drudgery. Rob's philosophy is that if the metal his robots rivet is the same in China as it is America, why send your metalwork overseas when robot labor is cheaper in Ohio and Michigan? Like Rob, I'd rather see those businesses take advantage of locally produced materials and build around local know-how. And as our small local businesses become more globally competitive with the use of automation, we have a chance to see those businesses both grow and add much-needed jobs across the country.

In the 2019 *New York Times* article "The Hidden Automation Agenda of the Davos Elite," tech columnist Kevin Roose argues that business leaders are making aggressive plans to use AI-powered automation to eliminate jobs on an unprecedented scope, scale, and timeline. It's a scary idea, and one of the principal anxieties that folks have about AI and the future of work right now. There have been numerous studies and books published by prominent institutions and authors showing just how many jobs AI can and probably will perform over the coming decades. While these are possible paths that the development of AI might follow, I see others: ones where the combination of human ingenuity and creativity with AI's ability to perform a broadening range of routine tasks creates new opportunities for workers, businesses, and society. Moreover, due to the nature of business and AI, I believe that the future of work will evolve in less extreme ways than either the most pessimistic or optimistic predictions, and that we will have time to help workers adapt to the changes that may come.

Why? Because no business has ever thrived over long periods of time by just optimizing its costs. If all folks are thinking about is using AI plus automation (AI + automation) as a way to lower costs and nothing else, then they are going to get their butts kicked by companies investing in people and infrastructure to support innovation and future business opportunities. If, on the other hand, businesses are thinking about AI + automation as a way to remove obstacles that are constraining them from better serving their customers and growing their business, i.e., using AI abundance to enhance their own creativity and productivity to create new types of value for their customers, then they are going to succeed. The former is cynical, degenerate, rent-seeking behavior that benefits no one—not even the rent-seeker—because markets reward growth more than cost-cutting. If we are smart, we'll figure out disincentives for this sort of thing, e.g., a very targeted version of Bill Gates's "robot tax." Gates proposed that if a robot takes a human job, "you'd think that we'd tax the robot at a similar level." You wouldn't want to do that universally because it would risk making the American robots more expensive than those in other countries, which could re-create some of the labor dynamics that result in offshoring that automation is now equalizing.

Employing AI to create business growth, on the other hand, requires enormous amounts of human creativity and human effort, not just to conceive of new ways to do business with AI, but to operationalize them. Moreover, in a healthy business, whenever AI automates something that a human was doing, the human becomes more productive because they are able to spend their time and energy on higher-value work. For all but the simplest of tasks, part of that higher-value work that humans are freed up to do might actually be overseeing the AI. The real world is an incredibly complex place, and AI-powered automation becomes increasingly brittle the more that it has to confront that human complexity. Navigating real-world complexity that is trivial even for a human toddler is still beyond the capability of AI. Consequently, for a huge number of business scenarios, AI is likely to assist rather than replace humans. This has been a consistent pattern in industrialization for years.

A computer numerical control (CNC) milling machine,

for instance, needs humans to program it to correctly make parts, and then in order for it to actually make parts, for humans to load raw stock or partly machined parts into the machine, make sure that everything is okay, start the machining cycle, and when the cycle is finished to inspect the part, potentially fix the mistakes that the machine has made, then remove the part, and repeat.

While the machine is doing its work, the human is free to do other things. The smarter the machine gets, the more time the human has to do higher-value work like designing new parts and fixtures, doing programming work for other jobs, figuring out ways to improve manufacturing processes, interacting with customers, up-leveling their skills, etc.

One of my colleagues at LinkedIn was the philosopher-economist Fred Kofman, author of *Conscious Business* and *The Meaning Revolution*. In the leadership development exercises that Fred ran at LinkedIn, he would often ask folks, "What is the job of the goalkeeper in a soccer game?" Most folks would respond, "To keep the ball out of the goal." Fred would smile and gently tell them, "No, it's to help their team to win." Some soccer games present situations where the team might lose if all the goalkeeper does is focus on the ball and the goal, instead of paying attention to the whole game and being willing and able to get out of position if the situation demands it. We know that modern companies are more likely to succeed when everyone is paying attention to the whole game, and when everyone is empowered and expected to be able to get out of position when the situation demands it.

This flexibility is critically important in a world of increasingly capable AI. As the smarter machine is able to do more work and free up humans to do more of what humans are awesome at doing, businesses and the humans they employ must be empowered and expected to very flexibly find new ways to leverage their precious ingenuity. Rigidly adhering to the way that you've been doing things for years, i.e., failing to empower everyone and having individuals unwilling or unable to get out of position to help the team win, means that both individuals and the company are going to lose.

Interestingly, small businesses inherently get this. From Hirebotics to my friend Hugh E's employer in Brookneal, Virginia, small businesses understand that more automation means that they can take on more ambitious work and lower their unit costs of production, both of which let them take on more and more valuable work, which in turn creates new jobs. The automation lets them do more with their human capital, which in turn produces a need for more employees. The risk for established businesses is that they might be tempted to imagine AI-powered automation as a way to reduce their costs, ignoring what they could do with a combination of AI and human ingenuity, and simply using AI as a way to eliminate jobs. Businesses that do that will be easy pickings for ambitious entrepreneurs running small, agile businesses who get the power of humans + AI.

This is a dynamic that software companies have understood for decades, and why you see so many start-ups competing so effectively with much larger companies. Each generation of technology allows you to do more, to innovate more quickly, for small groups of folks to build things that can compete and win against things that much larger companies have built from the previous generation. For big companies to stay relevant, they too must constantly invest in their own innovations, to make sure that they are using advanced technology and the best human ingenuity they can muster to grow. If anything, as AI-powered automation becomes more relevant across the breadth of business and industry, it is in a very real sense bringing this competitive dynamic with it. Which means that investment in just half of the AI + human ingenuity equation will leave you vulnerable to disruption.

The good thing about all of this is that companies have some time to figure it all out. AI-powered automation doesn't come as a Big Bang. Given the complexity of businesses and their real-world processes, and the current brittleness of AI, it tends to show up in businesses gradually. You introduce it as a way to help with the most straightforward tasks, slowly at first, experimenting, tuning, and refining until you have confidence that it can do a reasonable job on a simple task. As underlying AI technologies improve and as you have more confidence in and experience with them, you may be able to use them to achieve superhuman performance on the narrow tasks to which they have been applied, just like forklifts can carry more boxes than a warehouse worker, and spreadsheets can compute faster than accountants. In many cases the task that was automated was repetitive, mind-numbing, perhaps physically draining work, and the human is delighted not to have to do it anymore. They get to spend time on more enjoyable tasks, almost certainly more valuable work, and the company benefits twice: once from the higher productivity on the task that the AI is doing, and again from the higher productivity and freed-up ingenuity of the human who is no longer doing the task that has been automated.

With this confidence, AI-powered automation can then spread to other simple tasks. For each of these tasks, the economic benefit from this higher productivity isn't immediate, because AI isn't just a magical drop-in replacement for humans, even in the simplest of scenarios. Engineers and data scientists need to work with domain experts, in many cases the worker whose task is getting an AI assist, to train a model, to engineer all the interfaces from the digital world to the physical one, and to work out all the kinks. Engineering those interfaces to the physical world, as unsexy as it sounds, tends to be the most time-consuming part of applying AI to a task. When a customer hires a six-axis robotic arm from

Hirebotics to help with one of their processes, programming the arm usually takes a few days, while designing a task-specific manipulator, i.e., a hand that allows the robot to do the intended task, might take several weeks.

In other words, lots of human effort is required to deploy AI-powered automation. And even after the setup, given a relentlessly and unpredictably changing physical world, the work isn't done. The whole point of machine learning is not to have to anticipate every possible permutation of the current and future world. To really get a machine learning system to generalize well, you need to be constantly gathering new data as the world changes around it, and using that data to refine your ML models. And all of this requires human beings and the expertise that they have in their heads and hands. Even with very sophisticated reinforcement learning and emerging unsupervised learning techniques, it's very challenging to get humans out of the loop.

And that's just for the simple tasks. As your ambition increases and you want to use AI-powered automation for more complex tasks, all the things that you do for simple tasks must be done, but with more human effort.

Don't get me wrong. All of this is worth it, which is why this whole conversation is even worth having. AI is an incredibly powerful tool. It's just not one that can be dropped into a business, immediately works, and allows you to eliminate thousands of jobs in one seamless motion. Reality is far more complex. The amount of effort to deploy AI is higher than most folks—other than ones with experience deploying AI—realize. And to flog the proverbial dead horse, even if it were a Big Bang way to automate away a bunch of jobs, doing so probably puts your business at risk, even in the short term, as AI + human ingenuity is going to run circles around an operation that has used AI simply to automate what soon will be yesterday's work.

What is going to happen, and what folks should be concerned about, is a transition from, over time, a need for
workers to do repetitive physical or cognitive tasks with high
degrees of regularity. Those jobs are going away. The challenge that faces us is how to help workers doing these jobs,
with these skills, to find new work and purpose.

Another quirk of some of the current anxiety over AI and
the future of jobs is that some look at manufacturing, retail,
knowledge work, the service sector, and others as one big
monolith that AI will impact in the same way: a systemic
shift of rewards from labor, which we all have, to capital,
which only a few control. What will happen to "good jobs"
then? Here are a few considerations.

First, every segment of the job market is legitimately different, not just in terms of what it produces, what skills are
required of employees, etc., but also in terms of *maturity*, i.e.,
where that segment is in terms of its ability to fulfill the needs
of the population in the most efficient way possible. Each segment has a life cycle, and is on an inexorable march toward
reducing the number of folks needed to do that thing. That's
a good thing. It's what allows humanity to grow. It's the reason that we can support 7.7 billion people on the planet with
increasing standards of living, on average, for everyone. Even
though we have serious problems with the equitable distribution of nutrition to everyone, it's the reason that we can
grow enough food for the global population. It's the reason
that we can do this without climate change being worse than
it already is. It's the reason that we have more diversity of art,
music, literature, and a Cambrian explosion of ways for humans to express themselves, starting in the twentieth century
with new media, than at any point in human history. It's the
reason that bad stuff, like infant mortality, is down across the

board, and good stuff, like average life-span, is up. It's why we understand more about ourselves and the universe we occupy than at any point in history, and that our science and engineering is able to cure diseases once thought incurable, put the entirety of the world's information at our fingertips in our pockets, and on and on and on. It's what has allowed us to get to the point where every ten years so much stuff happens that we can't even imagine regressing to our lives ten years prior.

Second, as a segment of the job market matures, technology allows the segment to seek an *equilibrium* where fewer and fewer people are required to meet the demands of the job segment. (That's going to be obvious from looking at the data.) Economists might say that this is getting more output with fewer inputs, and call this productivity. Here's the controversial assertion: as a segment marches toward this equilibrium in a world without AI and increasingly cheap automation, globalization and conglomerates take an increasing share of the value being produced in the segment. Scale and cheap labor are hard to beat. But AI and cheap automation can change the whole notion of economies of scale and allow smaller-scale businesses to be economically viable and competitive. Running an AI or a piece of automated manufacturing equipment costs the same anywhere in the world. I believe that for segments already heading toward their low-employment equilibrium, AI and automation are exactly what we need to repatriate jobs and more fairly distribute the value being created in each segment.

The Southern comedian Jeff Foxworthy is known for his list of attributes, "You know you're a redneck when . . ." I have a different take. You know you're a geek when you love to watch YouTube videos of small manufacturing and entrepreneurship. One couple, for example, make small handmade products they sell on the Internet. They start small with each product but are prepared at any time to scale up as needed. They use design software to turn what's in their brains into manufacture-ready plans. They have 3-D printers and computer numerical control routers and grinders to turn those plans into products. Another awesome video shows how the German pen company Lamy uses precision technology and 350 workers to design and manufacture hundreds of thousands of the world's finest writing instruments. This is an example of Germany's wildly prosperous Mittelstand business approach, which leverages huge amounts of automation to make a leading product in a narrow vertical market. There are 3.3 million small- and medium-size companies in the German Mittelstand from which 48 percent of the companies leading a vertical market segment originate. The Mittelstand is why Germany is the largest economy in Europe and the fourth in the world behind the US, China, and Japan.

The role that AI plays and can play in making local, small, and midsize manufacturers successful is immense. Machine learning feedback loops will play an increasingly important role in machine controls. AI will play a huge role in the software that makers use to design, engineer, and test products before they hit the machines, making it possible for more and more of the physical product development cycle to exist in the digital domain where things are inherently cheaper and faster, and expose hitherto unimaginable possibilities for the sorts of things that folks can build at either small or large scale. AI plays a role in how products are marketed (ML is ubiquitous in online advertising), in making the e-commerce experience efficient (recommendation systems, fraud prevention, etc.), and even in the logistics of getting a product from the place where it is manufactured to the consumer (we can point to Microsoft Research work on using reinforcement learning to optimize container flows through shipping ports).

Because of all these efficiencies, it's easier than ever for someone to set up shop, make something, market it to potential customers, make sales, and deliver goods to consumers. An entire new segment of e-commerce is developing in direct-to-consumer, with companies like Warby Parker, Allbirds, Boll & Branch, Casper, etc., etc., who use some or all of these new efficiencies to build robust new businesses. And Germany is a prime example of what an economy can look like when you fully embrace the power of automation. Rather than having a few big businesses and consolidation to the point where labor markets start looking like monopsonies, you can have millions of businesses making a dizzying variety of things and providing a huge diversity of services, providing many opportunities for entrepreneurs to win and workers to find meaningful work.

In other words, let's worry less about AI being a bad thing for manufacturing or agriculture or any other mature job segment that's been on a long march toward efficiency. The disruption there is going to be net beneficial. Given this dynamic, we should encourage investment in AI that makes the whole product development-to-manufacturing-to-marketing-to-distribution chain as efficient as possible, and encourage business creation here in any way that we can. This is an enormous potential opportunity for the United States and for job creation.

Third, in job market segments where the efficiency curve is going up (larger percentage of population required to fulfill population demand over time) or has recently peaked, AI could potentially cause significant *acceleration* toward the efficient equilibrium. Retail is a good example. We saw retail employment peak in the early and late nineties, and have been moving downward since, likely because of the Internet. We are nowhere close to equilibrium here, and there is the possibility of losing many jobs very quickly due to AI being deployed in retail. My hypothesis is that many segments share similar curves to retail and also share other characteristics that make them vulnerable to AI disruption. If you think about broad swaths of the service sector—e.g., transportation, warehousing, etc.—it is low-skill work that exists because humans are the cheapest way to do the job, and other techniques for driving efficiencies, like globalization and consolidation, are either impractical or ineffective. This economic calculus changes with increasingly efficient automation and AI.

For these job segments, we should be encouraging as many workers as possible to re-skill, which we will address in the next chapter, because their jobs are going away, probably faster than they or anyone else expects. We should be thinking very carefully about policies that change the unit economics of this work before other work alternatives are available. The so-called Stop BEZOS Bill, introduced by Senator Bernie Sanders and Representative Ro Khanna in 2018, is a good example of well-intentioned if misguided legislation to help workers. According to *New York* magazine, "The Stop Bad Employers by Zeroing Out Subsidies (BEZOS) Act imposes a tax on large corporations equal to the value of the social spending—specifically, Medicaid, SNAP (food stamps), rental subsidies, and free or reduced-price school meals—collected by their employees. Its intent is to force these firms to raise their employees' wages high enough so that they no longer qualify for public assistance, in order to avoid paying the new tax."

I'm a huge believer in every individual having the opportunity to support themselves and their family through their work, and for a robust social safety net for those who can't. While I admire the spirit of what Senator Sanders and Representative Khanna are trying to accomplish for workers through this legislation, I worry that the incentive for businesses might not be the ones intended. When the cost of human labor increases—particularly that of low- and mid-skill repetitive labor—businesses with access to automation technology will do the math, and when projected labor costs exceed total cost of ownership for automation, automation will displace labor. We've seen this pattern play out over and over again, most recently with fast food restaurants replacing cashiers with kiosks in markets with high cost for low-skill labor. If the workers whom politicians are attempting to help are those in a logistics operation, for instance, the legislation may be pushing in the wrong direction on efforts already underway to fully automate those jobs. By making low- and mid-skill jobs more expensive and creating controversy around them, politicians may be introducing an additional incentive to accelerate automation efforts. Those automation efforts may impact all warehouse workers, not just ones who happen to be on public assistance. And there is a critically important balance to be struck in the speed with which automation rolls out, to allow workers to re-skill and businesses to retool to make new, creative uses of the labor freeing up from automated tasks.

Automation for many warehouse tasks already exists, all of which has been developed over just the past few years. If you go online and search for videos of a modern fulfillment center operating, you'll notice how few human beings are there. And you'll notice the nature of the work that the humans are doing. It doesn't require a huge stretch of the imagination to see how those remaining human tasks can be automated. The technology for doing so is more powerful and cheaper every day. These jobs going away is a matter of when, not if. That's not to say that we should do nothing for people who, despite their hard work, still must rely upon public assistance to get by.

Changing this dynamic is going to require more than a single piece of tax legislation, or politicians attempting to shame businesses. I don't think that means that we're helpless, and it certainly doesn't mean that we should abandon folks who are in vulnerable low- and mid-skill jobs who are struggling to find purchase and purpose in a world of relentless change. My perspective is that we should be figuring out how to create more high-skill jobs and high-margin businesses through any means necessary, to have the government become more active in the creation of new technologies (think the space program, or the New Deal's Tennessee Valley Authority) that will accelerate the creation of these jobs and businesses and, at the same time, can be used to lower the costs of subsistence (food, health care, housing, education, etc.), to invest radically more in K–12 education to create a workforce that can seize the opportunities presented by the AI and automation revolutions in which we find ourselves, and to invest in retraining and safety nets for low- and mid-skilled workers who will be temporarily displaced.

If you were ever going to do regressive AI regulation, applications of AI to the service sector are where you would want to do it. These would be the robots that you would want to tax. This is the stuff that you'd potentially want to slow down to allow time for folks to train for new jobs that AI is creating elsewhere. That said, I think that you would have to be extraordinarily careful about how you regulate things, and think just as much about what you want to incent as you are seeking to discourage. In the limit, just like every other job segment we've ever had, the service sector will trend to some very efficient equilibrium point so that the human capital and ingenuity trapped there now can flow to higher-valued things in the future.

Making that transition period unnaturally long results in twentieth-century India. When I was in my twenties working for that small electronic contract manufacturing company in Lynchburg, Virginia, Electronic Design and Manufacturing (EDM), I went with my boss to visit Lexington, Kentucky, where he had grown up, and where one of his friends had been in the contract manufacturing business a bit longer. We were hoping to learn from that business to improve our own. While we were there, we met another of my boss's friends, a professor of electrical engineering at the University of Kentucky, who told us a story about a sabbatical he had taken in India in the eighties. He had contracted with a local craftsman to make him a bathtub, which were uncommon there. The craftsman thought that he was crazy for wanting a tub, but agreed to make him one out of teak. It was going to be a true work of art. They shook hands, some payment was exchanged, and work got underway. After what seemed to the professor like a very long while, he still didn't have his tub, so he went to the craftsman's shop to see how he was progressing. The tub was there, still partly complete. As they were discussing why it was taking so long, the professor noticed that there were all of these power tools on the shelves with the cords cut. Puzzled, he asked the craftsman why the tools had cut cords. "Because if I used power tools, what would my workers do?"

While good for workers in the short term, potentially, the global ramifications of this sort of thinking are horrifyingly bad.

CHAPTER 9

Politics and Ethics

In the spring of 2019, several dozen politicians had either announced or would soon announce their candidacy for the presidency of the United States. Over the long and likely contentious campaign, each will issue a barrage of statements and policy proposals related to the future of jobs and technology. And one of the first stages, as always, will be Iowa.

My wife, Shannon, was born in Iowa, so when I was asked to speak in the little town of Jefferson, not far from her childhood home, we decided to make a family trip out of it. After a tour of her hometown, the kids' description of what they saw was as plain as the landscape—cold and flat. Back in the hotel room on that Friday night, the Victoria's Secret lingerie show competed with televangelists on local cable. RFD-TV (a reference to the nineteenth century's rural free delivery mail service) also was part of the cable package. RFD's *The Farm Report*, which looks at crop prices and advertises weed control and seeds, was investigating the *E. coli* outbreak that had halted sales of romaine lettuce, agricultural news that distressed Caesar salad lovers everywhere. President Trump, the commentator reported, had stopped implementing an EPA recommendation to test irrigation water for fecal matter. "We could do better," the reporter deadpanned.

On the front page of the *Des Moines Register*, the Hawkeyes prevailed over the Cyclones in college basketball, 98–84. There was worry about unfunded pension liabilities for public employees. And the newspaper announced it would partner with CNN to produce polls leading up to the 2020 Iowa caucuses.

"It may only be four weeks since the midterm election, but the 2020 presidential cycle is already well underway," Sam Feist, the Washington bureau chief of CNN, was quoted as saying.

Linc Kroeger, a fiftysomething Iowan, engineer, and entrepreneur, had invited me to speak at the opening of his company's first rural "Forge," a satellite office that will train, develop, and employ young software developers in an unlikely place: a nineteenth-century farm town of about four thousand people. His software company, Pillar, had been acquired recently by Accenture, and was throwing a party in the central Iowa town to attract both local and national attention for the venture. He calls it R3: revive, rebuild, and restore. Several tech colleagues; a congressperson from Silicon Valley, Representative Ro Khanna (D-California); and an unusually large contingent of reporters would be in attendance.

"There's something special about growing up in a small town—where hard work, hospitality and heritage are ingrained," Linc writes on the rural Forge website. "Yet countless young people don't see a future in the rural communities they love—especially those dreaming of a career in technology. Many feel they have no choice but to move away from their homes and families in search of more attractive jobs, taking with them the future of their community's economy.

R3 aims to bring an end to all of that by reviving, rebuilding and restoring rural communities."

On the Saturday morning of the launch in Jefferson, Linc sits in the Forge's Des Moines office. It's a stylishly updated warehouse with exposed brick and old wooden beams. In the front, young African American leaders who immigrated to Iowa are discussing community development plans. In a nearby conference room, an entrepreneur from San Francisco has flown in to locate a remote office in Iowa for one of his clients.

Linc is the youngest of three from Independence, Iowa. Growing up, he was always struck by the fact that his older brother and sister left the state after college and never returned. He joined the air force in 1986 to take advantage of the GI Bill for college. He learned FORTRAN while also making his contribution to Operation Desert Storm. After the military he worked in software—Cintas for fifteen years, and then Pillar, a consulting firm he had hired while still at Cintas. By his own admission, he drank their Kool-Aid on human-centered design, and opened the Des Moines Forge. He loved their mission to unleash the potential of people. He recognized that robots and AI will have an increasingly important role in the workforce, and concluded that people in his community needed to focus on cultivating what makes us all human in order to compete—passion, love, directness. We must lead with being personal and expert. His boss at Pillar recognized his commitment and would frequently ask him, "What is your dream?"

"I want to do this in rural areas because most of us that work here are from rural areas," he said. "We're already doing our work for people elsewhere. All we need is a place to work, and broadband."

There are seventy-two people in the Des Moines Forge, and Linc estimated half are from rural areas.

The CEO agreed to let him pursue the first rural Forge. He gave him financial guardrails, told him to keep the Des Moines business on track, and gave him lots of autonomy.

The question became where to start. The location needed to be within ninety miles of a major city, have broadband connectivity, and have a community college to help prepare workers. The engineer who designed the Forge building in Des Moines was from a little town about sixty-five miles northwest of Des Moines. "Why not Jefferson?" he would ask.

Linc agreed to look into it and discovered that Jefferson Telecom had had the foresight to build fiber (high-speed Internet) and would soon introduce redundant fiber, a critical element in maintaining a business's connectivity. The problem was, Jefferson did not have a community college.

Recognizing the opportunity, however, the citizens of Jefferson, and of Greene County, voted for a $35 million bond that would finance a new high school and an adjacent community college. The new high school and community college will have a career academy that, collectively, is designed to create a career ladder for the development of a skilled workforce for the Forge and other surrounding employers.

The community's vision is a ladder in which junior high students can see the job opportunity of working for the Forge or another software-based business, and take the right classes leading to those jobs. If students are hired, the Forge will invest an additional $5,000 to further train graduates and offer them apprenticeships so they get the training they need on their way to "software artisanship." Linc contends these students will emerge without debt and with the same training you would get in a state university's computer science program.

The idea captured the imagination of Representative Khanna when he was leading a rural workforce development initiative for President Obama, and it excited President Trump's then secretary of labor, Alexander Acosta.

Later in the day, on the beautiful drive through the countryside to Jefferson, we pass a sign proclaiming, "Prayer Changes Everything." Ahead, the grain silos and water towers that have long broken up the monotony of slow rolling hills and agricultural fields now are dwarfed by rows of enormous wind power turbines and the occasional solar panel. The freshly plowed fields, grazing pastures, and picked-over corn rows that are so familiar to me from back home are perhaps recognized by many Americans as brown squares, rectangles, and circles from the windows of jets at thirty-two thousand feet above on the flyovers.

We enter Jefferson on Route 30, the Lincoln Highway. It was America's first transcontinental roadway stretching from Times Square in New York City to San Francisco, California. We're smack-dab in the middle. I learn later that Silicon Valley pioneer and cofounder of Intel Bob Noyce is from this part of the country.

We stop for burgers with the kids at the A&W, and later gather in a hollowed-out building downtown. Built in the late 1800s, this was once a meeting hall for the local Independent Order of Odd Fellows. Soon it will become the first rural Forge. It's hardly been occupied for decades except for the occasional marginal enterprise—a tumbling gym for toddlers, most recently. Yet you can see the pride well up inside Linc and Jefferson's community leaders as they survey the potential. By the next year Forge employees will be building and testing software. Python and Java user groups will convene. Linc and local leaders cobbled together nine different sources of revenue, including tax credits and incentive grants, to fund the venue.

"We could have built a new building but then this one would just sit here and continue to rot," Linc thinks out loud.

As we tour, I meet Madhu Chamarty, a serial Silicon Valley entrepreneur. His latest venture is BeyondHQ, which he describes as expansion-as-a-service for high-growth companies. He works with tech start-ups like Michael Bloomberg's Bloomberg Beta that are growing rapidly and need workers who are ready to start and are affordable. He serves as a sort of chief people officer.

At the event, Madhu tells the crowd he'd never been to Iowa before but felt he knew it well. In a previous job he had studied satellite imagery of Iowa to predict corn and soybean production.

I get a few laughs when I tell everyone Jefferson looks like the nearest big town to where I grew up. I share that I had wanted to stay in Virginia, but was forced to leave in order to pursue a career. I say that I hope this night is not just a success for Jefferson because I hope it spreads to rural communities everywhere.

A. J. Whatling gets the biggest round of applause when it's learned that he is the Accenture software engineer moving from Des Moines to Jefferson to commence operations. He came from a town of 150 people. He couldn't play football or soccer but learned that he liked programming. The problem was that the only programming class he could take in high school was available his final year, as a senior. In Jefferson, his job will be to train students to write software and develop products, to recruit and retrain people, and "to bring AAA projects to Jefferson." It starts to feel real when he announces that the Forge's first project will be for the San Francisco 49ers of the National Football League, who happen to be playing the local favorites, the Denver Broncos, the next day.

Everyone quiets down for Lindsey Kitt, a student at the local high school, who says she and her classmates can see the Forge for what it is—opportunity. She took a coding class and fell in love, but she wanted more. There was none. Now those who follow her will have more opportunity, though she estimates fewer than half want to stay in Jefferson. That could change, though.

The head of Des Moines Area Community College calls this the start of a revolution. A community planner who leads what he calls "creative place-making," he says rural America is now the place to pioneer. Cities will become saturated, and the ideal place will be ninety miles outside of those saturated cities. Des Moines, he argues, will be saturated by 2030 like other great cities with a lot of assets. He says there are a lot of myths about rural America—you need money to make change; there are no good-paying jobs; we need more tech jobs. But, in fact, it's becoming harder and harder every passing year to find jobs that don't require workers to use technology in some way. If every business and every job depends upon tech, every community and every organization will need equal access to tech, which begins with access to broadband.

The 2020 campaign was about to begin. Meanwhile, in Washington, President Trump signed the Farm Bill into action after months of its lingering in a congressional committee. He entered the signing ceremony to a recording of him singing "Green Acres" years earlier. But the *New York Times* reminded us that the rural question is no joke. A Sunday essay, "Abandoned America," spread across the entire front page, promising to tell us "the hard truths of trying to 'save' the rural economy." It concluded that most rural communities have very little to offer economically. Perhaps it would be better if rural people simply relocated. Meanwhile, on the very same day, another *Times* article, this one in the technology section, reported that "wooing workers to rural areas" might help to fill the 2.4 million skilled jobs that might go unfilled over the next decade. Our national dialogue about rural America is confused, and that's not a great place to start when thinking about how to make the economy of the future work there.

Brad Smith, Microsoft's president and chief legal officer, sat with me in his office just before the holiday break in late 2018 and reflected on this conundrum. I had just returned from my Iowa trip to help kick off the rural Forge in Jefferson, and Brad had just returned from Washington, DC, where he had provided policy makers with an update on a rural broadband initiative he'd kicked off a year earlier.

"Broadband and skilling are prerequisites for growth in rural areas," Smith told me. Earlier in the year he had launched a massive effort both to learn about these challenges and to help make a difference. "If one builds it, will the jobs come?"

Back in DC a few days earlier, nearly two hundred people gathered in the Ronald Reagan Building and International Trade Center for Brad's briefing. He told them that there are two Americas: one urban and one rural. In Ferry County, Washington State, for example, unemployment is always double-digit and has reached as high as 18 percent.

"Almost every state has a Ferry County."

Then there is urban America. In nearby King County, home of Microsoft, unemployment stands at 3.2 percent.

"Some people are being left behind and we need to ask why. The answer lies in technology and connectivity and data."

It's not a problem that some people in America can watch YouTube videos uninterrupted and some cannot. Inadequate access to the Internet is far more serious. In the summer of 2017 wildfires raged across Ferry County. To stop the fire, data was needed to understand what was happening.

The only people who could download the data were in the county seat, not on the front lines. To get the data where it was needed, someone had to download it onto a thumb drive and then drive it to the front of the fire.

Unfortunately, this is not isolated to Ferry County. More than 25 million Americans lack access to broadband. An estimated 19 million are in rural areas—officially, that is. Almost certainly the problem is larger. Microsoft's own data indicate 162.8 million people do not use the Internet at broadband speeds—the speeds you and I likely enjoy. Because we're in the business, we can see download speeds, and we've found half the country is still not using the Internet at the same speeds businesses in the city use. Qualitatively this matters more and more—to agriculture, small business, education, and health care. In order to leverage the power of computing, to work with big data, and to build and even use modern software incorporating AI, you must be connected. Even attracting the right employees to your business is harder without high-speed Internet. Workers who have put in the hard work to get high-tech skills, by and large, expect modern Internet connections in their homes, and will choose to live in places where they can get these services.

Brad points out to audiences that there is no TV gap. TV and color TV use shot up after its introduction. Television united the country during the space race. Conversely, broadband coverage made it to 70 percent or so, but coverage growth has been flat since 2012, even though we've spent $22 billion to expand it over the past five years.

In my own personal experience, I've always had to rely on wireless service delivery because wireline systems simply didn't and don't provide adequate coverage in the places I've lived. Growing up, we didn't have cable TV, and I'm old enough that there was no Internet back then. In the late eighties, though, my dad had a good year at work, and we got one of the big, old satellite dishes that preceded DirecTV and Dish

Network. For the first time, my brother and I could watch MTV! I can still recall exactly what it felt like to sit there in the living room and to have our world of content explode from three channels to hundreds. Three decades later, I live in a house, in the heart of Silicon Valley no less, that doesn't have access to cable TV or wired broadband. Thankfully modern satellite TV is quite good, and I'm lucky enough to live within line of sight to a wireless broadband provider.

As Brad says, "If we are going to go faster, if it's an urgent problem, we will not serve the public with a wire."

To accomplish this, Microsoft announced its Airband Initiative, which will rely on a mixture of available technologies, including what is known as TV white space. According to a white paper by Paul Garnett and Sid Roberts, two of the leaders of Airband Initiative, "These are frequencies that have not been assigned or are otherwise not being used by broadcasters and other licensees in the VHF and UHF broadcast bands." The TV white space is in lower-band frequencies and signals that can travel over longer distances and penetrate many obstacles. Because competition by wireless companies for lower-band spectrum is so fierce, TV white space availability is somewhat limited. Internet connections using TV white space are typically 10 Mbps or slower, similar to 3G and 4G Internet connections on your mobile phone. Not the fastest, but certainly better than the 300 Kbps that my aunt gets through her wireline connection back home.

Microsoft is reinvesting any potential profits of the Airband program into expanding Internet access for all, with the goal of building a self-sustaining market that works for everyone. The Farm Bill did include some funding for rural broadband, but Brad pointed out that "it will take far too long if we are going to wait on federal dollars." To succeed, the effort will require partnerships with the Federal Communications Commission and other public agencies more broadly by targeting some of the existing spending on wireless, and on lower-cost devices, thus helping to drive lower-cost endpoint devices for farmers and others in rural America.

Public agencies are important, but so is the private sector. Microsoft is partnering with Future Farmers of America; 4-H; and broadband providers serving rural customers, like Declaration Networks Group in Maryland and Virginia. CEO Bob Nichols told us the story of bringing small businesses into the digital age. One business customer in rural Garrett County, Maryland, would go to coffee or lunch when they sent a contract or images to customers, because the speeds were so slow.

"With broadband the company is now talking about doubling the size of their company. It's transformative," Nichols said.

Cory Heigl of Packerland Broadband in Wisconsin tells the story of a medical transcriptionist who had to drive long distances to do her job. When her husband became ill she was not sure what the future would bring. With Airband, high-speed broadband could reach her home, her employer offered to reimburse the costs, and she could largely work from home, enabling her to work and care for her husband. "She wept when she saw the connection," Heigl said.

Renowned sci-fi author William Gibson coined the term *cyberspace* in 1982, and two years later used it in his book *Neuromancer*, which had an enormous impact on a generation of young technologists, me included. "The future is already here—it's just not very evenly distributed," Gibson is often quoted as saying. This unequal distribution of the future and the prosperity it holds, between the developed and developing world, between urban and rural, between those with access to capital and expertise and those without, is one of the defining issues of our time.

Much about the world is better now for a larger proportion of the global population than it has ever been. Steven Pinker's *Enlightenment Now* and Hans Rosling's *Factfulness*, among others, make the case that the world, in many ways, is demonstrably better than ever. It's a difficult experiment to run, but I think that even I would be better off as a poor kid in rural Virginia in 2019 than I was in the early eighties when I bought my first computer.

That computer, a RadioShack Color Computer II, affectionately known as the CoCo 2, cost $199.95 in 1984 and took me lots of odd jobs and crisp $5 bills from birthday and Christmas cards to pay for. That's equivalent to $480 in 2018, adjusted for inflation. For half that price today you could buy a laptop with 4 GB of RAM, a 32 GB solid state hard drive, an 11.6-inch high-resolution color touch screen, and a processor that's many, many orders of magnitude more powerful than the CoCo 2's 890 kilohertz MC6809E processor. (That's right, kilohertz!)

More important, in 2019, with the money that I saved buying a modern, almost incomparably more powerful computer, I would almost certainly buy a broadband subscription and connect my laptop to the Internet. With that broadband subscription, I would have access to search engines, repositories of general knowledge like Wikipedia and YouTube, and communities of specialized knowledge. For a curious kid like me, this would have been heaven. It would also have saved my parents a bunch of money on the *World Book Encyclopedia*, which I had spent hours reading cover to cover as a kid and that they purchased on a payment plan. Beyond satisfying my curiosity and giving me a way to learn what I couldn't at school, access to the Internet and its resources would perhaps have connected me with advice, mentorship, and community that could have made my meandering path to professional stability a bit easier and quicker.

Unfortunately, none of these analyses about how good we have it now, nor any of my musings about a childhood that could have been, are all that helpful in figuring out how we move forward. It's plain to see that the future really isn't evenly distributed. Whether you call it the ethic of reciprocity that you studied in philosophy class or the Golden Rule that you learned in Sunday school, it's equally plain to see that we owe it to one another to ensure that we all have a fair shot at a great future of our own, our shot at the American dream.

Exactly what this means is a question broader and deeper than this book, and is something deserving of conversation in communities, campuses, and campaigns. What this book can contribute to the debate is the idea that AI will be an important part of our future. It will be a tool to help address some of our most challenging issues. It is intertwined with the American dream. AI's development, from today forward, must be principled and aimed at getting more quickly to a future where we are all equitably empowered to achieve our full potential.

Microsoft has articulated six principles for AI development: fairness, inclusiveness, reliability and safety, transparency, privacy and security, and accountability. These are important and rigorously thought through. As an engineer and a citizen, I envision four pillars of principled AI development:

- AI must be a platform that any individual or business can use to enhance their creativity and productivity, and that can be used to solve the biggest of the big problems that confront us as a society.

- We must ensure that anyone—ideally, everyone—can participate in the development of this AI platform, and can intelligently engage in critical debates about how the platform evolves and is governed.

- In our push to advance the state of the art of AI, to build new products, to automate processes, and to found whole new businesses empowered by AI technologies, we need to be constantly vigilant that all this energy is focused on benefiting people, all people.

- We must work to prevent—ideally, eliminate—negative consequences of AI development, and when they do happen, to work as hard and compassionately as we can to mitigate those impacts as quickly as possible.

This ethical framework and set of development principles must also recognize that each of us will play different roles. Five of the roles that are particularly important are the AI expert, the technology developer, the executive, the policy maker and regulator, and the citizen.

THE ROLE OF THE AI EXPERT

Of these five roles, perhaps the AI expert has the greatest ability to influence the future of AI, and concomitantly bears the greatest responsibility for the future AI may bring about. As Spider-Man's Uncle Ben said, "With great power comes great responsibility." AI, in a very real sense, would not exist were it not for the work of AI experts. Nor would AI be advancing at the rate it is without so many experts focusing so much of their creative energy and intellect into advancing the state of the art.

Given this power and responsibility, it's crucially important for AI experts not to be so focused on the details of what they are creating, so immersed in the science and practice of the next breakthrough they are trying to achieve, so gripped by the momentum of their work, that they are paying insufficient attention to the greater human context in which they and their work exists. I know how easy it is to allow intense focus on a complex task to blind you to everything else. Many of us, in fact, celebrate and seek out this ability, the purest expression of which is a psychological phenomenon called *flow state* by Mihály Csíkszentmihályi,[27] which can be so intense that an individual's perception of time is distorted when in it. As a young engineer, I would get frustrated calls from my wife asking me where I was. I would say, "I'm almost done and should have plenty of time to get to dinner on time," only to have my wife tell me that I was three hours late already.

Giving yourself the time to put your work in context, and to think about how it and the work to which it connects are impacting your fellow human beings, is just as important as getting into and staying in the flow state that your most complex work demands. Creating this balance is an important part of your responsibilities. Moreover, if we collectively can't find this balance and then act on what we learn, we will lose the tacit permission that we currently have from our fellow humans to be AI experts.

Acting on the balance is a matter of aligning our work to the four pillars of principled AI development, about creating more value than we take, about inclusivity, about orienting our work on creating benefits for humanity, and about taking responsibility for the disruptions that our work might create. For AI experts this means publishing work in a timely manner, making sure that the results of publication are reproducible, and finding opportunities to create tools that make our jobs easier, and then open-sourcing those tools or otherwise making them available for broader consumption.

Although we could always be better at these things, much of this way of doing AI is already part of the rhythm of our work. What's less obvious about the role of the expert is helping to educate the greater public, and drawing folks who may not be AI technical experts into a conversation about the nature of AI. Given how complex the field already is, and how fast things are moving, AI experts can more clearly see the AI landscape unfolding, and in many cases have clarity about the new directions that the field is taking months, or even years, before others do. I believe that it's incumbent upon AI experts to not just inform their peers about their work through papers and open source, but to make the conceptual core of their work more understandable and approachable for everyone. Often this exercise of simplifying things to their purest essence so that other folks can better understand yields some of the most interesting breakthroughs. According to Einstein, "The definition of genius is taking the complex and making it simple."

If you are an AI expert, please use your voice and your power to help ensure that AI serves the common good. AI can't be developed without you, and you have more power than you know. Whether you know it or not, your obligation to do what's right for your fellow humans is even more important than any desire you have to do what's intellectually stimulating or personally enriching.

THE ROLE OF THE TECHNOLOGY DEVELOPER

Over the course of the next decade, every technology developer will, to varying extents, become an AI developer. The techniques of AI will become part of your repertoire and will inform how you solve problems more and more every year. At Microsoft, we see this transformation sweeping across the company as the tools, techniques, and knowledge being created by AI experts are democratized across tens of thousands of developers, and as the AI tools and infrastructure we make available to the public start to be used by millions of developers across the world.

Just as you have an obligation to make software safe, secure, accessible, highly available, fast, reliable, and usable, AI will bring with it a new set of obligations. For instance, once a year, everyone at Microsoft is required to take a course called Standards of Business, part of which involves watching videos that present dramatizations of legal and ethical issues that may arise as we do our jobs. The story lines change year to year, and with AI becoming a more ubiquitous tool for product development, we recently added a new AI ethics story to the course. It portrays a rock-star-level AI developer who had just created an ingenious algorithm that was being celebrated in the hallway. His demo had captured the imagination of colleagues looking for game-changing approaches to solving customer problems. But the developer's former manager was suspicious that the results were too good to be true, and gently confronted the AI developer in a smaller group. Where had he gotten the customer data to train his AI model? Did he follow the company's legal and ethical guidelines? As the theatrical drama unfolds, we sense the developer is digging a deeper hole for himself as he confides in a colleague that he had trained his AI using data for which he did not have permission. He begs the colleague to give him permission to access the data one more time in order to fix a bug. He had already made a serious violation of company policy to obtain the data in the first place, and the colleague says no. The moral of the story: It's not great AI if it's unethical AI.

Across industry and academia, we are just beginning to define what ethical AI is. Given machine learning's insatiable appetite for data, a lot of the focus on ethical AI is on data. As I write these words, Europe's General Data Protection Regulation has provided a good regulatory framework for customer data handling to ensure transparency and privacy, and that provides customers with more control of their data. Microsoft has taken a stand on AI systems that can identify people from pictures that include their faces. Given the potential of this technology to violate a person's privacy and to be used in ways that could impact individual liberty, we believe that governments should take a stand on appropriate uses of this type of AI and pass legislation to regulate it.

For good or ill, it is likely that the capabilities of AI will outpace the ability of our democratically elected legislative bodies to grapple with those capabilities and regulate them where appropriate. For instance, it's taken fifteen or more years now for the negative side effects of attention-optimizing machine learning systems to become obvious enough that both industry and regulators feel an urgent need for change.

We can do better. And part of doing better is holding ourselves to a higher standard not just in doing the right thing in the moment, but spending cycles thinking about and debating what the right thing is. Doctors, lawyers, professional engineers, teachers, and many other professions have formal codes of ethics. The National Education Association, for instance, has a code of ethics[28] mandating a set of teacher responsibilities to the student and to the profession, that includes things like "In fulfillment of the obligation to the student the educator shall not deliberately suppress or distort subject matter relevant to the student's progress." With AI, we as technology developers have obligations to our profession, to our employers and their shareholders, to the jurisdictions in which we provide products and services, to our coworkers, to those who use the work that we produce, and to the public good.

Since 2018, Microsoft has had a committee called Aether— AI Ethics in Engineering and Research—that helps to advise our senior leadership team. The Aether committee is a cross-functional, multidisciplinary group that focuses on six areas: bias and fairness; engineering practices for AI; human-AI interaction and collaboration; intelligibility and explanation; reliability and safety; and sensitive uses of AI. The work that this group does, led by AI pioneer Eric Horvitz, has informed all of Microsoft's major AI decisions since the group was formed. Moreover, members of the Aether committee are also involved with the broader community outside Microsoft, and have helped to establish groups like the Partnership on AI[29] and the Stanford Institute for Human-Centered Artificial Intelligence.[30]

In addition to participating in the conversation about what the formal code of ethics should be for practitioners of AI, and ensuring that you stay informed as the ethical and regulatory landscape surrounding AI evolves, as a technology developer, you're going to have to develop some commonsense patterns to govern the decisions that you make every day so that your work is striking the right balance among all the constituencies to whom you are obligated. Again, the four pillars of principled AI development can provide a good place to start in developing those patterns. Use, enhance, and if you can, build AI platforms that create more value for others in the broadest sense possible than for you, your product, or your company. Make sure that your work is inclusive, which in the case of technology developers means building products that are free of unintentional biases and that help users understand the ways in which AI might be influencing their interactions with your product. Make sure that the AI you employ in your products is human-centered. And think about the disruptive impact your product will have and figure out what you are going to do to mitigate the negative consequences of that disruption.

As a builder of AI things that will have an impact on other people's lives, you are on the front line making decisions every day about whether what you do will manipulate versus empower, whether you're playing a zero-sum game where AI is harvesting more value than it creates versus creating new non-zero-sum games where you are growing the size of the pie and benefiting everyone, and whether you are truly living up to the privilege and obligation of serving the public good with the things that you create. Choose wisely.

THE ROLE OF THE EXECUTIVE

The role of the executive in developing principled AI is simultaneously critically important and dead simple. It's the same as the rest of your job: build an environment where people can do their best work, and ensure that the work of individuals and teams results in products and services that make enough of a positive difference in the world that you earn the permission to continue to do what you do. Easy, right?

In all seriousness, AI brings challenges above and beyond those you might already be accustomed to facing as a leader. Building an environment for folks to do principled AI requires that you understand more than a little bit about what's going on across the AI landscape, and that you challenge your organization to take the sketch of principled development laid out here, or invent your own sketch, and fill in all of the details demanded by your particular set of business needs. That's no small thing. Done right, though, having a set of well-codified AI principles for your org, and ones that roughly reflect a determination to create more value than you harvest, to welcome everyone to the discussion about how you're using AI to benefit them, to focus your AI work on benefiting humans, their needs, and the broader public good, and to take responsibility for and work to mitigate negative impacts of your AI work, will earn you the permission to continue to serve the public.

The public doesn't have infinite patience for those who

don't take this stuff seriously. Abdicating your responsibilities to do AI in a principled way isn't really a choice that companies will be allowed to make in perpetuity. There may be short-term profitable arbitrage games you can play by disrupting inefficient marketplaces with AI-powered technologies, or by using AI to ruthlessly drive costs and labor out of your business processes. However, those companies taking this very myopic view of business opportunity are likely not to be the ones that create enduring value over many decades. The reality of strategies like these is that once you've harvested all the efficiency opportunities you can find, which can happen relatively quickly, you'll then need to find growth. And in the pursuit of these short-term opportunities, you'll most likely find that not only have you earned the scorn of a bunch of folks to whom you have obligations, but that you have also built the wrong AI development muscle. It could be the case that the very AI you deployed to eliminate jobs and become more efficient will itself become less effective over time when your business landscape evolves and you have too few machine teachers and too little training data to adapt.

Here again, thinking about the world in terms of who you are obligated to—your employees, your shareholders, your customers, and the public good—and searching for opportunities that are non-zero-sum instead of zero-sum are going to put you on more stable footing for long-term value creation. It might seem like the tougher path, but it is also the right one. We've already talked about how zero-sum-to-non-zero-sum thinking works in the case of automating customer service with AI bots. Zero-sum thinking says, "Customer service agents are expensive, so I'm going to cut my costs by replacing them with AI-powered agents." Non-zero-sum thinking says, "Customer service agents are a precious resource whose potential is being robbed by having them doing mind-numbing tasks, so I'm going to automate those tasks and free them up to create a more delightful experience for customers than would otherwise be possible."

In one case, the size of the pie stays the same: you generate a little bit more short-term profit for the company and its shareholders and you take away the livelihood of folks. You've made the world better in a small way for a handful of folks, a lot worse for another set of folks, and changed nothing at all for everyone else. There may be situations where this is the only decision you can make, but the calculus of zero-sum thinking with AI is grim.

In the other case, the size of the pie increases. You've made life better for your customers who are getting better service. You've made your customer service agents happier because they are doing less menial work and can use more of their potential to solve problems for customers. And as your customer satisfaction improves, your sales will likely increase. And you did all of this without spending more money.

Mind-set can make a tremendous difference when deciding how to leverage AI.

THE ROLE OF THE POLICY MAKER AND REGULATOR

Policy makers across the world are trying to wrap their heads around the impact that AI is having now, and the impact that it could have in the future. On one end of the spectrum, there is an enormous amount of concern and caution around AI and the companies that are developing these technologies. Is AI eroding privacy? Is it being used as an excuse to inadequately control harmful content on social platforms? Are people being fairly compensated for their data contributions to AI? Is AI manipulating people? What will we do about the jobs that AI will take? Is the AI in products like self-driving cars and autonomous drones safe? What do we need to do to maintain our national competitiveness in AI? Where should we allow AI to be used in the public sector? What do we do to control bias in AI? Which of the many dissonant voices claiming expertise in AI should we take advice from?

All of these are good questions, and I don't envy those grappling with them. I suspect that many more questions will arise over the next few years as the pace of AI advancement increases and as the use of AI in an expanding range of products and services means that more citizens are interacting, directly and indirectly, with AI daily.

On the other end of the spectrum, you have policy makers rushing to embrace AI. The Chinese government has developed a sophisticated AI policy and is investing hundreds of billions of dollars to develop itself into an AI superpower. Russian president Vladimir Putin declared in 2017 that "Artificial intelligence is the future, not only for Russia, but for all humankind. It comes with colossal opportunities, but also threats that are difficult to predict. Whoever becomes the leader in this sphere will become the ruler of the world."[31]

Blessed or cursed, we live in interesting times.

Policy makers play a unique role in guiding the principled development of AI and ensuring that AI becomes a part of our collective future prosperity rather than a harbinger of dystopia. Perhaps the two hardest things for our policy makers to do as they grapple with AI is to get as informed as possible, as deeply as possible, as quickly as possible, and to develop a set of first principles that will guide them to answers on the many questions AI raises, rather than starting at ground zero as each question arises.

First, on getting informed. Our policy makers have incredible convening power, and in the past have used this power to focus the attention of experts on important topics and themes in science and technology. From 1972 until 1995, Congress funded the Office of Technology Assessment (OTA), which served the House and Senate by providing technical expertise and technical assessment of complex questions in science and technology. The OTA was defunded in 1995 in a round of budget cuts. Subsequently, the Government Accountability Office (GAO) has built a Technology Assessment capability. Either reviving the OTA or increasing funding to the GAO's Technology Assessment program and using either office to build a world-class, dispassionate technology advisory team with deep expertise in AI is critically important to our future. Without a world-class group of bipartisan experts providing advice and analysis to our lawmakers, we will have a hard time making world-class policy on AI.

Second, on developing a set of principles and taking inspiration from the pillars of principled AI development, I submit the following as potential starting points:

Zero-sum to non-zero-sum thinking. The biggest opportunity that lawmakers have to benefit citizens through the development of AI is to find big social or national interest challenges where finite resources make all the questions about the allocation of resources hard and contentious, and to imagine how those challenges could be transformed into non-zero-sum games by AI. We are faced with such challenges in health care, climate change, demographic shifts, and agriculture, to name just a few. With health care, could we find ways to use AI to provide everyone with higher-quality care and better health outcomes with lower cost? With climate change, could we find ways to use AI to optimize the generation and consumption of power, to reduce the costs of deploying renewable sources of energy in a way that lowers carbon emissions? Could we use AI to help optimize how we plant, tend, and harvest our crops so that we can feed a growing population in increasingly challenging growing conditions? And as the populations of the industrial world age, could we use AI to supplement our workers as the working-age population contracts, so that we can avoid economic contraction? I think the answers to all these questions might be yes, if our policy makers can help create incentives to get these public-good investments to start happening faster than market forces might provide.

Disincentivize strictly zero-sum AI investments. Despite it being bad long-term business strategy, lots of folks will be tempted to make a quick buck with AI by using it to harvest efficiencies without reinvesting any of the savings into things that produce new value. Designing such incentives can have unintended consequences, so you must think very, very carefully about what you're doing. You can probably tell if you're on the right path by thinking about these disincentives as sources of strategic friction to discourage harmful behaviors and encouraging beneficial ones, not as new sources of revenue for the government. For instance, one of the reasons that folks might look to harvest efficiencies is because of short-term pressure from Wall Street. If you thought that these short-term pressures were encouraging bad behavior, you could reduce them by introducing something like a highly progressive capital gains tax: 90 percent if you hold an investment for less than a month; 75 percent for less than a year; 50 percent for less than two years; 25 percent for less than four years; and 5 percent if you hold for ten years or longer.

Be deliberate. When you're contemplating a piece of policy like a new disincentive, thinking not just about the intended effect, but the whole game theory around its unintended consequences, is crucial. For instance, one of the suggestions about how to deal with job losses that might potentially arise from automation in manufacturing is "Tax the robots!" Doing that, without any additional conditions, is probably a bad idea. Why? Because automation is being used in small and large manufacturing operations to make US manufacturing more competitive, lowering their unit costs of production and expanding their capacity, which means more work and more jobs, particularly as work is repatriated. Taxing those robots would simply could put us back into the situation where work gets sent overseas not just because they have cheaper labor, but because the robots are cheaper too! That's not to say don't tax the robots. It's just that if you do, either be prepared to carve out exceptions to reduce unintended consequences or be prepared to accept those consequences head-on.

Another class of unintended consequences will invariably rise from well-intended labor protections where the protection increases labor costs above the cost of deploying automation. For instance, raising minimum wages for workers in fast food restaurants is absolutely the humane thing to do. For a business with short-term margin pressures from investors and inelastic pricing (i.e., the consumers won't pay more), a natural response to these wage increases is to replace some of those workers with kiosks and automation. This isn't a theoretical concern; it's already happening in fast food restaurants in Europe, where labor costs are already high. Without some sort of offsetting disincentive for the automation, or changes to structural incentives around profit margins, the unintended consequences for these sorts of labor protections could entirely undermine the intent of the protection.

Reimagine education. Many of the characteristics of our modern education system have roots in the Industrial Revolution. As the new millennium gets properly underway, it should come as no surprise that what worked in the nineteenth and twentieth centuries might need a tune-up for the twenty-first. Even though I spent a significant chunk of my life in school, have taught computer science at two universities, have developed and managed a handful of corporate training programs, and have a family foundation and wife who are very active in education, I don't consider myself an expert in pedagogy. Even though I have a bunch of opinions about what we should do to make education better for children who will most likely enter a workforce profoundly transformed by AI, and for workers who will need to be lifelong learners and constantly acquiring new skills in order to adapt to a changing workplace, I'll keep those to myself, and simply state some of the challenges that we will need to solve in the not-too-distant future.

The notion that a skills gap was a significant part of higher unemployment following the 2008 financial crisis in the United States is a bit controversial. In their article "Unemployment, Schools, Wages, and the Mythical Skills Gap," Richard Rothstein and Lawrence Mishel of the Economic Policy Institute argue that the existence of a gap isn't borne out by economic data and doesn't even make intuitive sense. Data does, however, seem to indicate that local skills gaps, an imbalance between employer demand for skills and the supply of workers with them, are present and unsurprisingly concentrated in the coastal, urban innovation centers where the job growth is highest.[32] Having access to training for these skills obviously matters for folks living in these urban innovation centers. For workers with the ability to relocate, having access to this training wherever it is that they live also matters, even if there are no local employers with jobs requiring their new skills.

I've anecdotally seen several cases where small businesses requiring technical skills in places outside of urban innovation centers, like Boydton and Brookneal, Virginia, have the desire and opportunity to grow, but can't find enough skilled workers in or near their small communities. The skills gaps that exist in these small communities now may be for things like welding, machining, and IT. A few years back, I was listening to a report on the radio about the job market, and heard an interview with a woman in Southern California who was a single parent and had lost her job in construction. She knew that there were even better-paying jobs open that employers couldn't fill for welders, but because she was out of work and didn't have money, she couldn't afford to get a welding certificate at her local trade school. The idea that $600 was the thing standing between this woman and re-newed economic self-sufficiency for her and her kid seemed insane to me. But, for many, this is reality.

Being unable to train residents in the skills needed by local businesses is a huge lost opportunity for residents, businesses, and their communities. In the future, the nature of the skills gap is likely to evolve because of AI and its increasing capa-bilities. There will be fewer and fewer opportunities available for those with a high school diploma, and fewer jobs defined by repetitive, well-defined tasks, no matter how complicated they may seem from the vantage point of today. Being un-able to provide ongoing training for the skills of the future for the residents of communities outside of urban innovation centers will mean that these regions will continue to fall be-hind. Government has a big role to play in ensuring that this doesn't happen.

How do we provide the right educational opportunities for children so that they will be ready to do the jobs of to-morrow? This is something that my wife and I are actively grappling with for our children, both in elementary school as I write. Many of our fellow parents are anxious about preparing their kids to take standardized tests and to mas-ter twentieth-century cognitive tricks that AI itself is on the cusp of mastering. It may very well be the case that these things are a good exercise for the brain, and help you master modes of thinking that are less likely to be superseded by AI. The things that likely will continue to matter, or matter even more in a world of highly capable AI, are the ability to effectively communicate and connect with your fellow human beings, entrepreneurship, empathy and compassion, creative problem solving, and collaboration. The liberal arts are likely to be even more important in the future as we seek to better understand the essential nature of our selves, the past, our present condition, and our aspirations for the future. And I do believe that art will continue to be a fundamentally human activity, and among other things, a mechanism that we use to explore things that we barely know how to express, and the connections that we have between each other and with the world around us.

It should also come as no surprise that I think we should be providing our children with great technical education, providing a strong foundation in math and science, with an emphasis on both as tools to be used to understand and create, not as bodies of knowledge to be committed to memory for easy recall. We should be training our children about technology, about engineering and computer science. Learning to program is an important part of computer science and engineering, and the way that many of us express our craft. However, it is far more important to learn to think algorithmically and to build a foundation that allows one to adapt as the nature of programming itself changes.

The role of policy makers in all this should be to encourage a robust discussion about how we should be preparing citizens for the future, and investing in training for both the workers of the present and the future so that they can attain the skills they need to lead prosperous, fulfilled lives.

Get the basics right. There are still table stakes, like access to broadband Internet, that communities and their residents need in order to fully participate in the economy of the future. Alongside access to training, making sure that all our communities have access to modern digital infrastructure is vital. This infrastructure is not only the lifeblood for modern business, but is also required to attract and retain talent.

Go big. In 1962 President John F. Kennedy gave a historic speech at Rice University outlining goals of the Apollo program.

> *We set sail on this new sea because there is new knowledge to be gained, and new rights to be won, and they must be won and used for the progress of all people. For space science, like nuclear science and all technology, has no conscience of its own. Whether it will become a force for good or ill depends on man, and only if the United States occupies a position of preeminence can we help decide whether this new ocean will be a sea of peace or a new terrifying theater of war. I do not say that we should or will go unprotected against the hostile misuse of space any more than we go unprotected against the hostile use of land or sea, but I do say that space can be explored and mastered without feeding the fires of war, without repeating the mistakes that man has made in extending his writ around this globe of ours.*
>
> *There is no strife, no prejudice, no national conflict in outer space as yet. Its hazards are hostile to us all. Its conquest deserves the best of all mankind, and its opportunity for peaceful cooperation may never come again. But why, some say, the Moon? Why choose this as our goal? And they may well ask, why climb the highest mountain? Why, thirty-five years ago, fly the Atlantic? Why does Rice play Texas?*
>
> *We choose to go to the Moon! We choose to go to the Moon . . . We choose to go to the Moon in this decade and do the other things, not because they are easy, but because they are hard; because that goal will serve to organize and measure the best of our energies and skills, because that challenge is one that we are willing to accept, one we are unwilling to postpone, and one we intend to win, and the others, too.*

If you change just a few words in the first paragraph of the speech, Kennedy's words could easily be spoken about AI. What the president did in this speech wasn't just fund the primordial moon shot but give permission to hope for generations of storytellers. He defined why this incredibly technical, abstract, expensive, and risky undertaking was worth trying. We need the same for AI, to make a rallying cry around it. We need to make the provocation that as a fundamentally curious species, AI is perhaps the worthiest problem that we have ever attempted to solve because of its complexity and what it will reveal about our own human nature. And perhaps most important, we need to come together in some way to invest in AI that will have tangible, positive social benefit for all, so that beyond our curiosity, everyone has a stake in the future.

In the United States, we have had many examples of great public works programs where we invested heavily to accomplish some audacious goal, where we came together to create things that defined entire industries and changed the future of our country and the world. Policy makers should consider creating the moral equivalent of the Apollo program for AI in service of the public good. We've already identified a number of social-good problems that could be tackled with AI, and we already have several agencies through which such a program could be run, namely the National Science Foundation or the Defense Advanced Research Projects Agency. An Apollo-size program for AI would cost an estimated $200 billion, which spread over ten years would be 0.1 percent of our annual GDP. Coupled with clever regulatory incentives, we could accomplish amazing things.

Consider, for instance, the challenge of delivering high-quality, low-cost medical care for everyone in the United States. This has been a contentious issue for politicians and citizens alike for years. If we look just at government spending on health care, spending under current law is projected to increase 5.5 percent per year from 2018 to 2027, which is faster than GDP growth has been in any single year since 1984. In a zero-sum world, this means that in order to fund this growth we must raise additional revenues (taxes), or cut spending elsewhere, or both. The only way to change this is to generate more GDP growth, or to lower the rate at which we are spending on health care. GDP is somewhat difficult to predict or control. And lowering spending on health care typically means degrading or denying service for some or all. This is the very essence of a contentious zero-sum game.

One way out may be with AI. AI diagnostics are already able to cheaply and ubiquitously diagnose a whole range of illnesses with clinical accuracy. As the sensors in our phones and watches and other devices that we carry and wear become cheaper, more ubiquitous, and more capable, and as AI advances, it's not a science-fictional thought to imagine a world in which everyone has access to a virtual doctor who can tell you when you are getting sick before you're aware that you are, and that can either prescribe a course of action autonomously or refer you to a physician when your illness is beyond the ability of the AI to help remedy. Diagnosing illness for near zero cost, for everyone, before they are symptomatic, when illnesses are cheaper to treat and more readily cured with less impact to the patient, could be transformational for the country and the world.

In addition to funding research in academia and industry to solve the AI problems inherent to a health-care revolution, the government could also use the incredible amount of money that it's already spending on health care to incentivize behaviors that would benefit an AI transformation. For instance, one of the real challenges in building AI for health care is that the data, which is typically very high quality, is fragmented across mutually incompatible systems and formats, much of it sitting in handwritten notes decaying in manila folders, sitting inaccessibly for AI in a gazillion filing cabinets and archive boxes in doctors' offices across the country. What if the law mandated that to do business with government, every provider of medical services, on behalf of patients, had to securely and digitally provide a record of the services rendered in a standard format into a medical record locker controlled by the patient, perhaps implemented using blockchain? The patient's locker would contain a complete transcript of their medical history, and they would be able to authorize providers to see some or all of their medical records as they are being treated. The patient could also allow AI systems to have access to some or all of the data in their medical locker: to read data for training, and to provide a place to store data as diagnoses and AI services are rendered.

Having a way for AI researchers and developers to get confidential access, with the patient's permission, in order to build AI that can more ably serve them, could accelerate the effectiveness of AI-rendered health care by years or decades.

Whether it's health care or a combination of health care and other grand challenges, we already possess the mechanisms to fund an AI Apollo program. All we need to do is summon the will to do it, and the results could be nothing short of extraordinary.

THE ROLE OF THE CITIZEN

If you've made it this far, thank you. I promise the work you need to do to prepare yourself and your family for an AI future is modest, but critically important. AI must, in the limit, serve you and your needs. In a modern democracy, it is from you that permission ultimately flows for the experts, the developers, the execs, and the policy makers to do their part in shepherding AI into the future and all of us with it.

But for you to exercise this ultimate power over how things are unfolding, you must engage.

The first part of engaging is to form an opinion about AI. As my mom and teachers might have told me, "I don't care" isn't a valid opinion on something as important as this. That's basically you abdicating your agency and the decisions about your future to someone else.

Getting an opinion about AI isn't the easiest thing in the world. My people (scientists and engineers) have not made it as easy as it should be to understand a complicated and rapidly changing bundle of technologies. I'm sorry for that, and my decision to write this book is a first and certainly neither complete nor adequate attempt at changing that. I'm going to continue to do everything in my power to help make this stuff more accessible, and to call on my colleagues to do the same. It's the least that we owe you.

The second part of you engaging, once you have an opinion, is insisting that your elected officials are sufficiently technical to make good policy about AI, and that where they lack depth, they seek out the highest-quality technical counsel there is to be had. These elected officials are the folks whose job it is to make policy to protect you and your interests, and to ensure that the rules of the grand game that we are all playing are written in a way that you can have a prosperous career, take care of yourself and your family, and lead a fulfilling life should you so choose. They can't do their job in the age of AI if they are not able to grapple with some pretty complex technical issues and are able to get their most challenging questions answered when they hit the limits of their own expertise.

The third part of you engaging is learning to be a lifelong learner. I always want to apologize to folks when I say this, imagining that it might be some great imposition. I've never met anyone who isn't curious about something and willing to spend time satisfying that curiosity. You all have hobbies. If you are parsing this sentence, you're a curious reader. You listen to podcasts and watch YouTube videos. You spend time with your colleagues discussing new tools of your trade, with like-minded explorers in online communities and physical-world meetups. And some of you really love to go to school and enroll in courses all the time to challenge yourself to learn new things. If you just channel a bit of this into paying attention to what's going on with AI and into learning a new trick every once in a while to help you out in an AI world, you're going to do just fine. And when the thing that's blocking you is the expense of education and training, that's another opportunity for you to engage with your elected officials and to demand from those of us who are creating knowledge to package it up in ways that are cheaper and easier for you to consume.

Finally, be hopeful. For those who know me well, or who understand the mind-set of engineers, that may sound peculiar. I think of myself as a short-term pessimist, and a long-term optimist, which is how many engineers view the world. By training and disposition as an engineer, you are constantly surveying the world for what's broken or what has opportunity for improvement, then trying to figure out what you can do to make things better. That is the very definition of our job. And sometimes it makes you see the world through a pessimistic aperture. But even though you might see a dozen things a day that are frustratingly broken, there's always that faith that better is within grasp. I'm so confident that better is within our reach. We are, after all, the stories that we tell, so if we all have that hope, that belief that we can make things better together, and that insistence that we support each other in bringing about a better tomorrow, we might actually get what we hope for.

Conclusion

———

By the time I return to visit my hometown in the early summer of 2019, Microsoft has seen an unprecedented resurgence fueled by cloud computing and an ambitious vision for artificial intelligence. Tech is restless, and so is the world it serves. With another presidential election getting underway, a lot of new energy is going into winning rural votes, including proposals to improve everything from USDA programs to rural broadband. While I'm back in Virginia, the *New York Times* carries a full-page ad from T-Mobile and Sprint proclaiming the time has come to close the digital divide. "Too much of America has been overlooked, underserved, and left out of the digital revolution," according to the copy that overlays a pastoral photo of farmland that could easily be Campbell County, Virginia. As regulators ponder whether to allow the merger of these telecom companies, a message speaking to rural America seems now to be their emphasis. A few pages later the newspaper focuses on how President Trump's ban on Huawei Technologies, the Chinese telecom giant, "dashes farmers' cellular hopes."

The premise I set out to write about, that technology is going to be more boon than detriment to the rural economies, seems even more relevant today.

On this morning, I speak with David Reid, a delegate in the Virginia state legislature. I learn that these same issues—the divide between rural America and high-tech America—is also playing out in Richmond, where politics are only a little more civil and productive than farther north in Washington, DC. David represents suburban Loudoun County, but was born and raised in rural Buena Vista (pronounced Buoo-na Vista down here) not very far from my hometown. He has a personal calling to rural policy issues because of his birthplace, but he also sees helping rural Virginia as a means of helping urban Virginia. He also knows that with the right infrastructure and skills, anyone can work in tech from anywhere.

"I look at it not just from an altruistic standpoint of view where it's the right thing to do, but also from a selfish northern Virginia standpoint of view. The more things that we can do to actually help the rural areas of the state be able to attract new businesses to keep people in those areas, it means that there's less demand for them to want money from northern Virginia to support their efforts."

David was part of the "blue wave" of Democrats elected to the Virginia General Assembly on the heels of the 2016 Trump election. During his 2017 campaign, David noted that for approximately every dollar that comes out of northern Virginia and goes to the state capital, only about twenty cents comes back. The rest of that money, he said, gets reallocated to other parts of the state that struggle to sustain themselves, subtracting resources from northern Virginia that might otherwise be deployed to improve schools and transit. He sees no way out of America's broken political system until, geographically speaking, there is more economic equity.

So-called flyover communities and states need to "be seen and lifted up." In other words, urban, high-tech America depends on rural America's revival as much as rural America depends on the growth and consumer demands that comes from thriving technology-intensive regions.

Today's workforce can work from anywhere, so long as there is enough broadband connectivity. Ironically, one way to pay for that in rural Virginia is with funds derived from the national tobacco settlement, which prioritizes broadband infrastructure for former tobacco-growing areas like Campbell County. Christopher Ali is an assistant professor at the University of Virginia and has become a leading researcher and thinker on rural broadband. His op-ed for the *New York Times* in early 2019 called for a national rural broadband plan modeled after President Roosevelt's Rural Electrification Act of 1936. Over bacon and eggs at the Farm Bell restaurant in Charlottesville, Professor Ali tells me that even though the country has spent billions on rural broadband, it's a farce because the telecom companies are using copper wires, not fiber, and are erroneously calling slow-speed DSL high-speed broadband.

"DSL is considered 'good enough' for rural people," Ali said.

He sees rural co-ops as an important ally. Rock County, Minnesota, according to Ali, today has 100 percent fiber to houses and businesses thanks in part to bonds issued using credits from wind farms. The Farm Bill reportedly includes money for rural broadband. Ali shrugs, noting that rural communities qualify only if they can show 90 percent of households have no access even to slow speeds. Put simply, if the local provider supplies achingly slow DSL, that is good enough.

But it's not good enough. And the negative implications are immediately apparent as I sit down with Hunter Bass, the son of my classmate W. B. Bass, who now runs the sod farm with his brother Allan near my mom's house in Gladys. Hunter reminds me a little of myself at his age. After graduating high school in 2012, he attended university to study computer science. Unlike me, Hunter and his wife have chosen to remain in Gladys—at least for now—near family and friends. They earn a good living, with Hunter working as a software developer at a company in Lynchburg and his wife studying to become a nurse. But their ability to work from home, to start a family and a business, is imperiled by an Internet speed that, at 3 megabits per second, isn't adequate to fully connect to the opportunities of a digital now, much less those of an AI-powered tomorrow. His parents' nearby home gets even worse speeds. My aunt, who also lives nearby, is lucky to get 300 kilobits per second.

It's easy to overlook disparities like this when you're living in an urban innovation center like Silicon Valley or Seattle or New York City, and especially easy when your job in high tech focuses all your attention on the very frontier of technological possibility. In our conversations and debates about the future of AI technologies, it's easy to forget that equitable access to technological basics is just as important, perhaps more important, than the next machine learning advancement, the next AI-powered business, or our debates about how we push the technological frontier forward. As technology continues to advance at such an incredible rate, and as business and individuals increasingly depend upon it for their success, the digital divides that we now have will only serve to amplify inequality in the future.

Hunter is optimistic, though. He is pinning his hopes on the dream that his family home in Gladys might one day offer the same infrastructure—the same foundation of opportunity—that he sees in other communities. Just down the road, for example, South Boston, Virginia, hit the jackpot when the

Mid-Atlantic Broadband Communities Corporation and Microsoft announced they would team up to build high-speed connectivity and a new tech hub. But we need more than hopes and dreams.

After saying goodbye to Hunter, I stopped by the Governor's School campus, which was in its final week of the 2019 session. When I was a teenager, my hopes and dreams led to Central Virginia Governor's School for Science and Technology, which was a launching pad for my career as a computer scientist and technologist, and a foundation of opportunity for me and my classmates. The building, nicer today than when I attended in the 1980s, has three hundred devices connected to excellent broadband for its 136 students. It buzzes with the staff's excitement for the school's mission. But despite the great work that the Governor's School does encouraging the curiosity and creativity of its students, and sending them out into the world with the skills and mind-set they need to be successful, the school remains underfunded. Steve Howard, who teaches programming languages like Python and C#, is training the people who will help create the future of artificial intelligence and the next-generation technologies we have yet to even imagine. In a recent senior class "science scenario," his students tell him their goal for one assignment is 100 percent efficacy for cancer treatment. Even though it's unlikely that a group of bright high schoolers is going to cure cancer now, one of them—with the right skills, a lifelong commitment to curiosity and learning, a determination to help others, and optimism—just might someday.

CVGS draws from schools in the region, including Appomattox, Lynchburg, Bedford, and Campbell County. I am curious if anyone from my hometown, about a forty-five-minute drive away, has followed in my footsteps. There is one, a young man named Joshua. He is a valedictorian who will go on to university to study prosthetics. I am moved by

Hunter's and Joshua's stories. Hunter told me he would have preferred to take computer science before his senior year, but there were no classes. At the Governor's School, twelve slots went unfilled this year. We can't afford to let gaps like this persist, particularly in our rural communities, places that need tech jobs and skilled workers to fill them.

It's been decades since I drove home from school. Even so, the turns and bends in the road from Lynchburg to Gladys feel familiar and bring back old memories. June is such a beautiful month in rural Virginia. The dogwoods, lilacs, mountain laurel, and honeysuckle are blooming. The cloudy skies turn purple and a thunderous downpour pelts the rental car. It feels comforting, rolling hills and glimpses of the Blue Ridge Mountains off in the background. The same houses on both sides of the road have been here since I was a little kid. It all somehow feels reassuring.

On these trips outside Silicon Valley, beyond the reach of the tech industry filter, I've been encouraged and even inspired by my old friends the Bass brothers in Gladys, and Hugh E and Sheri Denton in Brookneal. If we convince ourselves that we have a bleak future, then we will take a protectionist and defensive posture. And if we believe that we have a hopeful future, we will build things to make that hope a reality. I saw that with Hunter. Here's a kid who grew up in the same place I grew up. He went to Gladys Elementary School and then Rustburg High. He saw an opportunity for himself to go do something different, and not in the way where you're dismissing tradition in order to pursue your own path. He is telling himself, "No, this is my path and I can still respect my family's roots." I could hear in his voice a great admiration for what his family has done. He and most of his friends went off to college, which was not the case with my graduating class. But like me, many of Allan's friends left home to pursue other careers. I think that's good and bad.

Good because we know what the benefits of a college education are. College isn't the only path to a prosperous future, for sure. There are and should be a multitude of paths for folks to pursue. But we know that a college education brings concrete and tangible economic benefits for folks. The lifetime earning power of someone with a college degree is more than someone with a high school diploma. The bad thing is that Allan's friends had to go elsewhere because that's where they saw work and life opportunities. We really need to think hard about how to create more job opportunities for the work of the future here in rural America so people can choose to stay. It's why I'm so excited about the work that Linc Kroeger is doing to provide digital skills to those entering the workforce and in employment in rural Jefferson, Iowa.

There's this disinterested, even disdainful attitude that people can sometimes have about those who choose to live in different places, who choose to pursue different paths in life. It's very easy to surround yourself with the same news sources, the same political views, the same entertainment, the same activities, and the same culture as everyone else around you. With modern technology, with more of our time spent online and on our devices, and with more and more of our connections with one another mediated by social networks, it's hard to avoid becoming trapped in self-reinforcing filter bubbles and then not to have those bubbles exert their influence on other parts of our lives. Many of my friends and colleagues see those living in rural communities, people who live outside of the urban innovation centers where the economic engines are thrumming right now, in a very different light than I do. That's not just unfortunate. It's an impediment to making the American dream real for everyone. The folks I know in rural America are some of the hardest-working, most entrepreneurial, cleverest folks around. They can do anything that they set their minds to, and have the same hopes for their futures and the futures of their families and communities as those of us who live in Silicon Valley and other urban centers all do. They want their careers and their families to flourish, just like everyone else. Where we choose to live shouldn't become a dividing line, an impediment, to a good job and a promising future.

That's the American dream. And it's on all of us to make sure that it works, because in a certain very real sense, if it doesn't work for all of us, it won't work for any of us.

See the people. If you have flown from New York City or DC to Atlanta, chances are you've flown over my hometown. The next time you fly, open the shade on your cabin window and look down. See the fields and the infrastructure down below. Recognize those are communities. Notice the expanse and its commerce. Someone down there—intelligent, motivated, and ambitious, someone as intelligent, motivated, and ambitious as you—built that and is working hard to make the future better for themselves and those around them.

While this book was in production in November 2019, the Aspen Institute published a definitive study, *Rural Development Hubs: Strengthening America's Rural Innovation Infrastructure.* Aspen's Community Strategies Group painstakingly researched and wrote the report to help policy makers and other decision makers understand rural context and how to build a better rural development ecosystem. The study focuses on the role of a specific set of intermediaries, rural development hubs, that are doing development differently.

In a previous chapter, I proposed the idea of an Apollo space program—a moon shot—for AI. We need that level of unifying ideal. Driving through the back roads of Virginia, we listen to one of my favorite pieces of music, Dvořák's Symphony No. 9, "From the New World," which Dvořák composed during his stay in the United States. Neil Armstrong brought a recording of this symphony on Apollo 11. The music is full of optimism, anticipation, tension, and triumph. He was influenced by African American and Native American music, and by the open spaces of Iowa, which he visited at the turn of the last century.

I love classical piano to the point of obsession, and have since I was a little kid. No one in my family listened to classical music. We didn't have a piano at home. And I never really learned to play. Still, as a kid I was attracted to pianos as these great, complex machines. I was intrigued by the fact that some people could sit and coax it into making something beautiful. I was frustrated, and still am, that there was this gap, a gap that I could never seem to bridge, between making sound at the keyboard versus making music. And as I started to program, I've always seen a parallel between the journey of a pianist and that of a computer programmer. The pianist, sitting alone with his or her machine in an attempt to achieve a level of mastery that would enable the making of something meaningful. The programmer, who essentially is attempting the same thing with a computer.

My favorite piano composition is Chopin's G Minor Ballade, Op. 23, No. 1. I go through phases where it's the only thing that I listen to, multiple times a day for weeks on end. Sometimes I listen to recordings from different pianists. Sometimes it's different recordings from the same pianist. And sometimes it's just the same recording over and over and over. The G Minor Ballade is one of the few pieces of music I can listen to frequently and still have chills run down my spine during certain performances, most often when the pianist hits the double fortissimo at bar 106, which releases all the tension that's been building up since the double pianissimo in bar 68.

What's fascinating to me is that some performances, while note-perfect and played by extraordinary pianists, don't give me those chills, don't overwhelm me with an emotional response I find hard to describe. I can appreciate less over-whelming performances analytically, but the same raw, visceral emotion just isn't there. I have no idea why this is, and I doubt I'll ever be able to figure it out. Which to me feels like one of the great and joyous mysteries of being human.

AI can compose and perform music, even convincingly. But I've never felt from a computerized performance any-thing of what I feel when Murray Perahia plays the G Minor Ballade. I have a very hard time articulating why a Perahia or Vladimir Ashkenazy performance of Op. 23, No. 1, gives me this feeling, while a Vladimir Horowitz or Arthur Rubinstein performance of the same piece doesn't, even though I would score Horowitz and Rubinstein greater pianists than Perahia and Ashkenazy. I know for sure that other people react com-pletely differently to this music and these performances. A person's reaction to music is deeply . . . personal. I've always thought that the performance of music might be the purest way for one human being to communicate an emotional state to another. I don't see how an unsupervised machine could effectively create that same emotional connection, either di-rectly or as a broker.

More important, why you would want it to?

Build skills earlier. I am convinced everyone will need the skills to incorporate AI into their jobs, regardless of indus-try or sector—whether it's a computer science PhD that will allow you to get a job doing cutting-edge research, college or vocational training in how to build things with the AI in-frastructure that others are building, or the skills that we will all need to work with, reason about, and intelligently debate AI-powered products and services as they have an increasing impact on our lives. Students in Iowa, Virginia, and Wyo-ming all told me they wished that computer classes and train-ing had been available earlier, perhaps even through a 4-H or Future Farmers of America program. We need to provide a foundational level of technical capability to every person on the planet, just like we expect everyone to have some foundational level of math, science, and language skills, so that everyone has standing to participate in the development of AI. This will help to create prosperity for more people, and it will help to ensure that the creation of AI is more diverse and inclusive. The way we create technology is about to change because of AI on two dimensions. Smaller and smaller groups of folks will have more and more power to create highly impactful products and services, and the mechanism we use to make things with technology is going to change from programming computers to do things to teaching computers to do things. The combination of these two things means that technology creation can be more inclusive and diverse than ever, and that if we want the impact of technology to be directed by an inclusive and diverse group of folks, we need to use every tool in the kit to get folks trained in technology.

The magnitude and scope of potential change means that policy makers have a significant role to play. Government, industry, the academy, labor, and organizations promoting the social good must work together across nearly every discipline to develop policy that both encourages the fair development of these technologies, and to help mitigate the worst side effects of their adoption.

There are four overarching objectives that we should seek to accomplish: democratize access to AI technologies and ensure their fair and ethical use; encourage and incent the development of technologies that reduce the cost of human subsistence; help every individual find agency and purpose in an AI-powered future; and defend individuals from misuse of their data, and from harmful uses of AI.

To democratize access to AI technologies, we should consider providing incentives to research labs, universities, and industry to continue to pursue R&D that advances the state of the art in AI, with specific requirements that the technologists producing these technologies package them in ways that are easy for "ordinary" developers to use. We should specifically encourage the development of learning-to-learn and other technologies that seek to lower the barrier to entry to incorporating AI into new products and services. We should encourage students to study computer science, and provide vocational training and education for young people and midcareer folks alike to get training in digital skills for the AI jobs of the future. Moreover, we should make sure that data and AI ethics are a foundational part of both university and vocational training. Every person working with someone else's data or building systems making decisions that impact human beings should be able to answer the question, "What are my ethical obligations to those whose data I am handling, and whose lives my work impacts?"

Data are the raw materials feeding existing and future AI systems. Folks building AI-powered products and services will need fair access to the data required to train machine learning systems. Encouraging fair, liquid marketplaces for folks to trade data will be extremely important not just for businesses, but for consumers who should be fairly compensated for the data that they contribute to these marketplaces.

The markets are already working to encourage folks to develop technologies that reduce the cost of subsistence, particularly in health care. There is a policy role here as well to encourage the development of systems that reduce the cost of health care while increasing the quality of outcomes, that help reduce the cost of food production and distribution, that decrease the cost of building and maintaining our living and work spaces, and that help to reduce the cost and quality of securing our safety at the individual, municipal, and national levels.

Democratizing access to AI technologies and using technology to better provide for our basic human subsistence needs will both naturally help to provide agency and purpose in the future. Not having to slave away to provide for our basic needs will enable freedoms that humans have never had. AI also has the very real potential to create jobs that we can't yet imagine, and to unlock human creativity in unprecedented ways. As I write this, I'm envisioning the scene from *Star Trek: First Contact* where Jean-Luc Picard is walking a character named Lily through a Borg-infested *Enterprise*. Through the convoluted plot device of time travel, Lily and Jean-Luc are from periods in time separated by hundreds of years, and when Lily asks Jean-Luc about money he says to her, "The economics of the future is somewhat different. You see, money doesn't exist in the twenty-fourth century. . . . The acquisition of wealth is no longer the driving force in our lives. We work to better ourselves and the rest of humanity." This may sound like a bunch of horseshit to us twenty-first-century citizens confronted by the reality of current economic systems, but it's what I aspire to. And if we don't aspire to things, especially complicated ones, they won't materialize on their own. We are the stories that we tell.

As was the case in the Industrial Revolution, when a variety of technologies like the steam engine provided a substitute for human labor and fundamentally changed the nature of work, AI will cause disruption. Jobs will go away, and people will need new purposes and new ways to provide for themselves and their families. Accelerating the creation of subsistence technologies, and making sure that the cost-saving gains of those technologies result in lower prices, not wealthier elites, in conjunction with government subsidies and re-skilling, will ensure that the duration and magnitude of disruption are less than they would be otherwise. That said, we must strive to help those whose jobs are disrupted. How do we help them find a new purpose, and manage the personal strain of economic disruption as well as the loss of dignity that comes with losing a job? Government must have a role here, even if it is nothing more than changing the rules of our current markets to incent businesses to help disrupted workers navigate their personal, individual journey through change.

Government must also play a role in providing individuals and businesses with strong data rights and then ensuring that those rights are respected, as well as making sure that individuals, businesses, and governments do not use AI to cause harm to others. This will include developing the capability to detect and defend against AI-powered hacking and human manipulation. And it will include providing legal frameworks for accountability, liability, etc., for AI that interacts with humans.

Provide access to broadband and digital tools for all. If you are too young to remember dial-up Internet access, and maybe never experienced the futility of drip-drip-drip slow connectivity, then surely you've experienced these: traffic congestion that makes you late for work for a very important meeting, a slow drain in the kitchen sink when you're preparing a family meal, a broken chair or door that goes unfixed because you lack the proper tools or skills to fix it. Not having the right tools to build and sustain a business in the digital era is what it feels like for those outside of urban innovation areas. If you live outside of a bustling city, that helpless feeling of not being able to participate in the digital economy can be crippling. You lack access to speedy broadband as well as the digital tools and skills that are practically taken for granted in urban areas. Research comparing US and Chinese Mean Download Speeds by state and region shows real disparities. States such as Mississippi, Wyoming, and Iowa are at the slow end of the chart, while New York and Washington, DC, are at the fast end. China's slowest regions are still faster than our more rural areas. Reports indicate China's progress on 5G will eclipse that of the US.

Compensation. One of the thorniest principles to tackle will be how humans are compensated when machines undeniably take on more and more human capabilities and jobs. Some experts have proposed a universal basic income (UBI), which is a noble idea but a poor solution to the problem that it is nominally attempting to solve. That problem—how will people make a living when machines take away their jobs?—could be better solved using other techniques.

For example, my colleagues and I are researching an approach we call "data as labor." We explained it in early 2018 in a cover story for the *Economist*. Artificial intelligence is getting better all the time, and stands ready to transform a host of industries. But in order to learn to drive a car or recognize a face, the algorithms that make clever machines tick must usually be trained on massive amounts of data. Internet firms gather these data from users every time they click on a Google search result or speak with Cortana. People "pay" for useful free services by providing firms with the data they crave. Rather than being regarded as capital, data could be treated as labor—and, more specifically, regarded as the personal property of those who generate such information, unless they agree to provide it to firms in exchange for payment.

It requires a profound lack of imagination and no small amount of hubris to believe that the only human beings capable of leveraging AI to build great businesses will be AI experts and elite software engineers, and that the only way forward for everyone else is subsidies from the wealthy elite. If I had to bet, I would put very large amounts of money on the likelihood that AI will create more jobs and prosperity than any technology in history. The sooner that we stop viewing AI as a substitute for human labor and start imagining how it can be a force multiplier for human ingenuity, the better. Imagine a small-business owner with limited resources who will be able to realize her vision by employing AI technologies to give her the equivalent of a massive, supercheap machine workforce to do her "grunt work" and to complement her human workers, who will be freed to create more value than would otherwise be possible.

But let's assume that it takes a while for this new vision of work, entrepreneurship, and business to materialize, and that folks are going to face economic disruption as their jobs are replaced by machines. Some financial safety net is entirely appropriate and, in fact, necessary. Failing to take care of hardworking members of our community put out of jobs through no fundamental fault of their own is inhuman, inconsistent with faith-based teachings, and un-American. People need to be able to subsist. They need food, clothing, shelter, health care, access to training and education, and the basic means to participate in the workforce. Universal basic income could help provide some of these things. But it is a blunt instrument that fails to address the underlying fact that several of these subsistence needs, specifically shelter, health care, and education, have costs growing faster than inflation or GDP, which means that it will be a struggle for universal basic income to keep up. Universal basic income in the context of free markets also has a ghettoization problem. For example—and perhaps most important, given the negative feedback loop forming around geographic skill-sorting that is resulting in low-skilled workers being displaced from the thriving economies of urban innovation centers—a fixed universal basic income (not indexed to subsistence costs) will result in folks who need UBI the most being pushed to less desirable locations, and potentially completely out of the geographies where, through re-skilling, they might have the most compelling future employment opportunities. If we index universal basic income to the costs of subsistence, then we have a bunch of thorny issues because some of those costs are growing exponentially because of supply-demand imbalances and unequal incomes.

Perhaps a better answer than just plain old universal basic income is UBI in conjunction with a set of technology and policy investments to reduce the cost of subsistence. For instance, it is highly likely that AI and rapid advancements in biotech, like CRISPR-Cas9, will dramatically lower healthcare costs while significantly increasing the quality of outcomes. There is a huge focus among start-ups and big businesses to develop AI technologies that can detect and diagnose diseases early when they are easier and much cheaper to treat, and before they can have impacts that reduce quality of life and/or life-span. These new techniques and technologies are already showing tremendous promise. AI, fitness sensors, and ubiquitous mobile computing will be able to lower the cost of routine checkups and diagnostics. And technology may be able to improve the quality of end-of-life care, helping the elderly, mortally ill, and their families make better decisions; improving the agency, dignity, and quality of life of the patient; and reducing costs at the same time. A large percentage of all medical expenses in the US comes in medical care provided in the last twelve months of life. We could spend 100 percent of GDP and the outcome would be no different in the limit. There is no cheating death. There is a role for policy here too, both in paving the way for deployment and adoption of these technologies, as well as ensuring that our insurance marketplaces are functioning as efficiently as possible.

HOPE IS NOT A STRATEGY

Hope is perhaps one of the most important things that we as human beings possess. The belief that there can be a better tomorrow is the foundation of progress. Hope fuels our resolve to push through the obstacles of the now to reach whatever that future is. And the absence of hope is a bleak thing indeed.

I can't tell you the number of times after launching an idea, a paper, a piece of art, some software, a complex project, or a company, that I've asked myself or those I've been lucky enough to work with, "Now what?" When the response comes back, "We've done all we can do, and now hope for the best," the reply that I've learned from decades of painful experience is, "Hope is not a strategy." Hope alone cannot make the future what we want or need it to be.

With the future of technology, particularly advanced automation and AI, there is much to be hopeful about. Hope is monumentally important. But it's just a down payment on a commitment that we must make to each other to do all the work necessary to redeem our hope with a future that uplifts everyone.

Acknowledgments

Perhaps the best things about writing this book have been all the interesting conversations that I've had with so many smart, passionate folks and the opportunity that writing has given me to reflect on all the people who have influenced me. When I told Satya Nadella, my boss at Microsoft, that I was thinking about writing a book, he didn't hesitate to offer encouragement and support. Beyond telling me to go for it, he connected me with Greg Shaw and shared what he was learning as he finished writing his book, *Hit Refresh*. My colleagues at Microsoft are amazing, and I've learned more from them over the past few years than I believe I've learned in my entire life. I've shared many interesting conversations with Eric Horvitz, Saurabh Tiwary, XD Huang, Yuxiong He, Ranveer Chandra, Doug Burger, Jaime Teevan, Umesh Madan, Luis Vargas, Mat Velloso, and Eric Boyd that have been particularly helpful for this book. Brad Smith and the work that he and his team at Microsoft are doing on privacy, AI ethics, and access to technology means a great deal to me as an individual, and I'm glad for the conversations we've had and the work we're able to do together on these important issues.

I've had the privilege of working with some truly amazing folks over the years, most recently with an incredible team at LinkedIn. For several of LinkedIn's most intense years, Mohak Shroff, Bruno Connelly, Igor Perisic, Dan Grillo, Sonu Nayyar, and Alex Vauthey worked with me to build an engineering and operations team and culture that I will always love. I learned so much from each of them and can never express enough gratitude for all their hard work, sacrifice, commitment, mentorship, humor, and grace.

My colleagues on LinkedIn's executive team were a fantastic band of brothers and sisters to be in the trenches with. Deep Nishar, with whom I worked earlier in my career at Google, was my link to LinkedIn, and was a great product partner for my first years there. David Henke, Erika Rottenberg, Mike Callahan, Shannon Brayton, Steve Sordello, Pat Wadors, and Mike Gamson cared more about one another, and about what we were trying to do together, than any team I had worked with prior. When I joined LinkedIn, I reported to David Henke for a bit and then was his peer on the executive team for a few years when he ran technical operations and I ran engineering. David is the best operations leader I've ever worked with (although his protégé, Bruno Connelly, is a very close second), and he taught me more about ego-less leadership, intensity, brutal honesty, and operational excellence than I've learned from anyone else. I've missed David's company since the day he retired.

When I read the words that I've written in this book, I can very clearly hear Jeff Weiner's voice and feel his influence almost everywhere. I was, and am, a pain in the ass to manage. Consequently, Jeff may not fully appreciate how much I learned from him. I'm grateful to him for his patience as a manager, his generosity with advice and help when I needed it, and for him genuinely caring about my well-being, not just for the work that I was producing. I'm glad to call him, and my other colleagues from LinkedIn, friends.

When I joined LinkedIn, Reid Hoffman was already a very big deal. I have to say that I was too intimidated to try to get to know him at first. That may be one of the biggest personal mistakes I've ever made. Reid is one of the smartest folks I know. Sometimes, folks as smart as Reid, who choose to think as broadly as he does, can be very difficult to connect with. Their minds move so fast, and in such peculiar ways, that simple things, like having a conversation with them, can be challenging. But Reid is also approachable, compassionate, truly thoughtful, and a sweet human being. Much of this book is influenced by Reid, partly from the many conversations that we've had about shaping the impact of AI so that it serves the public good, and partly from taking cues from him to try to engage in a public debate of ideas, even when that debate can be uncomfortable.

I couldn't have written this book without my family and old friends. My mom and dad, my brother, my aunt and uncle, my cousins, and my grandparents have shaped the way that I think about the world and have always been unfailingly supportive of me and the crazy things that I've wanted to do. They have always had this faith in me, and that faith has been the bedrock of my confidence to try new things, and to persist when they invariably prove to be hard and frustrating. In retrospect, I don't know why they've always had so much faith in me. But I'm grateful for it, and I wish that everyone, everywhere, had more of that in their lives. When folks believe in you, I think that it's easier for you to believe in others. And that's one virtuous cycle that the world could use more of.

As anyone who has ever read a book's acknowledgments section knows, writing a book takes an especially heavy toll on one's immediate family. In my case, my day job already takes quite a bit of time away from my family, and writing a book on top of that has meant many nights, weekends, and vacations spent typing away at my laptop instead of doing all the things I love doing with my family. But the thing is that this book, the hope for the future that it's trying to encourage, and the work to earn that hope that we need to do, is the mission that my wife, Shannon, and I have been on together since 2002. She more than anyone in my life gets it. But, beyond getting it, Shannon, with her tireless desire to help other people even when it reduces her to exhaustion and tears, is the reason that I've kept pushing year after year, and the main reason why this book exists. She also spent many of her own precious weekend hours scrutinizing drafts of this book and providing amazingly helpful feedback. I love her very much and wonder every day how I got so lucky.

My coauthor, Greg Shaw, is one of the luckiest breaks I've caught in my long series of lucky breaks. When I started thinking about writing a book, I didn't have the slightest idea how to make it happen. Putting together a few hundred pages of hopefully coherent thought seemed daunting, and I knew absolutely nothing at all about the publishing industry and how to navigate it. Greg is a pro, having been through this process several times, and in addition to being a great writing partner and editor, he helped to connect me with my agent, Jim Levine, and with my editor at Harper Business, Hollis Heimbouch, both of whom have provided thoughtful and incredibly valuable feedback that I would have been lucky and grateful to have even if this book never saw the light of day. Rebecca Raskin and the entire team at HarperCollins made the finished product so much better and the experience more fun. Greg and I have worked so well together, in fact, that both of us experienced a bit of melancholy as we drew close to the finish line. I'm already thinking about our next project, just so I can continue to spend time with Greg.

—Kevin Scott

My hometown in Cotton County, Oklahoma, is 1,313 miles from Kevin's home in Campbell County, Virginia. Thirteen is a lucky number. You'd pass through Memphis and Nashville to get there. Yet the first time we sat down to lunch with a plate of chicken and *Phaseolus lunatus*, we immediately fell into a conversation about whether our families called them lima beans or butter beans. It didn't matter, in rural America these flat little green beans are a signal we're eating out fancy. The moment I knew a fellow Southern techie wanted to write a book about AI and rural America, I was all in. I cannot thank Kevin enough for the opportunity.

Many people informed and inspired us along the way, and most are cited in the text of this book. But I do want to thank a few who are not:

At Microsoft, Mary Snapp, Jennifer Crider, Mike Egan, and Mike Miles are leading important work to support access to rural technologies. I am incredibly appreciative of Peter Lee's thoughtful explanation of "dropout theory" in chapter 7.

Kitty Boone at the Aspen Institute and Janet Topolsky at the Aspen Institute's Rural Development Innovation Group provided helpful connections. My good friend David La-Furia, a partner with Lukas, LaFuria, Gutierrez & Sachs, is encyclopedic about laws and regulations surrounding rural broadband. Rob Shepardson, my friend and colleague who cofounded SS+K with Lenny Stern and Mark Kaminsky, produced a gorgeous documentary about rural values that I hope will one day be available to everyone. Special thanks to the Microsoft Library team, Kimberly Engelkes and Amy Stevenson, for their review of the manuscript and for producing the section on "citations and further reading."

Finally, my passion for this topic was made possible thanks to both sets of grandparents from Cotton County, Oklahoma, a sparsely populated rural farming community near

Notes

1. Semil Shah, "Transcript: @Chamath At StrictlyVC's Insider Series," Haystack, September 17, 2015, http://haystack.vc/2015/09/17/transcript-chamath-at-strictlyvcs-insider-series/.

2. The Turing test is one of the oldest proxy tests for machine intelligence. It asks a human chatting with someone or something they can't see to guess whether they're conversing with a human or a machine. If the machine can fool the human, it passes the Turing test.

3. A Winograd schema challenge is a more difficult proxy test for machine intelligence. In such a challenge, you have a sentence like, "The city councilmen refused the demonstrators a permit because they [feared/advocated] violence," and you ask the machine to correctly determine the antecedent of the pronoun for both possible completions of the sentence. For a human being, who the *they* refers to in this example is usually immediately obvious. With *feared*, the *they* is the councilmen. With *advocated*, it is the protesters. This is particularly challenging for a machine because you need greater context, and some degree of commonsense reasoning, to correctly determine the antecedent.

4. Paul Triolo, Elsa Kania, and Graham Webster, "Translation: Chinese Government Outlines AI Ambitions through 2020," New America, January 26, 2018, https://www.newamerica.org/cybersecurity-initiative/digichina/blog/translation-chinese-government-outlines-ai-ambitions-through-2020/.

5. Federal Ministry for Economic Affairs and Energy (Germany), "SMEs Are Driving Economic Success: Facts and Figures about German SMEs," March 1, 2018, https://www.bmwi.de/Redaktion/EN/Publikationen/Mittelstand/driving-economic-success-sme.pdf?__blob=publicationFile&v=4.

6. Paul Petrone, "The Age of AI Is Here. Here's How to Thrive in It," LinkedIn, September 17, 2018, https://learning.linkedin.com/blog/advancing -your-career/the-age-of-ai-is-here--here-s-how-to-thrive-in-it-.

7. Timothy J. Bartik and Brad J. Hershbein, "Degrees of Poverty: The Relationship between Family Income Background and the Returns to Education," W. E. Upjohn Institute for Employment Research, March 2018, https://doi .org/10.17848/wp18-284.

8. Anthony P. Carnevale, Jeff Strohl, and Michelle Melton, "What's It Worth? The Economic Value of College Majors," Washington, DC: Center on Education and the Workforce, Georgetown University, 2015, https://cew.george town.edu/cew-reports/valueofcollegemajors/.

9. Steve Case, "The Rise of the Rest," Revolution, September 11, 2012, https://www.revolution.com/the-rise-of-the-rest.

10. Agricenter International, http://www.agricenter.org.

11. Wikipedia, "Green Revolution," https://en.wikipedia.org/wiki/Green _Revolution.

12. Clayborn Temple, https://www.claybornreborn.org.

13. "Breakthrough in Quality, Translation and Efficiency," Soundways, https:// www.soundways.com.

14. Wikipedia, "Filter Bubble," https://en.wikipedia.org/wiki/Filter_bubble.

15. Economic Graph team, "Workforce Report: August 2018: United States," LinkedIn, August 10, 2018, https://economicgraph.linkedin.com/resources /linkedin-workforce-report-august-2018.

16. Vaughn Grisham and Rob Gurwitt, *Hand in Hand: Community and Economic Development in Tupelo* (Washington, DC: The Aspen Institute, 1994), https:// assets.aspeninstitute.org/content/uploads/files/content/docs/pubs/Tupel o_0.pdf.

17. "Executive Order on Maintaining American Leadership in Artificial Intelligence," The White House, February 11, 2019, https://www.whitehouse.gov /presidential-actions/executive-order-maintaining-american-leadership-artificial -intelligence/.

18. Microsoft, "Airband Initiative," https://www.microsoft.com/en-us/air band.

19. Li Yuan, "How Cheap Labor Drives China's A.I. Ambitions," *New York Times*, November 25, 2018, https://www.nytimes.com/2018/11/25/business /china-artificial-intelligence-labeling.html.

20. John McCarthy, Marvin L. Minsky, Nathaniel Rochester, and Claude E. Shannon, "A Proposal for the Dartmouth Summer Research Project on Artificial Intelligence," *AI Magazine*, Winter 2006, https://aaai.org/ojs/index.php /aimagazine/article/view/1904/1802.

21. Wikipedia, "Behavioral Modernity," https://en.wikipedia.org/wiki/Behav ioral_modernity.

22. Peter Sterling and Simon Laughlin, *Principles of Neural Design* (Cambridge, MA: MIT Press, 2015).

23. Patrice Y. Simard et al, "Machine Teaching: A New Paradigm for Building Machine Learning Systems," arXiv, July 21, 2017, https://arxiv.org/abs/1707.06742.

24. Joan Gordon, "Winsome Ghosts in the Machine: Joan Gordon's 'The Lifecycle of Software Objects,'" *Los Angeles Review of Books*, April 27, 2012, https://lareviewofbooks.org/article/winsome-ghosts-in-the-machine-joan-gordons-the-lifecycle-of-software-objects/.

25. Judy Estrin and Sam Gill, "The World Is Choking on Digital Pollution," *Washington Monthly*, January/February/March 2019, https://washingtonmonthly.com/magazine/january-february-march-2019/the-world-is-choking-on-digital-pollution/.

26. "OpenAI Charter," OpenAI, https://openai.com/charter/.

27. Mihály Csíkszentmihályi, *Flow: The Psychology of Optimal Experience* (New York: Harper & Row, 1990).

28. "Code of Ethics," National Education Association, http://www.nea.org/home/30442.htm.

29. Partnership on AI, https://www.partnershiponai.org.

30. Stanford Institute for Human-Centered Artificial Intelligence, https://hai.stanford.edu.

31. "'Whoever Leads in AI Will Rule the World': Putin to Russian Children on Knowledge Day," RT, September 1, 2017, https://www.rt.com/news/401731-ai-rule-world-putin/.

32. Economic Graph team, "Workforce Report: April 2019: United States," LinkedIn, April 8, 2019, https://economicgraph.linkedin.com/resources/linkedin-workforce-report-april-2019.

Further Reading

———

Introduction

Harari, Yuval Noah. *Sapiens: A Brief History of Humankind*. New York: Harper, 2015.

Lee, Stan, and Steve Ditko. *Doctor Strange Omnibus*, vol. 1. New York: Marvel, 2016.

Menzel, Donald H. *A Field Guide to the Stars and Planets: Including the Moon, Satellites, Comets, and Other Features of the Universe*. Peterson Field Guide. Boston: Houghton Mifflin, 1964.

Puchner, Martin. *The Written World: The Power of Stories to Shape People, History, and Civilization*. New York: Random House, 2017.

Vance, J.D. *Hillbilly Elegy: A Memoir of a Family and Culture in Crisis*. New York: Harper, 2016.

Chapter 1: When Our Jobs First Went Away

Abernathy, Gary. "Our Town's Newspaper Was Mocked for Endorsing Trump. Here's What We Think Now." *Washington Post*, June 7, 2017. https://www
.washingtonpost.com/opinions/our-towns-newspaper-was-mocked-for
-endorsing-trump-heres-what-we-think-now/2017/06/07/3365e17c-4acb-11e7
-9669-250d0b15f83b_story.html.

Brandt, Allan M. The *Cigarette Century: The Rise, Fall and Deadly Persistence of the Product That Defined America*. New York: Basic Books, 2006.

Federal Ministry for Economic Affairs and Energy. "SMEs Are Driving Economic Success: Facts and Figures about German SMEs." Berlin: Federal Ministry for Economic Affairs and Energy, 2018. https://www.bmwi.de/Redaktion/EN/

Publikationen/Mittelstand/driving-economic-success-sme.pdf?__blob=publi cationFile&v=4.

Fischer, Paul M., Meyer P. Schwartz, John W. Richards, Adam O. Goldstein, and Tina H. Rojas. "Brand Logo Recognition by Children Aged 3 to 6 Years: Mickey Mouse and Old Joe the Camel." *Journal of the American Medical Association* 266, no. 22 (December 1991): 3145–48.

Hernandez, Daniela. "How to Survive a Robot Apocalypse: Just Close the Door." *Wall Street Journal*, November 10, 2017. https://www.wsj.com/articles /how-to-survive-a-robot-apocalypse-just-close-the-door-1510327719.

"The History of Boydton Virginia." Town of Boydton, Virginia. 2019. https:// boydton.org/history/the-history-of-boydton-virginia/.

Medeiros, João. "Stephen Hawking: 'I Fear AI May Replace Humans Altogether.'" *Wired*, November 28, 2017. https://www.wired.co.uk/article/stephen -hawking-interview-alien-life-climate-change-donald-trump.

Stone, Peter, Rodney Brooks, Erik Brynjolfsson, Ryan Calo, Oren Etzioni, Greg Hager, Julia Hirschberg, et al. "Artificial Intelligence and Life in 2030: One Hundred Year Study on Artificial Intelligence: Report of the 2015–2016 Study Panel." Stanford: Stanford University, September 2016. https://ai100 .stanford.edu/2016-report.

Vance, J.D. *Hillbilly Elegy: A Memoir of a Family and Culture in Crisis.* New York: Harper, 2016.

Chapter 2: The Career Choice I Made

Bartik, Timothy J., and Brad J. Hershbein. "Degrees of Poverty: The Relationship between Family Income Background and the Returns to Education." Upjohn Institute Working Paper 18-284. W. E. Upjohn Institute for Employment Research, Kalamazoo, Michigan, March 2018. https://research.upjohn .org/cgi/viewcontent.cgi?referer=&httpsredir=1&article=1302&context=up _workingpapers.

Carnevale, Anthony P., Jeff Strohl, and Michelle Melton. "What's It Worth? The Economic Value of College Majors." Washington, DC: Center on Education and the Workforce, Georgetown University, 2015. https://cew.george town.edu/cew-reports/valueofcollegemajors/.

Dunbar, Robin I. M. *How Many Friends Does One Person Need? Dunbar's Number and Other Evolutionary Quirks.* London: Faber and Faber, 2010.

Chapter 3: Stories of Revival

Case, Steve. "The Rise of the Rest." Revolution, September 11, 2012. https:// www.revolution.com/the-rise-of-the-rest/.

Ford, Sam. "Future of Work Initiative in Kentucky." Lecture, University of Kentucky, Lexington, March 28, 2018. https://www.as.uky.edu/video/future -work-initiative-kentucky-lecture-sam-ford.

Hoffman, Reid, and Chris Yeh. *Blitzscaling: The Lightning-Fast Path to Building Massively Valuable Companies.* New York: Currency, 2018.

Moretti, Enrico. *The New Geography of Jobs*. Boston: Houghton Mifflin Harcourt, 2012.

Posner, Tess. "Artificial Intelligence for All: A Call for Equity in the Fourth Industrial Revolution." Our World, United Nations, October 29, 2018. https://ourworld.unu.edu/en/artificial-intelligence-for-all-a-call-for-equity-in-the-fourth-industrial-revolution.

Reinhart, R. J. "Most Americans Already Using Artificial Intelligence Products." Gallup, March 6, 2018. https://news.gallup.com/poll/228497/americans-already-using-artificial-intelligence-products.aspx.

Wykstra, Stephanie. "Developing a More Diverse AI." *Stanford Social Innovation Review* 17, no. 1 (Winter 2019): 7.

Chapter 4: The Intelligent Farm

Brynjolfsson, Erik, and Tom Mitchell. "What Can Machine Learning Do? Workforce Implications." *Science* 358, no. 6370 (December 22, 2017): 1530–34. https://www.cs.cmu.edu/~tom/pubs/Science_WorkforceDec2017.pdf.

Economic Graph team. "LinkedIn's 2017 U.S. Emerging Jobs Report," December 7, 2017. https://economicgraph.linkedin.com/research/LinkedIns-2017-US-Emerging-Jobs-Report.

Grisham, Vaughn. *Tupelo: The Evolution of a Community*. Dayton, OH: Kettering Foundation Press, 1999.

Hawksworth, John, and Richard Snook. *UK Economic Outlook*, PricewaterhouseCoopers, July 2018. https://www.pwc.co.uk/economic-services/ukeo/ukeo-july18-full-report.pdf.

Neel, Phil A. *Hinterland: America's New Landscape of Class and Conflict*. London: Reaktion Books, 2018.

Post, Todd, ed. *The Jobs Challenge: Working to End Hunger by 2030*. 2018 Hunger Report. Washington, DC: Bread for the World Institute, 2018.

Chapter 5: AI: Why It's Needed

Piketty, Thomas. *Capital in the Twenty-First Century*, trans. Arthur Goldhammer. Cambridge, MA: Harvard University Press, 2014.

Richardson, Ken. *Genes, Brains, and Human Potential: The Science and Ideology of Intelligence*. New York: Columbia University Press, 2017.

Chapter 7: How Models Learn

Chiang, Ted. *The Lifecycle of Software Objects*. Burton, MI: Subterranean Press, 2010.

Clarke, Arthur C. *Profiles of the Future: An Inquiry into the Limits of the Possible*. New York: Harper & Row, 1962.

Gerrish, Sean. *How Smart Machines Think*. Cambridge, MA: MIT Press, 2018.

Hinton, Geoffrey, Simon Osindero, and Yee-Whye Teh. "A Fast Learning Algorithm for Deep Belief Nets." *Journal of Neural Computation* 18, no. 7 (July 2006): 1527–54.

Chapter 8: AI: A Threat or Boon to Jobs?

Kofman, Fred. *Conscious Business: How to Build Value through Values.* Boulder, CO: Sounds True, 2006.

Kofman, Fred. *The Meaning Revolution: The Power of Transcendent Leadership.* New York: Currency, 2018.

Thiel, Peter A., and Blake Masters. *Zero to One: Notes on Startups, or How to Build the Future.* New York: Crown Business, 2014.

Chapter 9: Politics and Ethics

Kennedy, John F. "President Kennedy's Special Message to the Congress on Urgent National Needs." Speech delivered before a joint session of the US Congress, Washington, DC, May 25, 1961. https://www.jfklibrary.org/archives /other-resources/john-f-kennedy-speeches/united-states-congress-special -message-19610525.

Pinker, Steven. *Enlightenment Now: The Case for Reason, Science, Humanism, and Progress.* New York: Viking, 2018.

Rosling, Hans, Ola Rosling, and Anna Rosling Rönnlund. *Factfulness: Ten Reasons We're Wrong About the World—And Why Things Are Better Than You Think.* New York: Flatiron Books, 2018.

Additional Reading

Agrawal, Ajay, Joshua Gans, and Avi Goldfarb. *Prediction Machines: The Simple Economics of Artificial Intelligence.* Boston: Harvard Business Review Press, 2018.

Banerjee, Abhijit V., and Esther Duflo. *Poor Economics: A Radical Rethinking of the Way to Fight Global Poverty.* New York: PublicAffairs, 2011.

Daugherty, Paul R., and H. James Wilson. *Human + Machine: Reimagining Work in the Age of AI.* Boston: Harvard Business Review Press, 2018.

Gray, Mary L., and Siddharth Suri. *Ghost Work: How to Stop Silicon Valley from Building a New Global Underclass.* Boston: Eamon Dolan Books, 2019.

Jasanoff, Sheila. *The Ethics of Invention: Technology and the Human Future.* New York: Norton, 2016.

Schwab, Klaus. *The Fourth Industrial Revolution.* New York: Currency, 2017.

Index

About the Author

KEVIN SCOTT is executive vice president and chief technology officer of Microsoft and has held executive and engineering positions at LinkedIn and Google. He built and led the technology team of pioneering mobile advertising startup AdMob, which was acquired by Google in 2010. He has received a Google Founder's Award, an Intel PhD Fellowship, and an ACM Recognition of Service Award. He is an adviser to several Silicon Valley start-ups, an active angel investor, the founder of the nonprofit organization Behind the Tech, the host of the Behind the Tech podcast, and an emeritus trustee of the Anita Borg Institute. Scott holds an MS in computer science from Wake Forest University and a BS in computer science from Lynchburg College, and has completed most of his PhD in computer science at the University of Virginia. A native of rural Virginia, he lives in Los Gatos, California, with his wife and two children.